Vikrant Pande has to date translated twelve Marathi works into English, including Vishwas Patil's *Sambhaji* and Kaka Vidhate's *Duryodhan*. His recent book (co-authored with Neelesh Kulkarni), *In the Footsteps of Rama: Travels with the Ramayana*, was published in 2021. Vikrant's translation of Girish Kuber's Marathi work, *Tatayan, The Tatas: How a Family Built a Business and a Nation* won the Gaja Capital Best Business book award of 2019. Vikrant is a graduate of IIM Bangalore.

'The absolutely fascinating story of India's largest bank from the nineteenth to the twenty-first century. Vikrant takes us on the long journey from the colonial period, through the socialist period to the re-emergence of India as an economy of global consequence; State Bank of India has been at the heart of it all. Written in a simple narrative style, it makes economic history accessible to a wider audience.'

—**Sanjeev Sanyal**, Principal Economic Adviser, Government of India

VIKRANT PANDE

THE SBI STORY

Two Centuries of Banking

First published in hardback by Westland Business, an imprint of Westland Publications Private Limited, in 2021

Published in paperback by Westland Business, an imprint of Westland Books, a division of Nasadiya Technologies Private Limited, in 2024

No. 269/2B, First Floor, 'Irai Arul', Vimalraj Street, Nethaji Nagar, Alapakkam Main Road, Maduravoyal, Chennai 600095

Westland, the Westland logo, Westland Business and the Westland Business logo are the trademarks of Nasadiya Technologies Private Limited, or its affiliates.

ISBN: 9788196011888

10 9 8 7 6 5 4 3 2 1

Typeset by Jojy Philip, New Delhi
Printed at Saurabh Printers Pvt. Ltd

CONTENTS

PREFACE

27 January 2021. An appropriate day to visit the SBI Archive and Museum on the premises of the Kolkata Local Head Office located at 1, Strand Road. It was on the same day a century ago, in 1921, that the Imperial Bank of India was formed.

My journey into the world of the State Bank of India (SBI) was serendipitous. I first visited the Museum after reading a newspaper article sent by my editor, friend and mentor at Westland, Minakshi Thakur, describing the wonderful museum. The museum does not fail to impress. It was during the visit that I discovered the treasures it holds and decided to write a history of SBI for the layperson. My editor, Karthik Venkatesh, took an immediate liking to the idea.

A person entering the SBI Museum is greeted with an imposing twelve-feet tall fibreglass statue of 'Prince' Dwarkanath Tagore, one of the early clients of the Bank of Bengal. The archives display names of account holders like Motilal Nehru (current account in 1917), a joint account of Justice N.G. Chandavarkar, Pherozeshah Mehta and Dinshaw Eduljee Wacha, a loan account of Ishwar Chandra Vidyasagar (for 1873–74), a current account of Dinshaw Maneckji Petit in 1903, a current account of Dadabhai Naoroji in 1875, Ashutosh Mukherjee (the father of Shyama Prasad Mukherjee), Rabindranath Tagore, Jagadish Chandra Bose (securities account in 1928), M. Hidayatullah (from 1905 to 1992), Dr Rajkumar Amrit Kaur and many such stalwarts.

The museum displays, amongst many things, the scales used to weigh gold to exchange for coins. There is a treasure trove of interesting facts. The visitor can see in the gallery how India's banking system evolved from the time of moneylenders to the commercial banks of today. The 107-feet high mural on the face of Samriddhi Bhawan on Strand Road is the tallest mural in Kolkata and captures the evolution of the bank.

I was fortunate that the detailed and academic work done by Professor Amiya Kumar Bagchi and Mr Abhik Ray did not require me to delve into the archival material stored in another room. The archive collection is impressive—and a researcher's delight, if one is inclined to spend countless hours poring over old records!

That Professor Bagchi and Mr Ray had done remarkable, detailed and unparalleled research made it easy for me to pick nuggets from their voluminous work, which runs into thousands of pages. It is to them that I owe my gratitude. It would have been impossible without the extensive support of Mr Ray. Meeting Professor Bagchi and listening to his erudite yet humble conversation was a pleasure. Former bureaucrat and ex-chairman of SBI Mr D.N. Ghosh, who wears multiple other hats, recounted many stories with vivid clarity while I sat listening to him in the Bengal Club.

I was helped by my dear friend Anup Bagchi of ICICI Bank, who connected me with many senior persons in the bank. Anup, a special thanks to you.

Karthik Venkatesh and Sonia Madan, with their edits, have made the book eminently readable. I hope everyone enjoys it.

THE ORIGINS OF BANKING IN INDIA
AN INTRODUCTION

The history of banking began with the merchants of the world making grain loans to farmers and to traders who carried goods between cities. This was probably around 2000 BCE in Assyria, India and Sumeria. Later, in ancient Greece and in the Roman Empire, lenders based in temples made loans, accepted deposits and changed money. There is archaeological evidence that confirms the practice of money-lending as far back as in the ancient period in China and India. Evidence regarding the existence of money-lending operations in India is found in the literature of the Vedic times, i.e., 2000 to 1400 BCE, and of the Buddhist period, e.g., the Jatakas. The Sanskrit word 'ṛṇa' (pronounced 'rin', meaning debt) used in the Vedic period implies the presence of banking.

'The role of interest rates was recognised in ancient India. Interest rates were prescribed by almost all Hindu lawgivers—Manu, Vasistha, Yajnavalkya, Gautama and Baudhayana as also Kautilya. A common base number was 15 per cent per annum—what the banker-economist Dr. Thingalaya calls Hindu rate of interest. Incidentally, this is higher than current Prime Lending Rate (PLR) of many banks,' said Dr Y.V. Reddy, former governor of the Reserve Bank of India (RBI), in a speech.[1]

Chanakya's *Arthashastra*, while primarily about economic and military strategy, gives details of how the banking systems evolved. In the treatise, Chanakya says that the sons should pay with interest the debt of a deceased person or co-debtors or sureties. While a wife was exempt from her husband's debt, the husband had to pay if the wife had borrowed. 'Perhaps, this was the background in which one of the committees on rural indebtedness concluded that "the Indian farmer is born in debt, lives in debt and dies in debt"', said Dr Reddy. He jokes to say that in ancient India the people from the Vaishya community could take up banking and 'thus the caste system gave the licence; not the RBI!'[2] Incidentally, in ancient times, Brahmins were charged the least rate of interest.

During the Maurya period (321–185 BCE), an instrument called 'adesha' was in use. It was an order on a banker instructing him to pay the money of the note to a third person—or a bill of exchange, as we understand it today. Shreshthi Chandandas was a famous banker in Pataliputra, and the word 'shreshthi' thus became a surname of the descendants of bankers. It appears that during the Buddhist period, which predated the Maurya period, there was considerable use of various banking instruments. For instance, merchants in large towns gave letters of credit to one another. The common currency was cowries (sea shells generally imported from the Maldives), copper, silver and gold coins. Colloquially, the cowries were referred to as 'kaudis' and continued to be used in India till the early nineteenth century.

In the medieval period too, bankers were active. Ballal Sena in Bengal in the twelfth century was in debt due to wars with the king of Manipur and he approached one Vallabhananda Adhya, the richest banker then, for a loan of one crore rupees. The famed Jain temples at Dilwara were built between 1147 and 1247 CE. It is said that Vastupala, the prime minster of Gujarat in the thirteenth century, drew a hundi of ₹10 crores on a city banker (Nagar Sheth) of Ahmedabad for the construction of the temple complex.

⌘

Modern banking can be traced back to medieval and early Renaissance Italy. In fact, the word 'bankruptcy' has its etymological roots in the Italian phrase 'banca rotta', which literarily means 'broken bench'. In Italy, bankers or money dealers used wooden benches. When a money dealer ran out of money, their bench was broken.

No story about European banking or money is complete without a mention of the Rothschilds who, at one time, were the richest family in the world. Established by Mayer Amschel Rothschild in Frankfurt in the eighteenth century, the Rothschild banking empire grew rapidly during the French Revolution, with Mayer Rothschild facilitating payments from Britain for the hiring of mercenary soldiers. Then, in the early 1800s, Rothschild sent four of his five sons to live in Naples, Vienna, Paris and London, while one son stayed back in Frankfurt. The five branches, under his five sons, became, in a sense, the first bank to transcend borders. The Rothschilds made money by lending to governments for war-financing over the last few centuries. According to a long-standing legend, which though is not true, the Rothschild family owed the first million of their fortune to the successful speculation by Nathan Rothschild, the third son of Mayer Rothschild, about the effect of the outcome of the Battle of Waterloo (1815) on the price of British bonds. Even today, the Rothschilds continue to be one of the wealthiest families around.

The Bank of England too has its origins in war financing. It was incorporated by an Act of Parliament in 1694 with the immediate purpose of raising funds to allow the English government to wage war against France in the Low Countries (Belgium, Netherlands and Luxembourg). A royal charter allowed the bank to operate as a joint-stock bank with limited liability. No other joint-stock banks were permitted in England and Wales until 1826. This special status and its position as the government's banker gave the Bank of England considerable competitive advantages. It soon became the largest and most prestigious financial institution in England, and its banknotes were widely circulated. As a result, it became banker to other banks, which, by maintaining balances with the Bank of England, could settle debts among themselves.

In India, Gujarati bankers were active during Mughal times. During Aurangzeb's time, Virji Vora of Surat was a wealthy banker who had the courage to refuse an interest-free loan to the Mughal emperor, stating that it would set a bad precedent. Shantidas Jhaveri of Ahmedabad, a jeweller and banker, was a contemporary of Virji. As the Subahdar (governor) of Gujarat, Murad Baksh, the son of the Mughal emperor Shah Jahan, had granted Shantidas Jhaveri the village of Palitana in 1656. Palitana later emerged as a major pilgrimage centre for the Jains. The Lalbhai family of Ahmedabad, who founded the Arvind Group, traces its ancestry to Shantidas. Another name, yet again from Gujarat, is that of Travadi Arjunji Nathji of Surat, who, realising that the Mughal Empire was on the decline, sided with the East India Company. His acumen lay in his understanding of trade routes and exchange rates in various parts of the country. As the East India Company had ports in Gujarat (its first ship arrived in Surat in 1608), it was natural that many bankers operated there.

Haribhakti (named after the brothers Haribhai and Bhaktibhai Sheth), a famous banking house from Vadodara in Gujarat, supported Nana Phadnis, the minister for the Peshwas in Pune, in 1730. Pilaji Gaekwad, the ruler of Baroda, conferred the titles of 'Nagar Sheth' and 'Raj Ratna' on the Sheth brothers. In 1740, the largest banking house in the South was that of Bukanji Kasidas, who too hailed from Gujarat and was styled as 'Sarkar's sowkar and the chief shroff of the province'.[3]

The family of Jagat Seths can be traced back to Hiranand Sahu, a Marwari Jain from Nagaur in Rajasthan. Hiranand migrated to Bihar in the mid-seventeenth century in search of better prospects. In Patna, he made some money in the business of saltpetre, an essential ingredient for making gunpowder. During those times, saltpetre from India was much in demand in Europe because of its superior quality. It was also easy to carry on ships. So, the East India Company set up a factory in Bihar, for which they borrowed a considerable sum from Hiranand. While Hiranand had made these beginnings, it was his fourth son Manikchand who went on to earn glory for the family. The Mughal emperor Aurangzeb honoured Manikchand with the title of Seth. Later, Manikchand's adopted son, Fatehchand was given the title of 'Jagat Seth' by Emperor Farrukhsiyar (the Mughal emperor who ruled between 1713 and 1719).

Such was his prestige that no Mughal emperor dared to send the khillat (royal robes) to the Nizam of Bengal without sending one to Jagat Seth. The Jagat Seths were the Rosthschilds of India. According to some estimates, their wealth was around ₹14 crores in those times. One can only imagine what it would mean in current terms!

Gradually, trade started getting formalised and by the seventeenth century, there were agents (banias) in Calcutta. Agents existed in other parts of the country too, but were known by different names: in Madras, they were called 'dubashees', which literally means those who could speak two languages; in Bombay, which was the third important trading port in India at that time, they were called guarantee brokers or, simply, agents. As the credit needs of the East India Company merchants grew, the shroffs (traditional bankers) found it increasingly unsafe to invest large amounts in a trade of which they knew very little. The merchants had no recourse but to form agency houses and take up the business of banking and combine it with their commercial and trading activities. By the end of the eighteenth century, indigenous bankers had declined due to intermittent wars.

In the beginning of the nineteenth century, the British made attempts to introduce a uniform currency throughout the country. At that point in time, there were four types of rupee in circulation: the Murshidabad rupee, also called the sicca rupee, from Shah Alam's reign; the Arcot rupee coined at the mint of Fort St. George; the Surat rupee and the Lucknow rupee of the Nawab of Oudh. Besides, there were various gold mohurs. The business of money exchange was profitable and some communities exclusively dealt in it. They were called Poddars. The Poddars were different from the shroffs, or bankers, who were primarily Banias, Vaishyas, Marwaris and Chetties. The Marwaris, as the name suggests, came from the Marwar region (in present-day Rajasthan), while the Chetties operated in the region that is now Tamil Nadu. In Punjab, there were the Aroras and Khatris.

The 'banks' operating in India in the early nineteenth century were primarily performing the function of regularising the rates of conversion between different types of coins circulating in the East India Company's territory and regulating the rate of exchange for hundis or bills of exchange collected from various parts of India. Indian banking experienced a strong English influence in policies and practices of the banks which were established in the early nineteenth century. The Presidencies of Calcutta, Madras and Bombay had their own banks and while the charters of the Presidencies were similar, the variegated nature of the vast landmass of India and the local conditions made for different types of institutions to emerge with their own unique character. The amalgamation of the Presidency banks created the Imperial Bank in 1921. Later, the Reserve Bank of India (RBI) was formed in 1935, while the Imperial Bank was nationalised to form the State Bank of India (SBI) in 1955. The SBI thus has its roots stretching more than two centuries back.

PROLOGUE

Bijapur – April 14, 2018: Hon. Prime Minister Shri Narendra Modi today inaugurated State Bank of India's Branch at Jangla village during his visit to Bijapur District, Chhattisgarh, identified recently as one of the top performing 'Aspirational Districts' by Niti Aayog. Hon. Chief Minister of Chattisgarh Shri Raman Singh and Shri Amitabh Kant, CEO, Niti Aayog, were also present on the occasion. PM also interacted with a few beneficiaries of Pradhan Mantri Mudra Yojana and handed over loan sanction letters. State Bank of India has taken a lead role in financial inclusion in the tribal dominated Kanker, Kondagaon, Narainpur, Bastar, Bijapur and Dantewada districts by opening 5 new branches and 15 ATMs. All branches and ATMs located in interior unbanked areas have also become operational from today.

What this Press Trust of India (PTI) press release did not mention was a motley crowd attending the ceremony, most of whom were customers of the bank. Amongst those present were a prominent businessman of Chhattisgarh, who had been banking with the State Bank of India (SBI) for more than two decades, a farmer whose loan for a tractor had been recently approved by another SBI branch, a shopkeeper who had taken a working capital loan, a retired civil servant whose pension came into his SBI account, a descendant of a former Maharaja whose grandfather had a relationship with the bank since 1960s, and many others. From aristocrats to artisans, musicians to masons, owners of cement plants to casual labourers, princes to peasants, the State Bank of India (SBI) has been *the* bank. It is the most ubiquitous of all banks in India. Most people trust it implicitly as it stands for sovereign guarantee. While there are many other public sector units, among the public sector banks promoted by the Government of India, the SBI holds a special position in the minds of the people. Despite this, most people standing and listening to the prime minister of India would scarcely be aware of the origin of the SBI.

It all began more than 200 years ago …

1

THE TURN OF THE NINETEENTH CENTURY

It was the turn of the nineteenth century. After the fall of Mysore in 1799–1800, the Marathas were the only major power outside the ambit of British control in India. For much of the eighteenth century and even in the initial decades of the nineteenth, the Marathas were a dominant power in the subcontinent.

The Maratha Empire at that time consisted of a confederacy of five major principalities: the Peshwa (prime minister) located in the capital city of Poona, the Gaekwads of Baroda, the Scindias of Gwalior, the Holkars of Indore and the Bhosales of Nagpur. The internal quarrels amongst the Marathas notwithstanding, they were still a force to reckon with, when they teamed up to fight a common enemy. Lord Mornington (later to become Lord Wellesley and addressed as such from hereon), the governor-general of British India between 1797 and 1805, had repeatedly offered a subsidiary treaty to the Peshwa and Scindia, hoping to absorb them into the British sphere of influence, but Nana Phadnis, a prominent Maratha statesman, who often acted on behalf of the Peshwa, refused it vehemently. The years that followed these offers witnessed two Anglo-Maratha Wars (between 1803 and 1805 and then in 1817–18) between the combined armies of the Marathas and those of the East India Company.

It was an eventful time in India. The Vellore Mutiny on 10 July 1806 was the first instance of a large-scale and violent mutiny by Indian sepoys against the East India Company, predating the events of 1857 by half-a-century. On the financial front, at the turn of the century, the East India Company's government in Bengal was under severe financial strain largely on account of the wars unleashed by Governor-General Wellesley against Tipu Sultan. The Anglo-Maratha tussles that would follow in the next few years would also be an expensive affair.

Parallelly, there was a persistent demand from the Company headquarters in England for a regular share of Indian tax revenues. Raising loans from private sources, to fund the war efforts, had become increasingly difficult and costly for the government. Large-scale borrowings had already resulted in heavy discounting of government treasury bills and a steep rise in interest rates.

Calcutta, as Kolkata was called then, was the centre of trade, banking and, more importantly, the capital of British India between 1772 and 1911.

Bankers were known in India since antiquity. At the time the British began establishing their political supremacy over the whole subcontinent, an extensive network of Indian banking houses, connecting all cities and towns which were commercially important, existed. Inland bills of exchanges known as 'hundis' or 'hundees' were the main medium of transaction between the Indian bankers with trans-regional connections. These bankers lent money to other bankers, landlords and princes; they financed the movement of commodities and, in times of war, the movement of armies, often sharing the spoils of conquests. They were not necessarily acting as safekeepers of deposits but rather as custodians of treasuries of whole states and they also had the privilege of minting money in the name of the Emperor of Delhi or the local ruler.

During the eighteenth and the early nineteenth century, a structure of European-controlled banking had also grown in India, primarily under the auspices of European agency houses. The agency houses accepted deposits, lent money to merchants, shipowners, ship managers, planters and governments and generally helped finance external trade. They issued bank notes, which were sometimes accepted even for public payments. Such banks, however, were almost never real joint-stock banks; the capital was not subscribed by a large number of independent persons nor did the bank proprietors enjoy limited liability. It was only Act VII of 1860 that conferred limited liability on join-stock banking companies operating in British India. More about that later.

It was in the settlement at Fort St. George in Madras that the East India Company first began to exercise effective territorial sovereignty within the geographical limits of India. Madras was also the biggest source of the Company's exports to Europe, closely followed by Surat. The first attempt to set up a bank by the officers of the Company seems to have been in Madras in 1683. Most likely the bank did not issue notes. It was a bank of deposit and discount. Not much is known about the bank. Later, institutions such as the Carnatic Bank, Madras Bank, the British Bank, the Bengal Bank, the General Bank of India and Asiatic Bank were set up in the late eighteenth century.

Before these banks were set up, it was the establishment of the Bank of Hindostan in Calcutta in 1770 that marked the arrival of European banking in India. Set up by Alexander & Co., one of the leading agency houses of Bengal, it was the first bank to introduce paper money in India with notes ranging from Sicca Rupees 4 to 1,000. Some more banks were soon set up by agency houses in Calcutta and other presidency towns. Their resources consisted of deposits from European civil and military servants, the capital subscribed by the principals and the loans given to them by the shroffs. All these banks were, however, extended partnerships and mostly fly-by-night entities that thrived on military and political exigencies created by the operations of the British in India and did not survive for long.

The Asiatic Bank was set up in 1804, a time when many private Europeans and servants of the Company had prospered as they were involved in trade and other activities, some of a dubious nature. The pockets of well-placed Europeans were lined further with the wars against Tipu Sultan and the Marathas unleashed by Lord Wellesley. This gave a fillip to banking enterprises as there were wartime exigencies like the provisioning of a huge army, the safekeeping of the prizes of the officers of the army and the settlement of the vast expanse of territory acquired by the Company. The government had to borrow from private banks (in which many senior officers had a stake) to finance such activities. This led to the Governor of Madras, Lord Clive (son of the legendary Robert Clive), proposing the setting up of a bank under government patronage. The Bank of Madras would be formed much later on 1 June 1843.*

---

* The prosperity of the Europeans in Madras was also associated with what is called as the 'ramp of Arcot'. This helped raise Sir Thomas Rumbold and several senior and junior civil servants in Madras to the status of wealthy 'Nabobs'. It so happened that the Nawab of Arcot (Carnatic), Muhammad Ali, known as Nawab Wallajah, found himself deprived

The origins of the bank which subsequently became the Imperial Bank (and later the SBI) can, however, be traced back to Calcutta.

The Role of the East India Company in the Development of Early Indian Banking

The East India Company represented the British authority in India and had been granted monopoly over trade between Europe and Asia.* This monopoly had been renewed in successive charters which specified that the Company was to act as a trading organisation and could not acquire any territories. That, of course, changed as the Company gained possession of certain territories in the late seventeenth and early eighteenth century.

By the beginning of the eighteenth century, the Company was, for administrative purposes, divided into the three Presidencies of Fort William (Bengal), Fort St. George (Madras) and Bombay, each having its governor

---

of all effective political power while still in nominal possession of a large territory. On being pressed by the Company for large tributes, he took the path of least resistance. In order to pay to the Company, he borrowed huge sums from anybody prepared to lend to him. The lending, of course, happened at exorbitant rates of interest and all Europeans who could exploit this situation did so. This continued even in the reign of his son Umdat ul-Umarah. When the support stopped after Umdat ul-Umarah died in 1801, the territory was formally annexed by the Company. Fake bonds flooded the market and creditors tried to get payment for non-existent debts. After fifteen years of investigation, the Commissioners charged with the settlement of the Carnatic debt scaled down the claims totalling 30 million pounds to 2 million pounds only. It was a severe blow to the European gentlemen in Madras!

One example of how the Nawab was looted is that of the House of Binny and House of Parry. Thomas Parry and John Binny, the founders of the two biggest British firms operating in Madras at the time of independence, had at one time or another been in the employ of the Nawab of Carnatic and his creditors. Parry seems to have engaged in some dubious transactions, such as presenting a forged Carnatic bond for settlement and acquiring a house from the Nawab of Carnatic (no less than the premises of 'Parry's Corner'—the headquarters of the firm) on the basis of a rather dubious title. It is yet another example of the financial morality of the British traders and some top government officials in Madras at that time.

* The Queen granted a Royal Charter on 31 December 1599 to the East India Company. The charter awarded the newly formed company a monopoly on English trade with all countries east of the Cape of Good Hope (southern Africa) and west of the Straits of Magellan (southern South America) for a period of 15 years.

or president. But in 1773, with the passing of what was called the Regulating Act by the British Parliament, two things happened: the presidencies of Madras and Bombay were subordinated to Bengal and the Company's government subordinated to the British Parliament. The Act was provoked by the application of the Company to the British Parliament for a loan to tide over its financial difficulties. This was the first public recognition that while the Company was thriving as a territorial power, it was in difficulties as a commercial body.

In 1784, the British Parliament passed the India Act (sometimes labelled Pitt's India Act as William Pitt the Younger was the prime minister of Britain at that time). Under the Act, a Board of Control was set up to oversee the East India Company's administration in India. This had no effect on the corruption in the government of the Company as the then British Parliament itself was full of nepotism and corruption. Lord Cornwallis, who was appointed governor-general in 1786, separated the functions of the revenue collector and the civil judge though the collector continued to dispense criminal justice. Cornwallis also prohibited private trade by all officials of the Company. The eventual establishment of British dominion in India under Lord Wellesley laid the foundation for scuttling the monopoly privileges of the Company and the installation of unbridled European private enterprise in India.

In 1793, the Company's charter was renewed for another twenty years. It was also decreed that as the Company was not the sovereign ruling over Indian territory, it could not insist on a monopoly over trade and could not prevent other Europeans from trading. Many Company officials exploited this loophole and traded privately. The changes initiated by Lord Cornwallis did not minimise the growing conflict between the interests of private traders and the commercial interests of the Company. Powerful agency houses had been founded on capital amassed by free traders and entrusted to these houses by the Company's servants for accumulation through the channel of 'country trade', which was trade between the regions east of the Suez Canal, and for eventual remittance to England. This remittance business was not easy as it meant tackling fluctuations in the rates of exchange or prices of commodities which acted as vehicles of remittance.

The Birth of the Bank of Bengal

Apart from the Bank of Hindostan, at least two other European banks were in operation for various periods in eighteenth-century Bengal: the Bengal Bank (different from Bank of Bengal) and the General Bank of India. None of these banks enjoyed limited liability nor could they be considered proper joint-stock banks as most of the capital was owned by a few individuals and the banks were managed by a few men. In legal terms, they were partnership firms with unlimited liability on part of the owners. There were numerous schemes for setting up of state-backed banks in Bengal but they did not bear fruit.

By the beginning of the nineteenth century, a clear functional division between the general administration and supervision of the Company and the private commercial affairs of agency houses and other European merchants, with the active support of the Company's servants, was taking shape. The need to set up a provisional bank that could take up the intermediate ground between the private and public interests of the Europeans in India, without fear of being a mere department of the Company's government or a mere tool in the hands of fly-by-night adventurers, was felt. The provisional bank, called the Bank of Calcutta, came into existence with its first board of directors constituted on 27 March 1806.

In the *Calcutta Gazette* of 3 April 1806, the government announced the appointment of government directors to the Bank of Calcutta, one of whom was Henry St. George Tucker. The Bank of Calcutta was wound up to form the Bank of Bengal. While the Bank of Bengal was formed on 1 May 1807, it opened for business with the public only on 2 January 1809. So, in effect, the Bank of Calcutta existed from 27 March 1806 until the very end of 1808. The arrangement for the Bank of Calcutta could only be provisional because it had to be ratified by the Court of Directors, who had on earlier occasions disapproved of any proposal to extend government support to any bank. The government had originally announced its intention to establish the full-fledged Bank of Bengal by 1 May 1807 or wind up the provisional bank after that date, if the Court of Directors disapproved of the government's plan. Eventually, the consent of the Court was not received until the end of 1808.

The first meeting of the board of directors of the Bank of Calcutta was held on 9 April 1806. The first item was the recording of a letter from the Government of India informing the directors that no servant of the Company was allowed to hold shares in the proposed bank. Those who had already subscribed to the bank were instructed to withdraw.

Maharaja Sookmoy Roy, grandson of Lakshmikanta Dhar, banker to Clive and the Company, was a director in Bank of Bengal, representing the interest of the Indian collaborators of Europeans. Roy died on 19 January 1811 and his place was filled by a European. It would take another century before an Indian became a director of the bank.

After Sookmoy Roy's death, his eldest son, Ramchandra Roy, was made the khazanchee (chief cashier). The bank started issuing notes with a limit for them not to exceed four times the capital. With the capital fixed at ₹50 lakhs, the notes worth ₹2 crores were issued by the bank. While the Bank of Bengal became operational on 2 January 1809, it took the government nearly two years before it could announce that the Court of Directors had approved the establishment of a bank in the presidency of Bengal. One reason for the delay was the legal uncertainty regarding whether the Company had the power to grant charters to establish banks within the territory of its government. This uncertainty was removed by the enactment of a special law, '47, George III, C.68' by which it became legal for governments in India to establish banks with perpetual succession, provided that prior approval was obtained from the Court of Directors subject to the control of the Board of Commissioners for the Affairs of India. In the charter for the bank, the liability of any shareholder was limited to the amount of capital subscribed by him. This included the government as a shareholder, so that the government did not pledge its own security as a guarantee to the bank. Due to the clause, the government escaped the liability for the collapse of the bank beyond the loss of most of the capital that it had subscribed.

When we study the history of banking in India, it becomes clear that the setting up of institutions like the Bank of Bengal was clearly not an attempt to modernise India's economy but a response to a compulsion to satisfy the needs of local European commerce. Very few Indian borrowers could take loans from the bank and the few who did were all highly affluent individuals.

Several early innovations in banking methods and organisation took place with the birth of the Bank of Bengal. Two important ones among these were the use of a joint-stock system for raising capital and the conferring of limited liability on the shareholders of the bank by means of a charter. The

Bank of Bengal had imposed explicit limits on the amount of credit that it could extend and the kind of securities it could accept. Such measures would pave the way for future banking rules in India.[*] There were also provisions for regularly changing the board for making decisions and a formalised office organisation for carrying on day-to-day business.

The Bank of Bengal, India's first large bank and the earliest predecessor of the present-day SBI, was the brainchild of Henry St. George Tucker, the Attorney General of the government of Bengal who eventually became chairman of the East India Company.[†] In putting forth a scheme for setting up the Bank of Bengal, he referred to the precedents of the Bank of Amsterdam and the Bank of England. There was, however, a clear difference in the constitutions of the Bank of England and the Bank of Bengal: the former was purely a private body which managed the finances of the governments whereas in the latter, the government was an important shareholder from the very beginning.

For the curious reader, as a matter of comparison, the gross revenue of the Presidency of Bengal in 1809–10 was approximately 9 million pounds sterling, while the total resources of the Bank of Bengal, including cash, government securities, private bills discounted and others were 8 lakh pounds, less than one-tenth of the revenues of the government.

---

[*] On 2 February 1837, George Udny, the secretary and treasurer of the Bank of Bengal, stated at a weekly meeting of the bank directors that the bank did not have a record of its history. It is then that the bank started maintaining records and a history of record-keeping emerged.

[†] An interesting story related to Tucker would surprise HR practitioners today. When Tucker was sentenced to six months' imprisonment and a fine of ₹4,000 for attempted rape on an English lady, Mrs Dorothea Simpson, it hardly affected his official status. The minutes of the bank for the supposed meeting he was to attend simply shows him as 'absent' and he continued to be the Director of the Bank of Calcutta even after his conviction. In another case, one Sir Thomas Turton, the registrar of the Supreme Court and past acting advocate general of the Government of India, was found guilty of defalcations of property of widows and intestate persons to the tune of ₹15 lakhs, a massive sum in those days. He was an officer of the Crown and the East India Company had no jurisdiction on him. He was let off with a few months in jail. Directors of companies which borrowed from the bank were on the board of the bank, thus looting without compunction. The directors of the Bank would even approve loans for their own businesses. In fact, many of those working in the bank believed they were above the law.

Among the big Indian borrowers when the bank began operations were well-known banking firms, such as Gopaul Doss and Hurry Kishen Doss, and members of the early trading communities of Calcutta, such as Sibchunder Bysack, Chintamoney Pyne and many others. Tucker had specified in the charter of the bank that the entire sum of debts of the bank, whether in form of bonds, notes or otherwise, should not exceed the capital of the bank which was then fixed at ₹50 lakhs. Any director infringing the limit would be held personally responsible for the excess.

⊗

A magnificent statue of Prince Dwarkanath Tagore greets us as we enter the present-day SBI Museum at its Strand Road premises at Kolkata. Tagore was one of the famous borrowers of the bank and had borrowed ₹60,000 on 21 July 1816 on deposit of Company's paper at a rate of interest of 9 per cent per annum. The loan, as usual, was for three months or less. His name appears frequently as a borrower from 1824 in the record books.

Another famous borrower was Bystamdoss Mallik, a cousin of Nilmani Mallik, who was the father of Raja Rajendra Mallik (who built the famous marble palace at Chorbagan). Many such stalwarts borrowed regularly from the bank.

The purpose for which the customers borrowed money from the bank on deposit of Company's paper is not recorded in the minute books of the bank. But the Company actively promoted the entry of private European business, especially in indigo and opium. Opium was contraband in China and the Company could not directly land the drug there but it did everything short of that to facilitate the export. Another commodity which was in great demand was indigo. One of the first persons to start indigo manufacture was John Prinsep, father of James Prinsep, the great Orientalist. Dwarkanath Tagore too borrowed presumably to start his own indigo factory at Silaidah in 1821.*

The Bank of Bengal, supported by high government officials, many of whom had served as secretaries or directors of the bank, helped to sustain the indigo boom of the 1820s. Another item for which people borrowed money

---

* Carr, Tagore and Company, of which he was a senior partner, in time, came to own seven indigo factories. The company borrowed regularly from the bank.

was the trading of salt. Salt was produced under a government monopoly system and then sold at certain selling outlets called salt 'golas' or 'gollahs'. Since it was a seasonal business, loans for this purpose were taken during specific times of the year. More than a century later, Mahatma Gandhi's march to Dandi for his famous Salt Satyagraha would result in questions being asked about the monopoly system.

The bank treated large borrowers like Tagore quite deferentially as they were adding to the bottom line. But that was not the case for the ordinary customers, whose treatment was similar to the callous attitude shown towards the 'natives' in general by the British.

The period beginning with Lord William Bentinck as governor-general (1828) and ending just before Lord Dalhousie became governor-general of British India (1848) is one of the most eventful, not to say most dramatic, epochs in the history of the Bank of Bengal. The period witnessed the fall of most of the agency houses, the very ones which had helped the wealthy British to transfer funds abroad.

During the early 1820s, agency houses had borrowed money from the bank at low interest rates and invested it largely in indigo concerns—the crop being the only profitable means of remittance in Europe. The crisis multiplied when newly formed agency houses, besides investing capital in their own indigo concerns, fiercely competed with the old houses and made indiscriminate advances to indigo planters, paying little regard to the actual state of the market. Excessive demand of indigo fuelled the prices in the mid-1820s and encouraged increased production of the commodity, which eventually led to a glut in the market and sharp decline in its price. Many agency houses collapsed as a result as their loans went bad.

It was natural for the Bank of Bengal to be concerned about the fall of the agency houses as the partners of these houses were on the bank's board and also their large customers. The top civil servants and even the governor-general, Lord William Bentinck, were too closely interested in the fortunes of the agency houses to pass up any opportunity to salvage them.

While the bank was salvaging the losses of the agency houses, a famous fraud took place in 1834 in the name of one Rajkissore Dutt. A regular borrower, Dutt used forged papers and looted the bank to tune of ₹3.15 lakhs. The precise amount noted in the Bank ledgers is 315509-2-8, meaning ₹3,15,509, 2 annas and 8 pice. That year, the whole of the profits of the period were written off and no dividend was declared. Rajkissore Dutt was convicted. There were several more frauds within the bank. Forgery of notes was a common type of fraud; it, however, stopped once the bank lost its right to issue currency.

The bank dealt with speed and harshness when it came to Indian debtors but showed a great deal of consideration to the European principals. The latter were granted almost complete immunity from the cruel provisions of the usual British laws related to bankruptcy by the Relief of Insolvent Debtors in the East Indies Act passed by the British Parliament on 19 July 1828. The Act seems to have been passed in anticipation of many European businessmen going bankrupt in the near future. Some debtors evaded their creditors by going away to Britain or China. Only lucky ones were spared, like Raggooraam Gossain Banian of Palmer and Co. Banian who owed the bank ₹1.65 lac, but he could not be arrested as he resided in Serampore (Srirampur), which was under Danish rule. Defaults had their own victims and one such high profile victim was Lord Combermere, the commander-in-chief of the British Indian Army. He lost £ 60,000, which he had deposited with Alexander and Co. and had failed to withdraw in time.

The organisational set-up of the Bank of Bengal too favoured the white man. Here too the common Indian employee suffered. The common employee's views were either disregarded or taken very lightly. Standing on the banks of the Hooghly at 1, Strand Road, Kolkata, the zonal headquarters of the SBI, where the Bank of Bengal building once stood and which was razed a few years ago for reasons not clearly known, one can imagine the scene two centuries back.

It was not as glorious as one may want to envisage. One of the khazanchees had raised the issue of the safety of the treasury in the bank. He wrote that '... the Bank is on the border of the river and the only thing which divides it from public road is a low iron fence like a park railing. A small party of desperate robbers or sailors may scale it and take away the iron treasure chest which is just fifteen yards off the premises. There are only 10 sepoys to guard.'*

---

* He also goes on to talk of the road being used for open defecation by the employees and customers. But the proposals were summarily dismissed. The Secretary's reaction is worth noting. He writes, 'Well, this is the way Indian public offices are run and how Indian employees are treated everywhere....' The Secretary believed that 'cluttered tables and

The bank treated the Indian ordinary customer as it treated the small debtors—in a rude manner. This was unlike how it treated the wealthy elite of Calcutta. Quite clearly, the bank was not meant for ordinary people.

True to British tradition, the bank has maintained its records meticulously. An excerpt from the Complaints Register reveals an incident that occurred in 1889 when a customer, Potit Pabun Mitra, complained of a junior British officer, T.W.L. Bruce's rude behaviour. The complainant said, 'I am desirous of an apology from the assistant in the Govt. Account Dept. for alleged rudeness and that an enquiry should be conducted into the matter.'

The officer gave his explanation, 'I have no recollection, whatever, of the occurrence, and most emphatically decline to apologise in any way to this exceedingly "under-bred" person. His letter is composed of insulting sentences, and my only regret in the matters is that his age alone prevents my taking further notice of the occurrence.'

The matter was discussed and the noting said, 'The above is no explanation. Superintendent Govt. Acc. Dept. will please report on the matter for the Secretary's information.'

After what may be considered an 'enquiry' was conducted, the following was noted in the register: 'After enquiring into this matter, it would appear the cheque was presented just at the time the Passing Officer was commencing to enter his clearing, the Baboo however seemed to think his cheque should take precedence, and finding Mr. Bruce still continued entering his clearing cheques in preference to his, took umbrage and reported the matter. Mr. Bruce says he has no recollection of having used any such language, as imputed to him by the Baboo.'

The matter stood closed with the comment, 'As the Baboo's feelings have been hurt, doubtless unwittingly, Mr. Bruce having no recollection of the

---

overcrowded rooms' were a norm in sarkari offices in India and he dismisses the rant that the khazanchee had to use candles on rainy and cloudy days which was risky by commenting, rather dismissively, that 'it was the same in London too'. On the point of open defecation, he writes that 'there is a little pucka house by way of commode for the native establishment and also for the European and Christian assistants.' The Secretary did not bother to appreciate that one little 'pucka' house for 35 officials was far too inadequate. The Secretary had also condescendingly referred to tiffin service being available for less than a rupee per month not bothering to realise that even in the days of low-cost living of the early 1800s, one rupee mattered a lot to the Indian workers in the bank (A.K. Bagchi, *The Evolution of the State Bank of India: The Roots (1806–1876), Vol II* [Oxford University Press, 1987], p. 243).

matter, I am sure Mr. Bruce will say the injury was unintentional and express his regret for it.'

An important banking practice was introduced by the Bank of Bengal in 1833—that of cash credit. The system was evolved in Scotland nearly a century earlier (in 1728) by the Royal Bank of Scotland. A cash credit was a credit given to an individual by a banking company for a limited sum, upon his own security and that of two or three individuals approved by the bank who became sureties for its payment.

But as was the case with many existing banking practices, the cash credit was hardly a system for the common man. The rules of business of the Bank of Bengal published in 1841 specified a minimum limit of ₹500 for cash credit, a significant amount in those days. By 1845, the minimum limit for opening a cash credit account at the bank had been raised to ₹10,000, which was beyond the common businessman's capabilities.

In 1848, a competitor to the Bank of Bengal, the Union Bank, fell, leaving the Bank of Bengal in a practically monopolistic situation in eastern and northern India with the exception of the Agra and United Services Bank.

While many borrowers suffered in the fall of the Union Bank, Dwarkanath Tagore played a role in the expansion of the Bank of Bengal. Tagore had apparently become wary of the operations of the Union Bank and is quoted as stating that the bank had entered into transactions 'at variance with the proper practise of banking'.[1] He then systematically set about getting rid of his Union Bank shares.[*] By 1845, he had only a few shares left.[†] Dwarkanath Tagore founded the Calcutta Steam Tug Association, the Steam Ferry Bridge Company and the Bengal Tea Association while he dabbled in coal mining in Raniganj and salt manufacture. The last one was done through

---

[*] The fall of Union Bank had its own share of victims, especially the prominent Parsis. In the middle of 1848, Dadabhoy Rustomjee, son of Rustomjee Cowasjee, who was one of the promoters of the Bank of Bombay, and son-in-law of Cusetjee Cowasjee, went bankrupt with debts exceeding his assets by more than a hundred per cent. A crisis in Bombay also led to Dadabhoy Pestonjee Wadia, the promoter of the Bombay Chamber of Commerce and the Bank of Bombay, and who in 1848 was considered one of the richest men in India, being forced to sell his real estate worth more than ₹50 lakhs at that time for a far lesser value. A few years later, in 1885, the same property was valued at ₹3 crores. Dadabhoy Wadia died a poor man.

[†] He converted most of his wealth into zamindaris to be held for his sons in trust.

Carr, Tagore & Co.*, and managed by George Prinsep. All these were done with borrowings from the Bank of Bengal.

The agency houses had gone bankrupt due to the changed business scenario. (Indigo prices had suffered and money was scarce as the government had borrowed largely for the Burma War. This resulted in an increase in the rate of interest for borrowers.) Most of the partners of the bankrupt agency houses easily obtained their discharge from the Court for Relief of Insolvent Debtors and a large number of them soon went into business again. James Young, a partner in Alexander & Co. which failed in 1832, was secretary to the Union Bank in 1834 and the Sheriff of Calcutta in 1838. William Prinsep and his brother, George Prinsep, became partners in Carr, Tagore & Co.

In a series of complicated manoeuvres, European creditors and shareholders of the Union Bank, many of whom had been the leading culprits in defrauding it in various ways, succeeded in setting up a Committee of Management of the Union Bank in liquidation. This committee's task was to apportion the payments to be made by the shareholders of the bank for liquidating its debts. This it did in an arbitrary fashion, so that three wealthy Indian shareholders, the Dey brothers and Raja Nursingchandra Roy (the youngest son of Maharaj Sookmoy Roy), found themselves saddled with a total payment of ₹7,50,000 while Europeans were assessed at much lowers amounts and some of them even 'bought' their own debts at very low price.[2]

The failure of the Union Bank literally eliminated Indians from the list of the big borrowers of the Bank of Bengal. Wealthy Indian found mercantile operations as junior partners of European entrepreneurs much too costly.

The Bank of Bengal doubled its capital between 1835 and 1839[†] and it emerged stronger with the fall of the Union Bank, becoming the sole possessor of joint-stock banking in Calcutta. With the Bank of Bombay incorporated on 15 April 1840 and the Bank of Madras on 1 July 1843, all three presidencies got their own banks.

---

* Carr, Tagore & Co. was the first equal partnership between European and Indian businessmen and the initiator of the managing agency system in India. In essence, a managing agency is the vesting of the management of a joint-stock company in the hands of a firm of professional managers.

† This doubling of capital was proposed in 1822. The capital was increased to 75 lakhs in 1836 and further to 107 lakhs in 1838.

The Rise and Rise of Bombay

Bombay had been in the possession of the East India Company for centuries. In 1661, the port and island of Bombay had come in the possession of the King of England when his queen brought it as part of her dowry. It was transferred to the East India Company in 1669 to be held 'as of the Manor of East Greenwich' in free and common socage* of 101 pounds. Two years later, in 1671, the East India officials began to mint their coins. It is said that when some coins with the 'name of their impure king' were shown to Emperor Aurangzeb, the chief of the Bombay factory explained that the coins were current only in their jurisdiction.

While technically Bombay was under the East India Company, many parts of it were being controlled by the Marathas, Portuguese and the English over the seventeenth and eighteenth centuries. The Treaty of Salbai between the East India Company and the Marathas in 1782 gave Salsette, Elephanta, Hog Island and Karanja, all parts of Bombay, to the Britishers. In the same year, William Hornby assumed charge as governor of Bombay and initiated an engineering project to unite the seven islands of Bombay into a single landmass.

Bombay was gaining importance in trade slowly but surely, and opium played an important role initially. By 1830, regular communication with England had started with ships.

Bombay experienced a boom in its trade in the 1830s. There were several reasons for this. Malwa, the territory north of the River Narmada, was a big producer of opium and it was channelled through Bombay, under British control, rather than the Portuguese ports. Also, the rise in price of American cotton led to a demand for Indian cotton from 1832. Added to this was the fact that there were better roads built between Bombay and the country beyond the Western Ghats. The islands of Bombay had been joined and the continual expansion of the city limits with improvements in the Bombay harbour also served to increase the flow of goods and population from the Deccan to the port city.

The Bombay Chamber of Commerce was established in 1836 and four years later, in 1840, the Bank of Bombay was set up on the same lines as

---

* Socage refers to a feudal tenure of land involving payment of rent or other non-military service to a superior.

the Bank of Bengal. Unlike Calcutta, the leading capitalists of Bombay were opposed to the formation of the bank. Bombay had been a source of capital and the government treasury had been used as a bank of deposit. Remington Crawford and Co., Jamsetjee Jejeebhoy and Sons, Leckie and Co. and B.N. Hormasjee had addressed a memorial to the government of Bombay against the proposal to establish a bank. These firms had managed to retain their control over the credit market of Bombay, at least as far as financing of external trade was concerned. However, the cessation of the Company's trading monopoly in 1833[*] had led to the entry of new European firms and the accretion of new business to the second-class house of the agency. The private merchants had organised themselves to take advantage of the expanding trade and established the Bombay Chamber of Commerce.[†] The old capitalists like Remington Crawford and Co. and others were against a bank and contended that all that was needed was that the government should issue interest-bearing treasury notes in exchange for cash in times of stringency in the money market. They believed that no advantage would flow from the establishment of a bank, while numerous evils would arise from the issue of paper notes which were not representative of real capital. A lot of lobbying took place with the Bombay government and appeals were made to the government of India and to Lord Auckland, the then governor-general of India. Ultimately, Act III was passed in February 1840 which granted a charter to the Bank of Bombay. The bank opened for business on 15 April 1840 and the capital was fixed between ₹50 lakhs to 56 lakhs. The bank acquired 23 Rampart Row, belonging to Jehangir Nusserwanjee

---

[*] The British Parliament continued to control the East India Company by extending its charter for only 20 years at a time. Those granted in 1793, 1813, 1833 and 1853 successively whittled away the Company's commercial rights and trading monopolies. Its last remaining monopoly over the China tea trade was abolished in 1833. The British Parliament allowed the Company to maintain its political and administrative duties in India, but the charter of 1813 included a clause asserting the Crown's undoubted sovereignty over all of the Company's territories and required it to open up India to Christian missionaries. The 1833 Charter Act invested the Board of Control with full authority over the Company and further increased the power of the governor-general.

[†] The biggest business houses of Bombay, such as Forbes and Co., Remington Crawford and Co. and others were not involved in the organisation of either the Chamber of Commerce or the joint-stock bank. In fact, Forbes and Co. did not join the Bombay Chamber of Commerce till 1867.

Wadia, for its office. The composition of the board was similar to that of the Bank of Bengal. The government of Bombay appointed three directors and six were elected by the proprietors. The government had put in ₹3 lakhs as capital.

The bank was forbidden to deal in foreign exchange and this restriction led to the formation of two banks in the next five years—the Bank of Western India, which later became the Oriental Bank Corporation, and the Commercial Bank of India. The two banks became competitors to the Bank of Bombay.

Madras, That Is Chennai

Meanwhile, things were changing in the Madras Presidency too. Like Bombay, Madras too had been under the East India Company for centuries. There had been Company factories at Machilipatnam and Armagon since the very early 1600s. In 1639, the Company had purchased the village of Madraspatnam and a year later, it established the Agency of Fort St. George, precursor of the Madras Presidency.

The replacement of the Government Bank in Madras, founded in 1806, the same time as the Bank of Calcutta, by the semi-government Bank of Madras was the purest case of the triumph of local oligopolistic interests over those of the general run of traders and merchants. Private trade had been stagnating for almost two decades before 1840. The Madras Presidency had suffered a severe depression in the markets for commercial crops and goods. The depression had been aggravated by the famines in the 1830s. The move of the leading European merchants to set up a semi-government bank on the lines of the Bank of Bengal and the Bank of Bombay was both an opportunistic and a defensive manoeuvre—opportunistic, because the merchants wanted to take advantage of the wind blowing in favour of private enterprise in the halls of Westminster and defensive because they wanted to forestall some other private or semi-private institution setting up business in Madras. The move by the Madras merchants was made only after the Bank of Bombay had been formally launched. According to J. Ouchterlony of Ouchterlony & Co. the birth of the Bank of Bombay had been hailed as a 'panacea for the losses and suffering entailed by the opium crisis in China' and already, in mere infancy, 'it had driven stagnation from the commerce of the island'.[3] Ouchterlony referred to what he considered the decay of private banks in England and the rise of joint-stock banks which were better fitted to serve public needs.

The Bank of Madras

It took more than a year for the Court of Directors of the East India Company to formally approve the setting up of a bank on the lines proposed by the provisional committee for the Bank of Madras.

Managing the institution of the Bank of Madras turned out to be difficult as business in the city was seasonal. Very little activity was seen from August to November. There were variations from year to year, but eventually, the bank in the third presidency flourished.

The three presidency banks were now opening branches across India as per the charter of 1839. With expansion came risks. And frauds were never far behind.*

---

* Wherever authority is misused, the opportunity for frauds exists. While civil servants enjoyed high salaries as compared to the modest ones for military officers, many British officers made money in the business of procurement of supplies. There is an example is one Lala Joteepersaud of Agra, who was a contractor in the North-Western Provinces. We have heard in recent times of money being collected from government schemes for wells to be dug in rural India while the actual well existed only on paper! Lala Joteerpersaud seemed to

It was probably helpful that under these circumstances, the Companies Act of 1857 was implemented in India. The Act gave the concept of limited liability for shareholders of joint-stock companies.

While frauds and other misdemeanours continued, it must be noted with admiration that many of the officers and clerks of the Bank of Bengal followed rules both in letter and spirit. In 1850, a cheque of ₹18 drawn by one Colonel Gough was sent for payment. The postage of the letter, prepaid, was 14 annas and the cheque was returned to the drawer, accompanied by the information that the bank did not cash cheques for less than ₹50. This was as per the by-laws. A famous example of the bank sticking to its rules was when a cheque sent by Lord William Bentinck was returned, as 'it proved to be four annas beyond the sum of his credit'. Bentinck, rather than being miffed at his cheque being returned, praised the bank saying, 'This was the bank to do business with, which would not violate its rules in the smallest particular for the Governor-General himself!'[4]

A landmark event was to change the future of banking as well as the Company. It was the First War of Independence of 1857.

---

have done something similar back in 1850, when he billed the government for 'thousands of visionary bullocks, who never ate straw or yielded beef'. Unfazed by the case against him, he in turn filed a suit against the government asking for recovery of nearly 1.3 million pounds due to him for supplies furnished during the first Anglo-Afghan war and the two Anglo-Sikh wars! For lack of any concrete evidence, the case against him fell through while he was paid nearly ₹14 lakhs while his account was being checked for total dues!

2

BANKING IN THE BRITISH RAJ POST 1857

The year 1857 was a turning point for India. India formally became a part of the British dominion and ceased to be a territory of the East India Company. With this development, things would never be the same again.* The Government of India Act of 1858 dissolved the East India Company and transferred its ruling powers to the British Crown. An India office was created, with the Governor-General now called the Viceroy of India. In 1877, Queen Victoria, the queen of the United Kingdom of Great Britain and Ireland, took the title of Empress of India on the advice of Prime Minister Benjamin Disraeli.

With the East India Company no longer acting as an intermediary between the Government of India and the British Parliament, the right of

---

* The 'Sepoy Mutiny', as it is commonly referred to by Western historians, was actually a concerted effort at throwing out the English from India. It had its genesis in the British policy of 'Doctrine of Lapse' which allowed the East India Company to take control of a princely state if the local ruler died without an heir. This system was subject to abuse and the Company used it to annex territories in a questionable manner. The rebellions started on 10 May 1857 in form of the sepoys of the Company's army in Meerut. Soon, it spread to other parts of the country, with leaders like Nana Saheb, Tatya Tope and Rani Laxmibai of Jhansi leading the charge. The Scindias of Gwalior, Baiza Bai Scindia and Jiyaji Rao Scindia, played a covert role, while they showed their outwardly support to their English sahibs. While the rebellion was squashed with brutal killings and violence by the Company, it had succeeded in planting the thought of an independent India. But it would take another 90 years for that thought to materialise. The Mughal Emperor, Bahadur Shah was arrested and tried for treason for his role in the 'mutiny' of 1857 and exiled to Rangoon, where he died in 1862. With his death, the Mughal dynasty in India ended.

the presidency banks to issue notes was withdrawn. The full authority of issuing paper currency within the territories of British India now lay with the Government of India.

Alongside the drive to bring the whole of the Indian subcontinent under British rule was an attempt to integrate the conquered territories within a uniform fiscal and monetary system. The period also witnessed some rudimentary infrastructural development in British India in the form of irrigation and navigation canals, roads, steamboats and, most importantly, the railways. While this so-called modernisation was taking place, there were frequent crop failures and famines in many parts of the country. How many famines were the result of callous British policies is another story and much has been written about it already.

Despite the enthusiasm of people like Dwarkanath Tagore, most of the tea plantations, railways and other businesses like inland steamer companies were owned and managed by people from London. Indians had little share either in capital stock or in the management of these enterprises. It was the Europeans—more specifically, the British—who, under the political and social conditions prevailing at the time of the Queen's Government, were truly in charge.

The new enterprises rarely looked to the presidency banks for capital. The exchange banks and London-based transport and plantation companies neatly complemented one another to eat into the potential business of the presidency banks. The Indian banks did not get most of the business.

There were significant changes after the first war of independence in 1857. In 1858, Chartered Bank opened a branch in Calcutta—its first branch in India.[*] In 1860, George Dickson was made the secretary of the Bank of Bengal and, on 18 February in the same year, James Wilson presented the first Indian budget.[†] Wilson proposed that the government

---

[*] James Wilson was responsible for creating the Chartered Bank of India, Australia and China, when many European merchants protested that the Bank of Bengal was not willing to grant advances even when the merchants were willing to deposit government securities. Much later, in 1969, Chartered Bank merged with Standard Bank, which did business throughout Africa. The merged enterprise was incorporated in London under the name of Standard Chartered.

[†] Wilson, who was the Finance Member of the India Council that advised the Indian Viceroy, was also the founder of *The Economist* magazine.

issue a paper currency for India as a supplement to the silver coinage in circulation. He wanted the supply of this paper currency to be fully elastic with the demands of trade and to be against gold currency. He thought that the paper currency economised on capital locked up in silver and gold bullion and he abhorred the costs that a transition from silver to gold through a regime of bimetallism would impose on creditors and debtors. He expressed the wish that the three presidency banks be compensated in some way for the loss of their note circulation but did not specify how that should be done. Wilson was not in favour of the presidency banks being allowed to issue a paper currency which was the legal tender. To be really effective, the paper money had to penetrate into every corner of India. It would be impossible, he argued, for any banking establishment to extend its agencies over the greater part of India though the government had agencies throughout the country.

The Paper Currency Act was thus introduced in 1861. While the Act took away the right of the banks to issue currency, the presidency banks were allowed to manage the note issues of the Government of India. In response to this, on 27 June 1861, the Bank of Bengal directors informed the government that the bank was prepared to make immediate arrangements for the establishment of branches under the conditions and stipulations prescribed by the government, namely, the transfer to the bank of the Treasury balances and the management of the currencies at the following unoccupied stations: 'Benares, Farruckabad (Farrukhabad), Amritsar, Multan, Saugor (Sagar), Jubbulpore (Jabalpur), Patna, Mirzapore (Mirzapur), Dacca (Dhaka) and Rangoon'. The Bank of Bengal also offered to open branches in places such as 'Agra, Delhi, Lucknow and Umballa (Ambala)'.

The Cotton Boom and Its Impact on Banking

Events happening across the globe, thousands of miles away, had a dramatic impact on Indian banking and business. Abraham Lincoln was elected as president of the USA in 1860 and he supported a ban on slavery in all the states of his country. However, seven slave states in the South, with a cotton-based economy, decided against it, formed a Confederacy and declared secession. They were hoping that many European nations dependent on them for cotton would support them, but none of that happened. As Frank

L. Owsley Jr., an American historian, said, 'If slavery was the corner stone of the Confederacy, cotton was its foundation. At home, its social and economic institutions rested upon cotton; abroad, its diplomacy centred around the well-known dependence of Europe ... upon an uninterrupted supply of cotton from the southern states.'[1] The American Civil War was soon underway and this disrupted shipments of cotton from the US.

With the supply of cotton compromised, England suffered for a time, as its cotton mills in Manchester were dependent on it. It was nicknamed Cottonpolis. Nearly 600 million pounds of cotton was imported each year, mainly from the southern states of America. This is where India and Egypt stepped in, bridging the gap. It was boom time for cotton trade in India and the 1860s thus saw massive investment of British capital in India. The price of cotton soared from 10 cents a pound in 1860 to US$1.89 a pound in 1863–64.

The year 1861 would later turn out to be an important year for India in general and Bengalis in particular. On 7 May that year, Rabindranath was born in the Tagore family. This grandson of Dwarkanath Tagore would go on to influence millions of Bengalis and Indians in his later life.[*]

The development of railways, which catapulted transport of goods, and the setting up of cotton presses and mills, favoured both the English and rich Indian merchants in Bombay who rode the cotton boom. There were massive exports of jute from Bengal. Even tea plantations and coal mines were promoted and managed by Europeans. The only exception were the Assam Company and Bengal Coal Company, led by Dwarkanath Tagore as one of the major shareholders.

---

* Known later as Gurudev, Rabindranath Tagore made significant contributions in the field of literature, music, art and education. He is the only individual who has penned the national anthem of two countries—India and Bangladesh. A couple of years after Tagore's birth, in 1863, Narendra Nath Dutt, who would be later known the world over as Swami Vivekananda and who would take India to world stage when he gave the opening address in the Parliament of Religions in Chicago in 1893, was born. Mohandas Karamchand Gandhi would be born in 1869 and would occupy centre stage, many decades later. It is amazing that Calcutta had at the same time greats like Tagore, Ramakrishna Paramahamsa, Swami Vivekananda, Jagdish Chandra Bose, Pandit Ishwar Chandra Vidyasagar, Bankim Chandra Chattopadhyay, Michael Madhusudan Dutt and many others—all living within a few miles of each other.

Madras too saw large-scale businesses being controlled by European agencies like Arbuthnot and Co., Binny and Co., Parry and Co., which were involved in the trade of indigo and coffee. Thus, the period, from 1857 till the early 1870s saw an influx of British capital into colonial India.[*]

The 1860s also saw an important proposal put forward to merge the three presidency banks. It would take many years before the proposal saw the light of the day.

While Calcutta continued to be the capital of British India, the cotton boom and development of other industries saw Bombay emerge as the commercial capital. By 1860, the export of goods from the Bombay port exceeded that of Calcutta. The cotton boom surely played a part in exports touching £ 40 million in 1865 as against less than £ 18 million for Calcutta. With the end of the American Civil War in 1865, fortunes reversed and Bombay suffered a great loss due to the sudden withdrawal of imports from England. But Bombay, with its characteristic resilience, bounced back quickly. The Gujaratis, Parsis and Bohras, apart from the Europeans, continued to be the dynamic business communities.[†]

It is often said that those who don't learn from history are doomed. Business booms lead to unbridled expansion, a phenomenon we see even

---

[*] Silent revolts were taking place across India, one of the notable ones being the non-violent Indigo Revolt of 1859. Indigo planters, seeing the huge commercial demand of blue dye in England, were forcing ryots to plant indigo. The farmers were indebted owing to the loans they took even as they were getting meagre returns for the crop. By the Charter Act of 1833 , the planters were given a free hand to deal with the farmers leading to the eventual revolt. Thousands of farmers were brutally killed and hanged publicly. The government was then forced to form the Indigo Commission in 1860. In the commission's report, E.W.L. Tower noted that 'not a chest of Indigo reached England without being stained with human blood'. The Indigo Act in 1862 provided some relief to the ryots. Some historians consider the Indigo revolt as the forerunner of the non-violent passive resistance later successfully adopted by Mahatma Gandhi.

[†] In 1854, the first cotton mill was opened in Bombay by a Parsi, K.G.N. Daber. Soon thereafter, in 1861, a mill was opened in Ahmedabad. The two cities would continue to dominate the textile industry for a long time. Jamsetji Tata bought a dilapidated oil mill in Chinchpokhli and started a cotton mill naming it Alexandra Mill. Proximity to a cotton-growing area, cheap land and plenty of water and fuel made him open a mill in Nagpur, the Empress Mill. While a Marwari financier in Bombay dismissed the idea and likened the investment to 'taking out earth and putting gold into the ground', Jamsetji soon proved them wrong.

today. Businesses extrapolate the current situation and go for massive expansion and when circumstances change later, they go bust.

While the Bank of Bengal had a much larger area under it compared to the Bank of Bombay, the latter was more aggressive in terms of branch expansion. While the Bank of Bengal had opened only 16 branches till 1867, the Bank of Bombay opened as many as 21 branches during the boom time. Soon thereafter though, the Bank of Bombay collapsed due to a combination of decline in cotton trade, corrupt directors of the bank and a negligent and complaisant Government of Bombay.

The story behind the collapse of the Bank of Bombay has in it an important character named Premchund Roychund. In the early 1860s, a dapper and devout Jain in his early thirties, Premchund was known for his astute financial acumen. Everyone trusted him and he was called the 'cotton king' of Bombay. His father, Deepchund, was his guide. An intelligent and refined individual, Premchund was quick to fathom the weak moral character of the directors of the bank and used it to his advantage.

Premchund would procure attractive allotment of shares of upcoming companies for the managers of the Bank of Bombay. Buying and selling shares on their behalf, he could influence their decisions. He could get away with anything, which is not surprising. Even in today's times, when there are much stricter laws and more stringent processes, similar instances can be found—the several banking scams that have come to light in recent times are a testimony to this fact. The Bank of Bombay in those times was not being carefully supervised, unlike the Bank of Bengal and the Bank of Madras. In the words of James Blair, the secretary and treasurer of the Bank of Bombay, 'it was so expensive to send inspectors through India, that I fancy it was not necessary unless something was really wrong— because everything was going on well'.[2] Blair's attitude was akin to a modern-day CEO not visiting branches or having any contact with them and depending solely on trust without as much as an audit or any control over the business!

With the cotton boom, Premchund Roychund found ready buyers for the shares of companies floated during that time. He would act as a broker and allot the shares to willing buyers. He quickly realised the imbecility and weak moral character of James Blair and others and soon acquired great influence over him and his subordinates with complete command of the funds of the bank. But in all speculative schemes where Indians were involved, the dominant partners were generally Europeans.

A little background of Premchund's speculative investment merits a mention here. Bombay's population as well as its trade and commerce had been expanding for the last few decades, rendering the available space in the islands grossly insufficient. Reclaiming land from the sea was the only solution to the growing problem of congestion. Using this premise, in 1864, Roychund, promoted the first land reclamation company in Mumbai, the Back Bay Reclamation Company. Soon, the government recognised his importance and governor Frere appointed him a director of the Bank of Bombay. The shares with a face value of ₹5,000 each were put on an auction and sold for ₹26,500 per share.

The money was deposited with the Asiatic Banking Corporation, who were appointed as bankers to the Back Bay Company. Asiatic Banking Corporation was founded by Roychund himself and he had total control over its management. The cotton boom had given surplus money, which traders used to buy Back Bay shares expecting great returns. Taking lead from here, a large number of joint-stock financial companies also joined the party—floating land reclamation companies and adding to the speculation. The civil war ended and the news reached Mumbai on 1 May 1865. Traders realised that Britain would go back to sourcing cotton from America. This created a panic in the market and investors rushed to sell off the shares of reclamation companies, only to find that there were no buyers. This news was the needle that burst this bubble.*

At one time, Premchund had accumulated debts of more than ₹42 lakhs. With the fall in cotton prices, Back Bay shares, which had been bought for ₹55,000, could not be sold even for their original price of ₹5,000. Bank of Bombay shares, whose price tag was ₹2,900, could not be sold even for ₹500 each. When Premchund was asked to pay, he produced the documents he had furnished as collateral. The land which was valued at ₹26 lakhs was eventually sold for ₹5 lakhs or so. The jewels, also given as security, were

---

* In 1865, there were 25 banks and seven land reclamation firms in Bombay. The bank and other firms together had a paid-up capital of ₹30 crores with total premium paid on them to the tune of ₹38 crores. One of the most famous ones was the Back Bay Reclamation Company whose shares, par value being ₹5,000, were quoted at ₹55.000 before everything crashed.

valued at ₹15 lakhs. Later, a few well-known jewellers and an auctioneer valued the same at around ₹5 lakhs. Such was Premchund's influence that this word had been taken when the bank had asked for collateral, without as much as a thorough check of the true valuation. It is not surprising in hindsight that the said assessment of Premchund's jewellery, when he first produced as security, was written on a piece of paper with pencil! But such was Premchund's reputation that it was said 'there was not a bank manager in the place who was not eager for his advice'.[3]

As with the boom, the bust too began thousands of miles away when the American Civil War abruptly came to an end, when General Robert E. Lee of the Confederacy of Southern States surrendered to General Ulysses S. Grant of the Union. The total loss in Bombay cotton market was around ₹3 crores. No one was spared. The poor, rich and elite—all had participated in forward trading and they were all left bankrupt.[*]

As is the case with 'expert committees' and 'commissions' which are created to investigate a financial dispute, in this case the Jackson Commission, headed by Sir Charles Jackson,[†] pinned the blame for the affairs related to the loans advanced by the bank on Premchund Roychund. Premchund emerged as the main villain, while the Commission considerably played down the role of many English officers and businessmen. One such business was Ritchie Scott, a senior partner in Ritchie Stuart & Co., which was one of the biggest firms in Bombay at that time. Scott played a major part in the financial disaster of the Bank of Bombay. In 1866, when Ritchie Scott & Co. failed in all but in name, its liabilities were over ₹91 lakhs with assets under ₹58 lakhs.

Failures don't seem to have taught the banking community a lesson, and we continue to see financial scams even today. One of the biggest failures in mid-1865 was of the firm B.H. Cama owned by Byramjee Hormusjee Cama, one of the biggest Parsi merchant houses. When the cotton prices fell suddenly, Cama, the largest shipper of cotton, was unable to meet the redrafts from banks against their consignments. When the firm failed, it owed more than £3 million and it was estimated that only 15 per cent of that

---

* Premchund too was left bankrupt but he rebuilt his empire and later participated in various philanthropic activities.

† Sir Charles Jackson was judge of the supreme court of judicature in Bombay.

would be recovered. Despite the lesson learnt from B.H. Cama, the Bank of
Bombay and its directors granted a large loan to Dossabhoy Merwanjee &
Co. on security of land at Parel with maturity of 12 months.

It was obvious that due to such long-term loans, the liquidity of the bank
was likely to decline significantly in a panic situation or in a tight money
market. But most of the mercantile directors wanted to prolong the speculative
boom as long as possible to protect their own and their friends' interests.

Human greed is universal. Share market and stock prices rose gradually
when it was discovered that the end of the Civil War had not produced the
kind of output and supply of cotton from America. Seeing the happy turn of
events, in August 1865, one director Cowasjee Manockjee asked his fellow
directors and the secretary of Bank of Bombay to sell all shares deposited as
collateral for overdue bills in order to pay off debts or at least get an amount
equivalent of it. The directors were personally involved in speculation and
hoped for better prices. They were also afraid that if the bank sold so many
shares, the prices would come down. Thus, none of the directors agreed.
They believed they were following a policy of forbearance and in the end,
failed to realise the value of a single share. The secretary, A.D. Robertson,
was left holding a large number of shares. He took this opportunity to sell
off some of them and attempted to close his account with Premuchund. If
only he had done for the bank as he did for himself, the bank would have
saved a lot of money!

In the spring of 1866, the great panic which destroyed so many banking
institutions in England, also ended the commercial prosperity of Bombay.[4]

The Emergence of the New Bank of Bombay

The cotton boom and bust sounded the death knell of the Bank of Bombay.
The total loss in the years 1864 to 1866 stood at more than ₹2.2 crores. As
most enquiry commissions end, the Jackson Commission set up to enquire
into the failure of the bank failed to indict Sir Henry Bartle Edward Frere,
the flamboyant governor of Bombay. His extravagance with public money
was well known. For example, in place of a perfectly serviceable government
house at Dapoorie, he built a new one—the Ganesh Khind Palace, for
an enormous sum of ₹17 lakhs. It was also clear that the government as a
shareholder in a joint-stock bank was a disaster.

In January 1867, the shareholders of the bank decided to reduce their capital by half to reflect the true value of the net assets of the bank. A proposal to form a single State Bank for the whole of India was made. The idea of a 'great Central Bank for all India' abolishing the distinctive names of several banks and merging all of them into a new charter and new name was suggested. Unfortunately, this was not to happen as both the Bank of Bengal and the Bank of Madras did not agree to the idea. This led to the formation of New Bank of Bombay, which had the support of many capitalists who had made enormous wealth in the cotton boom and had not been ruined by later developments. The New Bank of Bombay opened for business on 14 January 1868. The opening of the bank with its reported coverage in the newspapers hinted at the end of the discussions on the merger. The New Bank of Bombay objected to the appointment of an agent by the Bank of Bengal in its territory. Though permitted by charter, it had been an unwritten rule that the presidency banks would not interfere in each other's territories. The Bank of Bengal justified its appointment of agent on the pretext that the earlier agent, the Bank of Bombay, had been dissolved.

The first board of directors of the New Bank of Bombay formed in December 1867 included, in addition to four Europeans, three Indians as well: Kessowjee Naik, Dinshaw Manockjee Petty (Petit) and Ahmedbhoy Hubibbhoy. This was noteworthy, even though the number of shares owned by Indians (2,609) was a small proportion of the total shares (9,788). The Government of Bombay too participated in the shares, with an option to 'withdraw from its connections as a shareholder with the bank in the event of its being found desirable to the position of the state with respect to the Presidency Banks.'[5]

The opening of the Suez Canal in 1869, coupled with expansion of the railways and the introduction of the telegraph, would also see a transformation in Indian trade. Many banks like the Chartered Mercantile Bank of India, London and China, Chartered Bank of India, Australia and China, Comptoir d'Escompte de Paris, National Bank of India and Hongkong and Shanghai Banking Corporation were opened around this time.

The New Bank of Bombay meanwhile succeeded in becoming profitable in a short time. As mentioned earlier, many of the industrialists began investing in cotton mills. In 1870, Morarjee Goculdass started the Morarjee

Mills. Soon, in a span of less than three years, nearly 15 such mills were launched in Bombay.

The Government of India, under the British Raj, had started controlling the princely states. While the royals retained their royal duties, the government, through the resident posted at the durbar, controlled most of the administration. There had been many disputes between the presidency banks of Bombay and Calcutta with regard to the management of the treasury for the Nizam of Hyderabad, who at that time was considered one of the wealthiest men in the world.

In the case of Baroda, where the Gaekwads ruled the state, in 1875, the government stepped in to remove Malhar Rao Gaekwad on the charge of maladministration. They appointed Sir T. Madhava Rao, who was earlier the dewan of Travancore, as the new dewan of Baroda state. The most serious charge against Malhar Rao Gaekwad was of having attempted to poison Colonel Robert Phayre, the British resident of Baroda.* Other than that, he was charged of financial mismanagement. The New Bank of Bombay was involved in winding up the affairs of the deposed king and it had asked the Bombay Police to seize the valuables deposited with the agents of the Gaekwad, namely Parvatee Kant and Nurseedas Luckmedass.† A few decades later, Sayaji Rao, Malhar Rao's successor and an able administrator,

---

* The colonel had apparently noticed some sediment in his sherbet glass which were later alleged to be a mixture of arsenic and diamond dust. A committee was set up to enquire into the matter. There were three Indians in the committee—Maharaja Jayaji Rao Scindia of Gwalior, the Maharaja of Jaipur and Sir Dinkar Rao Rajwade, who was earlier member of the Legislative Council. Two of the three Indians considered Malhar Rao innocent. Sergeant William Ballentine successfully defended Malhar Rao. He was, at that time, paid an enormous sum of ₹1 lakh for his services. While the commission did not hold Gaekwad guilty, he was nevertheless deposed and sent to Madras where he lived till his death. A young boy, Sayaji Rao, was adopted by Maharani Jamnabai as the heir to Khande Rao who had preceded Malhar Rao. Sir T. Madhav Rao was formally made the dewan. In his stay at Travancore he had known Raja Ravi Varma and it was Dewan Madhav Rao who would introduce the young artist to Sayaji Rao. Raja Ravi Varma was paid a handsome sum of ₹50,000 for the 14 paintings he made for the Lakshmi Vilas Palace built by Sayaji Rao in 1890.

† The police recovered from them 73 bags containing various European and other coins weighing 1,44,734 tolas, 42 silver ingots, 43 bags of gold weighing 6,868 tolas, 269 gold ingots weighing 8,415 tolas and many such items totalling to nearly ₹1.2 lakhs!

laid the foundation of another great institution, the Bank of Baroda, which opened in 1908.

Meanwhile, the racial prejudices against Indians by the presidency banks, which we had talked about earlier, continued. In the case of the Bank of Madras, it was noted by the accountant-general that the agents employed by the bank should be familiar with the local language and he cautiously suggested having Indians employed occasionally as an experiment. He believed that the Indians, selected carefully from the upper classes of native society, might help to build the business with their local knowledge. The Madras government found that the New Bank of Bombay and Bank of Bengal had not employed any Indians as agents nor were they thinking of doing so. The government had no intention of being the first to appoint 'natives' as agents and felt that it would not be considered right by most of the shareholders to appoint native gentlemen, since 'however respectable, educated and intelligent they might be,' they would not have had any training in the business of the bank. Using Catch-22 as a logic, the idea was trashed![6]

By 1876, the three banks were covering most of the important trade centres in India. They had branches, agents and sub-agents. The Bank of Bengal had 18 branches while those of Bombay and Madras had 15 each. By 1861, the Bank of Bengal had a branch in Rangoon too.[*]

The passing of the Presidency Banks Act in 1876 was a major milestone in the history of the three banks.

A lot of correspondence had been going on between the officials of the Government of India, the governments of Bombay and Madras and the directors of the three banks. The authorities were convinced that the government should cease to hold shares in the three presidency banks and much of the correspondence, apart from discussions on other issues, was about how the shares of the government would be disposed of. The correspondence between the Bank of Bengal and the Government of India in 1872 revealed certain problems. The other two banks were also facing similar issues. First, if the government sold the shares in the market, it would almost certainly lead to a heavy fall in the prices of the shares,

---

[*] Later, as part of bank nationalisation, the operations of the Rangoon branch of the SBI were taken over by the Peoples' Bank of Burma in February 1963. Things came a full circle when, in October 2016, the SBI became the first domestic lender to open a branch in Myanmar in the capital city of Yangon (Rangoon's new name).

thereby causing huge capital losses to the private shareholders. This problem was most acute in the case of the Bank of Bengal because the government shareholding in that bank was the largest; however, it existed in the case of the other two banks as well. In 1872, the government shareholding in the Bank of Bengal, Madras and New Bank of Bombay was ₹22 lakhs, 5.62 lakhs and 6 lakhs respectively.

If the government did not sell the shares in the market but instead sold them to the banks, to be disposed of in an agreed fashion, the question that arose was: at what price should the government sell these shares? In November 1875, the government ultimately took a decision to dispose of the shares, which resulted in a fall of the price of the shares. The directors then asked the bank to buy back the shares. In the case of the Bank of Madras, the government eventually accepted the proposal for the bank to take over the shares at a 10 per cent premium. The Bank of Bombay floated tenders for disposing of the government shares.

The Presidency Banks Act of 1876 marked the virtual end of experimentation with the structure and functions of the three banks. They all came to be governed by very similar sets of rules; their custody of government balances was subjected to stringent limits; their advances became subject to rigid limits again (through the Act and the approved bylaws); the securities admissible and terms for which loans and discounts could be granted were also defined quite strictly. Foreign exchange banking was made out of bounds.

The structure of the banks with a head office and numerous branches also became a settled affair.

❈

The basic system of Indian currency remained unchanged throughout the period from 1861 to 1920: the currency in circulation consisted of government notes, silver coins and coins of smaller denominations. Gold coins became legal tender after the passage of the Indian Act XXII of 1899, making the sovereign and half-sovereign legal tender at 15 rupees to the pound. Gold coins, however, remained a rather insignificant proportion of the total circulation till the First World War broke out. Paper currency also remained a rather small, though an increasing, proportion of the total circulation. Paper currency took a long time to become popular and common due to a variety of reasons. One main reason was the fact that the smallest denomination of paper currency was a huge ₹10 when the average person on the street, be it a skilled or semi-skilled worker, earned less than half a rupee daily. An unskilled worker, in fact, earned only a few annas per day. It was thus impossible for the common man to have any use for paper currency. Another reason was that the paper currency was legal tender at its full value only within its own circle (a defined geographical territory) and could only be converted into silver coins outside the circle in which it was issued under special circumstances. Earlier there were three circles with headquarters at Calcutta, Bombay and Madras; by 1900, there were eight.

By 1876, Britain had perhaps the highest per capita income in the world, and its incomes from the empire and from its stock of foreign investments were increasing fast enough for its rulers not to worry about the future of its economy. India, of course, had already become a backward country, thanks to a century of Pax Britannica. The presidency banks were severely restricted and their main function, as far as the government was concerned, was to help the latter to raise loans from time to time and to provide a degree of stability to the prices of government securities.

Today, there is a lot of talk about the need for 'independent directors' in a bank or any firm. The presidency banks rarely carried out such practices in those times. Most directors of the Bank of Bengal were regularly selected from a few firms. It was an unwritten convention that if a partner of a particular firm resigned before his term expired, another partner of the same firm would get elected. Some complaints regarding a 'clique' controlling the directorate were raised but were not given much importance. The same firms could be represented through different partners year after year. For example, in the case of the Bank of Bengal, Jardine Skinner & Co., Kettlewell, Bullen & Co., Gillanders, Arbuthnot & Co. and Bird & Co. were represented almost every year for many decades. In case of the Bank of Madras, Parry's, Binny's and, until its collapse, Arbuthnot, were almost certain to have a seat.

The Bank of Bengal remained the most racist amongst the three presidency banks and also the biggest of the three. It was closest to the Government of India as until 1911 Calcutta remained the capital of British India. The Bank of Bombay differed from the other two in having significant Indian representation on its board of directors. It also operated in a far more competitive business environment than the other two banks.

Indian businessmen were the predominant players in many sectors of the business served by it. The main industry in the Bombay presidency was the cotton mill industry and barring the control of Greaves Cotton & Co., most of the other cotton mills were controlled by Indian industrialists.

Like the cotton mills in Bombay, Bengal saw the emergence of jute mills, the first one being set up in 1855 by George Auckland at Rishra. It was a mill on the banks of Hooghly.* The banking system did not provide any support for these enterprises to flourish. The Bank of Bengal did not directly lend to most customers in the hinterland who had to depend on the local moneylenders. It was the bank's policy to never lend a large amount to an Indian borrower except through an intermediary of Indian banker.† The industrial rejuvenation, which seemed like a possibility, remained largely unfulfilled. There was lack of capital, no technical education and no domestic protection for the products produced. Large capitalists were happy to put money in land or in money-lending rather than in enterprise.

The Swadeshi Impact

The year 1905 witnessed a landmark event—the partition of Bengal. Calcutta saw a lot of revolutionary activity and the political sentiment was that of swadeshi.‡ It was not a mere rejection of foreign goods. It also sought

---

* Along the banks, both north and south of the city, jute mills at one time stretched for nearly 20 miles. Within a few decades, Calcutta would see more than 17 jute mills which were making money hand over fist. Unlike the Bombay textile mills owned by Indians, mainly Parsis, such instances were few in Calcutta. One fine example of a company manufacturing Bengali dhotis was the Banga Lakshmi Cotton Mills. Many top politicians and local industrialists came forward to support the venture. A hosiery factory, a match factory and a cigarette factory too made their appearance but the stranglehold of jute, tea and coal remained high.

† It is a different story though that the bane of the jute industry was the advent of plastics, apart from labour unrest, much later in the 1960s. Today, it is a sad sight, with most of the abandoned mills in a state of decay looking like ghost factories. Some are occasionally used for film shoots, like the picturesque Agarpara Jute Mill was used by Mani Ratnam for his Aishwarya Rai–Abhishek Bachchan starrer *Raavan* in 2009.

‡ The disastrous partitioning of Bengal on religious grounds in 1905, which was later annulled, created a series of effects in India. The national outrage created by Lord Curzon's 'divide and rule policy' provided an impetus for the freedom movement. The rallying cry of those times was 'Vande Mataram'. It also created a platform for further division of the

to encourage local industries and indigenous commercial services such as banking and insurance. The movement led to the rise to many banks.

The formation of Central Bank* on 21 December 1911 was one such example. The establishment of the People's Bank of India in 1901 and Indian Specie Bank Ltd in 1906 with head offices in Lahore and Bombay respectively were largely the outcome of the swadeshi upsurge backed up by profits arising out of a boom in agricultural exports.

The idea of swadeshi can also seen in the formation of the Punjab National Bank (PNB), which was established in 19 May 1894 in Lahore. Some of its prominent founders were Sardar Dayal Singh Majithia, Lala Harkishen Lal, Lala Lal Chand and Lala Dholan Das. It was their conviction that if India had to grow and progress when independence came, it should have its own institutions, more so, its own financial institutions.[†]

The idea was first mooted by Rai Mool Raj of Arya Samaj who, as reported by Lala Lajpat Rai, had long cherished the idea that Indians should have a national bank of their own. He felt keenly 'the fact that the Indian capital was being used to run English banks and companies, the profits accruing from which went entirely to the Britishers whilst Indians had to contend themselves with a small interest on their own capital'.[7]

Going even further back, the *Thacker's Indian Directory* of 1876 mentions Bengal Banking Corporation Ltd with a share capital of ₹2 crores and run largely by Bengalis. Referring to the bank, *The Statesman* of 18 February 1880 carried an article which said, '... the absence of banking in India has often been lamented. The country possesses no agencies for gathering together the sums, small individually but very great in the aggregate, which make up its unemployed wealth, and poor as the masses of the people

---

subcontinent on religious grounds, a thought which had been brought to the fore thanks to the division of Bengal.

* It was established by Sir Sorabji Pochkhanawala with Sir Pherozeshah Mehta as chairman and claims to have been the first commercial Indian bank completely owned and managed by Indians.

† Lala Lajpat Rai was actively involved in its administration and was the first to open an account in its first office opposite Arya Samaj Mandir in Anarkali in Lahore. His younger brother worked as a manager in the bank. Later, Lala Yodh Raj took over the command of the bank in 1943. It was his foresight that he shifted the head office from Lahore to Underhill Road in Delhi in June 1947 just before the Partition took place. It saved the bank as the funds were transferred to India.

are, no one can doubt but that the aggregate of the small hoards that are lying everywhere, unused and unfructifying, is immense. Everyone who has thought much on the condition of the people must sometimes have wished that a system of banking could established all over the country, so that the people might be taught to deposit their little savings at a small interest, that those savings, thus accumulated, might be employed in industry or trade, and that, on the other hand, the people might, when they had to borrow, be able to obtain money on equitable terms ...'

It would take more than half a century after the partition of Bengal for the SBI to emerge, in 1955, with its focus on small deposits, rural banking and lending to small and medium enterprise, including agriculture.

3

THE TURN OF THE TWENTIETH CENTURY

The Swadeshi movement in Bengal also resulted in the opening of the Bengal National Bank Ltd on 13 April 1907 with an authorised capital of ₹50 lakhs. It had on its board of directors Maharaja Rameswar Singh of Darbhanga, Maharaja Surya Kanta Acharya Chaudhari of Muktagachha (now in Mymensingh district of Bangladesh), Raja Sreenath Roy of Bhagyakul (near Dhaka, Bangladesh) and Prasad Das Boral, one of the seven founders of the Calcutta Stock Exchange which was incorporated in 1908. But the bank could not continue for long and went into liquidation on 31 May 1928. The Cooperative Hindusthan Bank Ltd., listed for the first time in the *Thacker's Indian Directory* in 1911, was set up in Calcutta with an authorised capital of ₹2 crore with Maharaja Manindra Chandra Nundy of Kassimbazar and B.K. Roychowdhury, zamindar of Gauripur (Mymensingh district of Bangladesh), as its main patron. The bank continued to operate till the mid-1930s.*

---

* Many of the swadeshi banks had been created and operated by men utterly ignorant of the most elementary principles of banking, finance and economics. Deposits gathered at unwieldy rates of interest made it impossible for money to be employed lucratively except in the most hazardous enterprises. One of the leading newspapers had warned that that if a bank allows a high rate of interest on its deposits, it can only make a profit by lending its money at an even higher rate to the public. It made common sense that people who had a good business would not pay a high rate for loans and hence the bank would land up funding businesses which were not sound to begin with. By 1913, the number of banking and loan companies registered under Indian Companies Act had risen to 451 and deposits had doubled from ₹12 crore to ₹25 crores between the years 1906 and 1911. Deposits had, in fact, increased 950 per cent in the 21 years between 1890 and 1911 and the dangers that

We had seen earlier the development and collapse of collaboration in business between European (mostly British) merchants and their Bengali business partners in the first half of the nineteenth century. While most had floundered by the middle of the century, the Bengali businessmen shifted their focus to investing in land. In contrast, the Indian businessmen, especially Parsis, had flourished in Bombay in various businesses including textiles. In Bengal, wee, therefore, see the rise of many such zamindari families like the Malliks, the Deys, the Dattas and the Tagores of North Calcutta who had large land holdings. The new breed of traders in Calcutta were mainly people from the Jodhpur-Marwar region, called Marwaris. They operated from Burra Bazar, which continues to be a trading centre even today. Most of the business houses from Calcutta were also owned by Marwaris, the largest being the Birlas. Thus, while the regions of Bombay and Ahmedabad saw Gujaratis and Parsis investing in enterprise, the large industries in Calcutta were mostly based on capital amassed by Europeans in India. By the second half of the nineteenth century, the Bengali businessman had been relegated to a position of insignificance and confined to 'barren clerkdom, petty speculation, short opportunism, peddling and merchandising'.[1] There were exceptions to this though. For instance, we see the involvement of the Tagore family in many areas.* Moreover, India's first pharmaceutical company, the Bengal Chemical and Pharmaceutical Works Limited, was set up by Prafulla Chandra Ray in 1901.† However, the business enterprises of the British in India had by then entered a period of 'maturity, prosperity and authority' and with it emerged a new racial caste in business.[2] British and European merchants controlled the shipping and insurance business, tea plantations, coal and other mines.

---

the public was exposed to were increasingly becoming clearer. Inadequate reserves against deposits, a precariously low percentage of cash to liabilities and an imposing capital with little of it paid up—this was a prescription for disaster. As expected, in around 1913, a total of 57 banks failed. The Anglo-Gujarati Bombay daily, *Jam-E-Jamshed,* on 8 October 1913 ascribed the collapse of the Credit Bank and others to 'the cliques which are running the banks making them the tools of their own gambling adventures'.

* Surendranath Tagore, son of Satyendranath Tagore (the elder brother of Rabindranath Tagore and the first Indian to join the Civil Service), was the secretary of Hindusthan Cooperative Insurance. Rabindranath Tagore was a founder in one of the companies.

† Even today, many people are fans of Bengal Chemical's Cantharidine hair oil and Lamp brand phenol.

The Swadeshi movement led to some positive changes in terms of the Indian enterprise. National Insurance Company was formed in 1906 and several other insurance companies were floated around that time in Calcutta, both in the categories of life and general insurance. National Insurance Company was followed by Eastern Life Insurance, the India Equitable Life Insurance and the Hindusthan Cooperative Insurance Society Ltd. Many of them survived the test of time. They were eventually absorbed when the nationalisation of life insurance business took place in 1956. The Life Insurance Corporation (LIC) was formed by merging 256 life insurance companies. Another example of the Indian enterprise are the Tatas, who too were part of the Swadeshi movement. They started the Tata Industrial Bank on 4 April 1918, which was later merged with the Central Bank of India in 1923.

A lot of laws passed during 1876–1920 had an impact on the banking industry. In 1881, the Negotiable Instruments Act relating to banking practices was passed. Under the Act, 'A "negotiable instrument" meant a promissory note, bill of exchange or cheque payable either to order or to bearer. When a promissory note, bill of exchange or cheque is transferred to any person, so as to constitute that person the holder thereof, the instrument is said to be negotiated.' Under the Negotiable Instruments Act, banking practices were covered and local governments were authorised to fix banking holidays. The Bankers' Books Evidence Act, 1891 was an important law about what could be tendered acceptable legal evidence in disputes. A significant change was the removal of stamp duty on cheques which gave an impetus to their use.

How the Bank of Madras Fared

Amongst the three presidency banks, the Bank of Madras remained the poorest. This was due to a combination of factors: repeated famines, the decline in exports of cloth and depopulation in many districts because of the famines. But with the spread of the railway and road networks, trade grew in the late nineteenth century. Cotton, oilseeds, grain, spices, tobacco, tea and coffee were some of the agricultural items traded. The leather industry improved while sugar and rice mills too proliferated. The Godavari, Guntur and Krishna districts were rice-growing areas and saw the emergence of rice mills. The plantation industry, which included coffee, tea, cardamom, pepper and rubber on the west coast and over the Ghats, were industries organised along scientific lines. The leather industry in Tamil Nadu has a long history going back to the middle of the nineteenth century. While India was a traditional producer of leather, export trade in raw hides and skins and leather began in the 1830s. It began to be recognised that India, with the largest cattle population in the world, could become a potential supplier to the world market. Initially, India exported only raw and cured hides and skins, but by 1850, it began exporting tanned hides and skins as well. This was due to a significant technical improvement introduced in the Madras Presidency. Usage of myrobulan extracts on avaram-bark-treated leather produced quality which was accepted internationally.

There was also the growth of Nidhis, which evolved from the centuries-old tradition of chit funds. Nidhis and chit funds were unique to the Madras Presidency.[*]

While many Nidhis proliferated, helping small businesses, they were not a competition to the Bank of Madras in the real sense. They financed

---

[*] Chit funds have existed in India from time immemorial. Often, they serve as microfinance organisations where people used the money for marriages and other such activities. A chit fund is both a savings and a credit product. Some people claim that chit funds or its equivalent existed in ancient times in China and developed into what is popularly known today as the Chinese lottery. There is also evidence to suggest that in earlier days, farmers took part in 'grain funds' (Dhanya Chittu), where grains were used instead of cash. Nidhis acted as local non-banking finance companies, giving small loans. The scene in lending was dominated by two groups, the Nattuukottai Chetties and the Kallidaikurichi Brahmins. The Chetties controlled lending and traded in timber, diamonds and pearls, among other things. They also funded the opium trade with Malaysia. Many of the Chettiars, as they were known, went on to become top bankers. The first finance minister of independent India was one R. Shanmukham Chetty. In 1937, M. Ct. M. Chidambaram Chettyar established the Indian Overseas Bank to encourage overseas banking and foreign exchange operations, primarily to serve the trade of Nattukottai Chettiars.

Kallidaikurichi or Kalladaikurichi is a small town in Tirunelveli district of Tamil Nadu and is home to Brahmin families who were involved in banking. Today we find many names like Easwaran Iyer of Easun Group, S.N.N. Sankaralinga Iyer of India Cements and Sanmar group, K.R. Sundaram Iyer of Royal Enfield and K.S. Vaidyanathan of Paterson & Co., all hailing from this small village. S. Anantharamakrishna of the Simpson Group and T.V. Sundaram Iyengar of the TVS group also belong to villages very close to Kalladaikurichi.

The other lending classes were the Labbai Muslims and the Nadars in Tamil Nadu and the Mapillas on the west coast.

businessmen and professionals and some agriculturists and thier focus area was localised to the region in and around Coimbatore and places where banking facilities were not present. Nidhis did not discount bills but were definitely competition to local zamindars and money lenders.

Local entrepreneurship would blossom much later. There was no opportunity to raise capital. The Madras Stock Exchange was founded in 1920 and Madras did not see big ventures like in Bombay and Bengal. The most significant development from the point of view of local joint-stock banking was the founding of the Indian Bank in 1907 with the financial help of S.M.A.R. Chettiar and S. Rm. M. Ramaswami Chettiar (Dewan Bahadur Satappa Ramanatha Muttaiya Ramaswami Chettiar). This was in response to the Arbuthnot crash in 1906 wherein Patrick Macfadyen, one of the partners, engaged in speculation, in the process losing huge amounts of the firm's money, apparently to the tune of £ 400,000. Macfayden committed suicide and the depositors approached an eminent lawyer, V. Krishnaswamy Iyer, who managed to get compensation for them from Arbuthnot Bank. Iyer was one of the founder-directors of Indian Bank.

Some of the noteworthy banks set up in this period were Nedungadi Bank in 1899, South Indian Bank in 1903 and Canara Banking Corporation of Udupi in 1906. Nedungadi Bank was set up by Rao Bahadur T.M. (Thalakodi Madathil) Appu Nedungadi.* People in Kerala were paying high rates of interest to the local moneylender, as was the case across India. This prompted a group of 44 enterprising men from Thrissur who contributed ₹500 each to the initial paid-up capital of ₹22,000 to form South Indian Bank. The idea was to take the common man out of the clutches of the local moneylender.

⚛

The presidency banks were not set up, with their typical British hauteur, to help the common man. The minimum initial deposit of ₹500 for opening a current account was rarely, if ever, waived off. The banks paid no interest on the amount deposited, a rule which other banks used well to their advantage,

---

* He is also famous as the first Malayalam novelist. He wrote the first Malayalam novel, *Kundalatha*. (After a scam, which nearly wiped out the bank in early 2000, Nedungadi Bank was merged with PNB.)

attracting deposits on which they paid interest. The business in the western and northern parts of India was dominated by Europeans and Bank of Bengal and other banks were primarily used for financing the operations of the European managing agency houses. Financing Indian trade and business was not a priority.

At times, Indian laws were not very helpful. For instance, the presidency banks, with their inadequate knowledge of the laws, were unable to collect money from their borrowers as the local laws did not allow legal means to be used. Then there was the Dayabhaga law, which did not give the sons any right to their father's ancestral property until after the father's death. This law was one of the main factors for the ruin of the Bengali businessmen in many crises of the 1830s. Under the Dayabhagha law, the male head could absolutely dispose of his property, and in such a case a debtor could not escape liability by pleading, for instance, that being the son or the grandson, he had a share in the ancestral property. European principals decamped or went scot free, while their Indian partners had to pay off the debts and lose everything in the process. Potential European insolvents operating in the presidency towns of Calcutta, Bombay and Madras had been granted almost complete immunity from the cruel provisions of the usual British laws relating to bankruptcy by the Relief of the Insolvent Debtors in the East Indies Act passed on 19 July 1828. It would almost appear that the Act was passed in anticipation of many European businessmen going bankrupt in the near future. While in theory this law applied equally to both British citizens and Indian subjects of the Crown, several provisions definitely discriminated against Indians as debtors or creditors—for instance, the *London Gazette* containing notice of the insolvency of the debtor involved was sufficient proof of insolvency; on the other hand, any Indian creditor, apart from the petitioning creditor, was barred from the choice of assignee. Some Europeans simply went away to Britain or China, thereby evading their creditors.

The Bank of Bengal needed to know the business of the Indians in order to make a profit by financing it. But the officers of the bank did not know the local language and their social arrogance and carefully cultivated social distance made them unfit to gather local intelligence. They thus needed the khazanchees who were engaged in business and would absorb any losses which the bank made through financing of Indian business. But after a series of conflicts over the duties and responsibilities of the Indian khazanchee in its Calcutta office, the bank decided to bring the whole cash department under European supervision assisted by an Indian. After 1881, there was no Indian khazanchee, as by then the Bengali business in Calcutta had reduced significantly. The Marwaris were becoming prominent but they had a long way to go. At the branches, however, the bank continued to employ the services of Indian khazanchees. The khanzancheeship was acquired by politicking among the Indian mercantile community.[*] At one time, the khazancheeship of the Cawnpore branch was offered to one Lala Joogelall of the Baijnath Ramnath firm. However, Joogelall wanted a salary of ₹500 per month whereas the average salary of the Khazanchees in the North West Provinces (roughly today's Uttar Pradesh) was only ₹225 and 5 annas. Incidentally, Joogelall was the founder of the Joogelall Kamlapat (JK) business house.[†]

The Bank of Bengal operated in a huge territory which was nearly half the area of the British empire of India and Burma and stretched from Moulmein (now called Mawlamyine) in present-day Myanmar to Lahore in the west and included Hyderabad and Nagpur. There were branches of the presidency banks in many towns now and they represented the prestige the banks carried.

The bank buildings of the presidency banks were deliberately planned edifices meant to transmit messages of opulence and grandeur—they were in a way celebration of the commercial spirit of the empire. A little deviation to talk of them deserves merit.

The presidency banks opened various branches post 1861. The branch offices that proliferated all over India did not, as a rule, plan their buildings, but acquired already existing constructions by hire or purchase. These

---

[*] One Lala Sheopersad held the khazancheeship of both Lucknow and Cawnpore branches of the Bank of Bengal and as per reports he was worth ₹3 lakhs in 1879, owned seven bungalows in Cawnpore and his father had bought a house which cost ₹1 lakh. His rental income was nearly ₹1,000 per month. He was later given the title of Rai Bahadur. His son was made the khazanchee when he retired. Later, his son was 'demoted'—he was given the title Rai Saheb as against the title of Rai Bahadur that his father had received.

[†] Lala Kamlapat Singhania, son of Joogelall, would go on to form the JK group business conglomerate. The first major business set up by him was Juggilal Kamlapat Cotton Spinning & Weaving Mills in 1921.

constructions deserve a closer look as illustrations of the tremendous cultural and climatic variations in the newly founded empire rather than as a significant architectural achievement in their own right. What is most fascinating about them is the richness of local styles that characterised many of these structures.

The branch at Cawnpore (Kanpur), for example, came into importance as the town became the military headquarters of the British troops. After the quelling of the First War of Independence in 1857, Cawnpore remained an important cantonment of British India. In northern India, it was an important commercial centre with the East Indian Railway, the Oudh and Rohilkhand Railway and the Indian Midland Railway systems converging there. Cotton mills and tanneries were the important businesses of Cawnpore. The branches at Allahabad, Lucknow, Benares and Agra too contributed to the business of the Cawnpore branch. Lucknow was the capital of Awadh but when the last Nawab was exiled to Calcutta, the artisanal industries faced a decline and Lucknow, once a proud capital of a semi-independent kingdom, was reduced to the mere headquarters of a division.

The Lucknow branch of the Imperial Bank of India

With its Doric-style six-column front surmounted by a bare pediment, the building of the Lucknow branch is a fine example of neoclassical style. The palatial building was built as an observatory on the initiative of Nawab Nasir-ud-din Haidar of Oudh and was popularly known as Tara Wali Kothi. During the First War of Independence, it was here that the Indian soldiers took refuge. The building, initially taken on rent by the bank in 1863, was eventually purchased in 1889 for ₹45,000.

The new building at Shimla was constructed in 1911 and expanded later. It is an English half-timber mock-Tudor affair redolent of the Raj ambience. It was earlier known as the Dalzell House estate. Being bankers to the Government of India in the largest presidency of British India, the directors wanted to remain in close touch with the Viceroy and his key officials, who had begun to spend the better part of the year in Shimla. The branch at Banaras with heavily rusticated porte-cochere, verandahs on all sides propped up by round arches and the usual wooden venetians, the balustrade on top with urns set at intervals, is a typical rich man's house of nineteenth-century India in the Anglo-Indian style. A statue set in the corner in a niche with rusticated pilasters on both sides is a stamp of this stylistic conception.

The Shimla Branch of the Imperial Bank of India

Each province put its stamp on the bank buildings. For example, the bank's branch in Calicut is characterised by its wide and airy verandah, thin columns which support rather than impress, and the porte-cochere with its terrace on top. The tiled roof with prominent bracket supports for the window shades in the building in Cochin has a characteristically local style. The same is the case with the branch at Madurai which has a local style with the verandah being a prominent feature. A hallmark is provided by the copy in stone of the pitcher-and-coconut motif on two sides of the arched entrance.

In Coimbatore, the one-storeyed building has rusticated walls and flat roof and thin square columns with the distinctive touch of a bungalow. The Dhaka branch is a typical example of dak-bungalow architecture—designed by the engineers of the public works department with no imagination to speak of! The same is the case with the Agra branch.

In Jalpaiguri, we find the influence of the tea-garden architecture complete with fixed wooden venetians on the upper part of the first-floor verandah and the gabled corrugated iron-sheet roof. The Moulmein branch in Burma had a sloping roof with corrugated iron sheet and a round arch on the ground floor in the modified Palladian style. Large windows on top floor complete the architecture. In places where the incidence of monsoon was high, like Rangoon, we find tall arches covered with wooden venetians.

The Rangoon Branch of the Imperial Bank of India

After Cawnpore, Banaras was the second largest city of the North West Provinces (later United Provinces and now mainly Uttar Pradesh) and a centre of pilgrimage, artisanal industry and Indian banking for a long time. Unlike Banaras, Patna, once a proud capital of a Mughal Suba, had long ceased to be an important banking centre though Jagat Seth and many such bankers had earlier set up kothis there to facilitate remittance operations between Dhaka, Murshidabad and Delhi.

By the last decade of the nineteenth century, Delhi was the richest town in the Punjab[3] and soon became the commercial capital for entire

The Chandni Chowk branch of the Imperial Bank of India

northern India. The branch at Delhi deserves a special mention. Enriched with hexastyle Corinthian columns, balustrade terrace, arched doorways, spiral iron staircase, old English lifts, and tinted glass windows, the building epitomises European architectural elegance. Eighty feet tall, and built in 1806, it is the oldest building of the bank in India and one of the largest in the country. The branch began operations in late 1866. It was originally owned by an Englishman, Dyke Sombre, and some of his associates. It is a four-storey building and was witness to a carnage during the 1857 massacre which took place in Delhi. The branch was called Samru Palace, a building named after its owner Begum Farzana Joanna Samru. Begum Samru was a Muslim woman of Sardhana who was of Arab descent. It is a heritage building today and houses a mini-museum of sorts. The manager George Berresford Esq. and his family consisting of his wife and their five daughters were killed by the freedom fighters in 1857. They are buried in the nearby St. James Church. The bank branch building was declared a heritage building in 2002.*

An important event would soon change the fate of Delhi forever. In a letter to the Earl of Crewe, secretary of state for India, sent from Shimla to London on 25 August 1911, Hardinge pointed out that it has 'long been recognised to be a serious anomaly' that the British governed India from Calcutta, which was on the eastern extreme part of the subcontinent. There was another reason for this observation—Calcutta was becoming hostile to Britishers and the calls for self-rule were increasing. King George V, the first British monarch to visit India, announced the reunification of Bengal and the move to Delhi in 1911. It would take another two decades for the architects Edwin Lutyens and Herbert Baker to construct the 'Lutyens Delhi' as we know it today.†

---

* The impressive buildings of the SBI, some a century (or more) old, continue to impress to this date. The author is lucky to have attended music concerts at Hopeville, part of the 12-acre property on St. Marks and Residency Roads, on the invitation of the CGM of Bangalore circle a few years ago. Modelled on the Greek Revival style, Hopeville had a spacious terraced porte-cochere and a balustered balcony that was semi-circular at the centre with twin Ionic columns. It was originally owned by Charles James Green, a retired Major General of the Madras Army.

† The third Imperial Durbar was held in Delhi in 1911. It had been held for the first time in 1877 to proclaim Queen Victoria as the Empress of India but it was largely an official event. The second Durbar was held in 1903. The two full weeks of festivities were organised

The Bank of Bombay Marches Ahead

The Bank of Bombay (and the Bank of Madras too) started opening branches around 1907. The Indore branch, closed for some time, was reopened. The Bank of Bombay also opened new branches in Hyderabad (Sind) and Sholapur to take over the treasury business there. The fortunes of the majority branches of the Bank of Bombay, unlike branches of the other banks, were determined by the ebb and flow of one product—cotton. They were also affected by changes in railway routes and trade routes. In all the three banks, there was one branch which outperformed all other branches. In case of Bank of Bengal, it was the Rangoon branch. For the Bank of Bombay, it was Karachi with the Ahmedabad branch coming a close second. For the Bank of Madras, it was the Colombo branch.

The Bank of Bombay was the first presidency bank to make a start in Indianising its officer cadre. There was a lot of pressure from Indian shareholders to do so. The first Indian auditor to audit the books of the New Bank of Bombay was Raghoonath Narayen in 1869, who was succeeded by a series of Parsi auditors.

Until 1899, the president of the board of directors for Bank of Bombay was always a European, till Ahmedbhoy Hubibbhoy, one of the founding directors—and the longest serving director of any presidency bank—became the first Indian president of the Bank of Bombay. Among the presidency

---

in meticulous detail by Lord Curzon, Viceroy of India. It was a dazzling display of pomp, power and split-second timing. Neither the earlier Delhi Durbar of 1877, nor the later one, could match the pageantry of Lord Curzon's 1903 festivities. The Durbar of 1911 was attended by practically every ruling prince and nobleman in India, along with thousands of landed gentry and other persons of note, to pay obeisance to their sovereigns.

An interesting controversy ensued when Maharaja Sayajirao III Gaekwad of Baroda approached the royal couple without his jewellery on, and after a simple bow turned his back to them when leaving. His action was interpreted at the time as a sign of dissent to British rule. The sentiment shown by the Maharaja was a representation of what was simmering across the nation. In a conspiracy hatched by Rash Behari Bose, a homemade bomb was thrown into the Viceroy's howdah on 23 December 1912, as a ceremonial procession moved through the Chandni Chowk. Although injured in the attack, the Viceroy escaped with flesh wounds. Basant Biswas, a young boy of 16 years, had dressed up as a woman and thrown the bomb. After the blast, Bose went back to his government job at the Forest Research Institute and even organised an honorary reception for Hardinge a few months later! When fingers began pointing at him, Rash Behari Bose escaped capture and later fled to Japan in 1915.

banks, the Bank of Bombay was an exception with Indian directors. In 1876, when the New Bank of Bombay was transformed into the presidency Bank of Bombay, there were seven directors, of whom three were Europeans. The other directors were: E.D. Sassoon, a Baghdadi Jew; Kessowjee Naik, a Dasa Oswal Jain from Kathiawar; Dinshaw Maneckjee Petit, a Parsi, and Ahmedbhoy Hubbibhoy, a Khoja. Quite surprisingly, Maharashtrians—Hindus or Muslims—produced very few big businessmen, except for Jagannath Shankarseth and his son. Ahmedbhoy Hubibbhoy continued as director from December 1867 until his death in 1914. He was succeeded by Fazulbhoy Currimbhoy, another Khoja, the son of Sir Currimbhoy Ebrahim, and possibly the first Muslim Baronet in India created by the British Government.* Kessowji Naik, one of the founder-directors of the bank and who had been continuously on its board, resigned in late 1878 when Nursey Kessowjee & Co. collapsed.† He was succeeded in 1879 by Vurjeevandass Madhowdass, a Gujarati Hindu. Upon his retirement in 1896, Vurjeevandass Madhowdass was succeeded by his son, Tribhovundas Vurjeevanas, who continued till the end of 1920. D.M. Petit, one of the original seven directors since 1876, retired in 1893 and his place was taken successively by his two sons, Framjee Dinshaw Petit (1893–1895) and Bomanjee Dinshaw Petit (1896–1914). When Bomanjee retired, he was succeeded by Sir Jamsetjee Jejeebhoy (1914–1920), who in turn was succeeded by N.B. Saklatvala (in the first half of 1920) from Tata Sons.‡ The Sassoon family too continued to hold the post of a director. Unlike the Indians, the European succession was not on family lines, as their families were not settled in India. The directors were generally from the top managing agency houses like Charles Forbes & Co., Greaves Cotton & Co., Killick Nixon & Co. and so on.

---

* Incidentally, an orphanage started by him in 1895 on Altamount Road, Mumbai was sold to Mukesh Ambani and it is the spot where his family residence Antilla, a 28-storeyed building, stands now.

† Kessowji Naik, a Dasa Oswal Bania by caste, floated the Royal Mill, a composite spinning and weaving mill, and was, therefore, one of the pioneers of the cotton mill industry. He possessed properties in the Kutch region which Gellabhoy Hurridass, the bank's cash keeper, was sent out to scout when Kessowji started defaulting on loans.

‡ Saklatvala was one of the few people outside the Tata family to head the Tata empire.

Today, we see a lot of shareholder activism in running organisations, where the shareholders have a voice and legal rights. They appoint the directors, can remove CEOs and have voting powers. But this was not the case during in the presidency banks.

The Presidency Banks Act of 1876 and its latter amendments gave enormous powers to the board of directors of the banks as against the shareholders. Once a board was in place, the directors could more or less choose their successors. The power of the shareholders was never brought to test except in the case of the Bank of Madras on the eve of the First World War, when the Indian shareholders put forward the name of an Indian as a director who lost against the official candidate.

All directors were men, without fail. If it were to so happen that the shareholders put a person on the board against the wishes of the incumbent directors, he would have to acquire the necessary shares. This would prove very difficult as the shares were traded within a narrow circle, especially in Madras and Calcutta. An ordinary shareholder, under the Act, had no right to demand information about a number of vital matters without which they could not intelligently or collectively intervene in the decision-making processes of the bank. There was no concept of an Annual General Body meeting of the shareholders at that time! The shareholders had no right in the appointments made by the bank. The AGMs thus were formal affairs, with only the directors, secretary and one or two shareholders in attendance. Quite obviously, all decisions made by the management were passed!

It was different when it came to running of the Bank of Bombay. For example, a special general meeting of the shareholders on 5 December 1877 was attended by six directors and 21 other shareholders. The meetings were quite contentious at times and there would be disputes over choice of auditors, issues of discriminatory treatment of Indian and European employees, the policy of the bank in lending to near-bankrupt firms like Nursey Kessowjee & Co. and other such matters.

Despite such open discussions in the Bank of Bombay meetings, the European officers continued to enjoy their special privileges. In 1915, for example, when Sir James Begbie retired as secretary and treasurer of the Bank of Bombay after serving for three decades, he was given a gratuity of ₹1.25 lakhs and a pension of ₹12,000 per month, which was significantly over and above the sum he was entitled to. This was simply because the directors thought he 'fully deserved it'.[4] There were similar instances earlier too when English officers were arbitrarily given benefits on the whim of the board.[*]

Bonuses had been paid before but was not an annual feature. In 1909, the Bank of Bengal paid a special centenary bonus constituting one month's pay to its staff, European and Indian. Similarly, in 1911, the bank paid a special bonus of half a month's pay to all Indian employees drawing ₹50 and under a month, on the occasion of the visit to India of George V.

We see exceptions in the favourable treatment of a few Indians. For example, in 1917, the retiring chief cashier of Bank of Madras, Parthasarathy Aiyangar, was conferred the title of Dewan Bahadur. The title, which while emphasising the Indianness of the conferee elevated him above other British Indian subjects of the King Emperor, must have taken place on the recommendations of the directors and the secretary, W.B. Hunter, who had been knighted the same year. This was not the only instance of Aiyangar receiving special treatment. In September 1907, the bank had given him an increment of ₹50 per month and he was granted another special increment of ₹100 per month in the following year. When he retired, he was given a bonus of ₹15,000 and his pension was increased to ₹500 per month, which was more than what he was eligible for as per the rules. He was also presented with a piece of plate with a 'suitable inscription' on his retirement.

In contrast, the lowest paid employees of the bank, two peons, C. Ramunni Nair and Rarappen Nair, who had resigned probably due to old age, were treated strictly in accordance with their lower status and granted

---

[*] In the same random manner, the bank would sometimes show largesse, as it did during the famine in May 1877, when a monthly batta of ₹1 was paid to two peons drawing ₹8 and ₹12 each in Dharwar as the grain prices had gone up. Subsequently, when the prices of grain fell, the batta was removed. In 1899, the bank directors granted an application from sepoys and hamals for an allowance on account of the rise in price of food grains owing to the famine; an allowance of ₹2 per month was given to each of them. The peons of the bank applied for an allowance to enable them to erect temporary dwellings away from the plague-affected districts and to meet expenses for travel from their huts to the bank and back. Not all applications for compensation on account of famine or plague were allowed. Some sort of dearness allowance system was followed for a temporary period. While European and British officers got bonuses and regular salary increases, the abundance of labour also tempted the bank to hire apprentice clerks who were paid no salary whatsoever. This was a practice being followed by other European firms as well.

gratuities of 12 months' pay amounting to ₹105 and ₹99 respectively. In contrast, Parathasarathy Aiyangar's loyalty and services were rated highly enough by the directors to nominate him as a prospective director of the new-born Imperial Bank of India. The extreme inequality in the salaries and service conditions which existed between Indians and European officers was carefully preserved! European officers, posted to India in 1906, received a monthly salary of ₹300 and were provided accommodation at the Bank House. If posted outside Madras, they got free accommodation or a housing allowance ranging from ₹50 to ₹250 in case of senior officers. Their salary too changed rapidly as they were promoted.

The First World War and Thereafter

The First World War and the famines saw a lot of banks folding up. By 1919, the decision to amalgamate the three presidency banks into one imperial bank was gaining ground. It had been an idea which had been around for more than five decades.

On 23 September 1919, Rao Bahadur Sir Bayya Narasimheswara Sarma moved a resolution in the Indian Legislative Council for the establishment of a State Bank of India. Sarma felt that the bank should be largely, if not wholly, controlled with regard to its general policy by the state for the improvement of Indian banking system which was 'woefully behind' the enormous progress achieved in other countries. He stressed the need for diverting unused treasury balances into general banking system to help trade prosper. Maharaja Sir Manindra Chandra Nundy supported the move and suggested that the functions performed by the government, such as note issue, holding of treasury balances and managing cash balances and portions of reserves, and regulating foreign exchange, should be handled by a State Bank as it would do it more efficiently. Sir Fazulbhoy Currimbhoy, who was the vice-president of the Bank of Bombay and who was anxious to see the implementation of the amalgamation, stressed the need for developing banking facilities in India which, with 165 towns having bank offices, was far behind the USA and Canada which had 9,138 and 4,000 branches respectively. He believed that a lot of money lying dormant in the country could be used for the purpose of trade. Madan Mohan Malviya, Sardar Vallabhai Patel and Sir Dinshaw Wacha spoke in favour of a bank that was truly a State Bank having all the support and resources of the government—one that would help industries and banking facilities across the country to grow.

Madan Mohan Malviya submitted before the Legislative Council the need for a Central State Bank. He explained: 'I submit that in a country like India with all its enormous sums which are available to the Government it is a pity that there should not be one Central State Bank which should serve as a reservoir in which all surplus revenue of the country should be gathered and which should be, so to say, the fountain to feed the different provinces and activities in different directions in different parts of the country ... we have to promote co-operative credit societies and co-operative banks, and we have to promote small industries, and all these mean an organised, sound and extensive system of banking in the country.'[5]

After a lot of debate and discussion, the Imperial Bank of India (IBI) Act, 1920 was enacted and would come into force on 27 January 1921.

One of its interesting features was the provision to allow scrutiny of the list of shareholders, which had also been included in the Indian Companies Act of 1913. As we saw earlier, the three presidency banks did not have such a provision and the bank denied shareholders access to the shareholders' list. A few people had tried earlier but they had been unsuccessful.[*] Under the Presidency Banks Act, the directors held all powers to appoint, remove and remunerate all officers and employees, and any changes to the conditions of work or conduct of bank's business could be carried out only after their approval. Section 55 of the Act specifically laid down that all resolutions of the shareholders' meetings would be valid and binding on the bank only so far as such resolutions were consistent with the provisions of the Act. Thus, it would appear that any resolution of shareholders objecting to the changes in the bank's staff and their conditions of work or the conduct of the bank's business by the directors had no legal force. The same provisions were repeated in the IBI Act.

---

* In 1881, the directors of the Bank of Bengal reluctantly provided the shareholders' list to Prasad Das Dutt. In 1906, the Bank of Bombay denied Suleman Sonji the right to scrutinise their shareholders' lists. Sonji filed a suit against the bank in the Bombay High Court but lost. Dissatisfied with the judgement, he appealed to the Appellate Court and his demand was upheld. But the bank then referred the matter to the Privy Council and managed to obtain a decision in its favour.

The Presidency Banks Act and the IBI Act apparently provided for remedies against the abuse of their powers by the directors. While the shareholders were empowered, in principle, to remove any director or governor (other than a government nominee), by a special resolution passed by a majority of the votes of shareholders holding in the aggregate not less than one-half of the capital, and appoint in his stead, a person who has the qualifications demanded of a director, it was a provision which was impossible to use. The majority of the shares were held by Europeans who were resident in Britain or some other country and were happy to leave matters in the hands of the bank directors who also acted, in many cases, as the custodians of approved securities owned by the non-resident shareholders. It was only in the case of Bank of Bombay that there were Indian directors on the board and real issues of policy could be considered in the shareholders' meeting. When the three banks were amalgamated, this Indian element was swamped by the European domination of the Bank of Bengal (which possessed the largest capital stock of the three) and the Bank of Madras. Thus, the Indian shareholders could exercise little control.

The Imperial Bank of India represented the victory of the imperial element as embodied especially in the management and business practices of the Bank of Bengal. The biggest of the three presidency banks had also proved to be the least dynamic of the three, especially after the Bank of Bombay had survived the turmoil of 1890s and the Bank of Madras had profited from the collapse of Arbhutnot & Co. Not only had the deposits and advances of the Bank of Bengal advanced more slowly than those of the other two, its branch expansion record was also the poorest among the three. The Bank of Bombay and the Bank of Madras had opened a number of new branches during the First World War while the Bank of Bengal had opened none. Finally, the Bank of Bombay also embarked on a process of Indianisation of its branch agents. Neither had the Bank of Bengal taken any steps in this direction, nor had it contemplated any, as is evident from its minute books.

The ethos of the Bank of Bengal is evident from the statement of R.M. Watson Smyth, the chairman of the first general meeting of shareholders of the Bengal circle of IBI held in August 1921. He claimed that 'the talk of Indianisation of the officer corps of the IBI was premature, since men of the right quality were not to found in Bengal!'[6]

Coming back to the amalgamation of the banks: the three presidency banks drew up a detailed memorandum for the Government of India for a merger. The banks wanted the 'intimate personal touch' with the government which had developed through the First World War.[7] The banks also felt that three banks shared common interests and that 'friendly, though informal cooperation' between them was necessary for mutual interest. Also, in view of the demand for more banking facilities in India, with access to London and privileges by the government, the merged entity would be in a better position to provide for a healthy banking development in India. The bank was to open 100 branches in five years.

The Imperial Bank of India was being set up against the backdrop of a series of calamities. The plague of 1917 had caused large number of deaths. Feeble monsoons had resulted in famines in many parts of the country. In 1918, an influenza epidemic spread across the entire country, which ended up wiping out in a matter of a few months practically the whole natural increase in population for the previous seven years.

In 1920, there was another famine in many parts of the country. The First World War from 1914 to 1918 had led to a 'massive plunder of Indian human and material resources'.[8] Indian economy suffered severe shocks while large recruitments in the Indian Army meant a colossal increase in defence expenditure, which could only be met by floating war loans and inflicting a stiff dose of taxes. There was a sharp rise in prices causing hardship to the labour class. A worldwide rise in labour consciousness saw its influence in India too, with strikes greatly increasing during this period. In 1920, during the first six months, more than 200 strikes involving nearly 15 lakh people took place and these included railwaymen, dockyard workers, postal employees, steelworkers in cities like Ahmedabad, Kanpur, Bombay, Calcutta and Madras, prompting Viceroy Chelmsford to describe the events as 'a sort of epidemic strike fever'.[9] The countrywide struggle laid the foundation of Indian trade union movement eventually giving rise to the birth of All India Trade Union Congress (AITUC) on 31 October 1920.

While the working class suffered on account of the rising costs of living, the war years saw a sudden rise in the demand for Indian industrial goods. Mill owners and industrialists benefited from windfall profits, with textile and jute manufacturers recording profits of 200 per cent or more.

The Gourepore Company, a leading jute mill of Bengal, for instance, paid dividends of 300 and 420 per cent in March 1918 and March 1920 respectively.

Against this background, the Imperial Bank of India began its operations in January 1921.

4

THE IMPERIAL BANK OF INDIA

When the Imperial Bank of India began its operations in 1921, the country was yet to recover from the recent shocks of war, drought and epidemic. Political and economic unrest on an unprecedented scale also threatened to overrun the country as it faced a declining exchange rate on the one hand and a massive flight of capital on the other. The war years, over and above the outbreak of plague and the influenza epidemics in many parts of the country, had led to a massive plunder of Indian human and material resources. Large recruitment in the Indian Army meant a colossal increase in defence expenditure which could only be met by floating awar loans and inflicting a stiff dose of taxes. Raising of the general tariff, imposition of, and, in some cases, increasing duties on certain imported items as well as select exports, and enhancement of income tax rates inevitably followed. A rising war expenditure, which included a gift of a hundred million pounds sterling in 1917 and a further 45 million a year from the Government of India to the British war efforts in addition to the usual 'Home Charges' (payment of tribute to Britain), coupled with the disruption of trade and a decline in imports had led to a steep rise in prices. It was probably an unpropitious time for launching an all-India bank.

The Indian Legislative Council passed the bill to constitute the Imperial Bank of India and the relevant Act (Act XLVII of 1920) was gazetted for it to come into force on 27 January 1921. On the appointed date, the new bank formally opened for business after taking over the undertakings and business of the three presidency banks of Bengal, Bombay and Madras.

The Imperial Bank Act was modelled on the old Presidency Banks Act of 1876 and shared many of the features of the earlier Act. The Act also provided for local head offices (LHO) to be set up in Calcutta, Bombay and Madras and at such other places in British India as the bank, with the previous sanction of the governor general in council, would determine. No other LHO, however, was created in the days of the Imperial Bank. The Act also provided for the establishment of an office in London, which the presidency banks had demanded ever since the question of their amalgamation was taken up with some degree of urgency. Thus an office was set up in London

The Act did not necessitate the formation of a central office but one was set up to manage the affairs of the three circles. It did not have a fixed location and revolved between the three LHOs. The Imperial Bank of India became the sole banker to the Government of India to hold all treasury balances at the LHOs and the branches of the bank. The new bank was to use the seal of the Bank of Madras and the share certificate of the Bank of Bengal, the latter with some necessary alterations. The authorised share capital of the Imperial Bank of India was ₹11.25 crores consisting of 225,000 shares of ₹500 each.

As we saw earlier, in the debate in the Indian Legislative Council, Rai Bahadur B.N. Sarma had brought into sharp focus the lamentable state of Indian banking. In 1918, India had altogether 96 bank head offices and 322 bank branches, including those of the three presidency banks, exchange banks and Indian joint-stock banks. A large part of the country was underbanked; nearly 75 per cent of towns with population of 10,000 or more and 21 per cent of those with a population of 50,000 or more did not have a bank branch. The presidency banks, which then had 68 branches and agencies and three head offices, accounted for 17 per cent of the total bank offices in India. The finance secretary assured Sarma that the government had realised the need for a very large increase in banking facilities in India and in the scheme of amalgamation, it had provisions for the opening of a branch in every district in India which would ensure 'as reasonably rapid a step on the way towards the extension of banking' as one could hope for.*

---

* Speech of H.F. Howard, financial secretary to Government of India on 23 September 1919 in *Proceedings of the Indian Legislative Council assembled for the purpose of making Laws and Regulations from April 1919 to March 1920 Vol. LVIII* (Calcutta, Supdt. Govt. Printing, India, 1920).

In the midst of all this, a significant event took place 160 kms away from the Kolkata office of the Bank of Bengal, even though not many Indians noticed it then. In December 1921, Rabindranth Tagore founded Visva-Bharati at Santiniketan, an institution that would go on to play an important role in education in India. Almost three decades later, in May 1951, it was declared a central university.

The Imperial Bank Act provided for opening of at least 100 new branches within five years of commencement of the bank. A quarter of them were to be determined by the government. In accordance with this charter, on 13 January 1926, the managing governors informed the finance secretary to the Government of India that 102 new branches, six new sub-agencies and 14 new pay offices had been opened. The demand for Indianisation of the cadre too was met.* The management trainee system that we see today began on an experimental basis with the recruitment of probationary assistants in 1921. By August 1925, the bank had 41 Indian officers, apart from assistants and probationary assistants. The acute shortage of European officers had evidently compelled the management to induct more and more Indians in managerial positions for running the increasing number of branches. The induction of Indians was thus more circumstantial than policy!

In order to spread banking education, an all-India bankers' institute was proposed. This saw the establishment of the Indian Institute of Bankers (IIB) in 1928.

In 1930, the issue of Indians being promoted as officers had been taken up by the Imperial Bank of India Indian Staff Association (IBIISA) through its mouthpiece, the *Bulletin*, where it had complained that '... it is well known that while graduates from the Universities having no practical experience and not the least pretensions to it either, are being appointed year after as Probationary Assistants, the employees of the bank who have put in years of ungrudging service and have even passed the examination of the Institute of Bankers, are being uniformly ignored ... the employees in the clerical service satisfy the conditions of having previous banking experience and have cleared the exam ... the members view with great alarm that the door to

____

* Sir Badridas Goenka, from one of the most influential Marwari families of Calcutta, was director of both the Imperial Bank of India and the SBI. For many years, he was the first Indian to preside over annual general meetings of the shareholders of the Imperial Bank.

promotion has been practically shut against them. Apart from the question of glaring injustice done to those who have already established their claim to immediate promotion, such a policy of persistent denial of legitimate rights and privileges is bound to remove all incentive to consistent effort on the part of those who are by means thereof are anxious to better their own prospects and serve the interests of the Bank.'[1]

Fast forward to a few years later, J.R.D. Tata, who was a member of the local bank's board in Bombay, spoke on the issue. He could not have been more pointed in his criticism. Tata drew the attention of the managing director to a decision taken by the bank's central board in January 1936, which stipulated that the recruitment of European and Indian officers in future would be regulated so as to result in due course in a 50-50 ratio in all grades between European and Indian officers. Yet, he added, probationary officers had continued to be recruited from the UK while recruitments in India stood suspended since 1931. He also observed:

> I have the highest regard for the ability, integrity and loyalty to the Bank of its European personnel, and I have had nothing but the most courteous and friendly treatment from all those with whom I have come in contact. My attitude is based solely on the following considerations: If the Imperial Bank, whose shareholders, clients and employees are predominantly Indian, is, as I believe it should be, considered an Indian Bank, it is desirable that its control and management should be in Indian hands. The complete exclusion of Indians in the past from all high positions in the Bank, and the insistence on reservation in the future of 50 per cent of the senior posts for Europeans, can only be justified by the assumption that Indians are inferior in ability to Europeans, or, if they have the ability, that they cannot be trusted. As an Indian I cannot accept either of these assumptions, and, unless, therefore I felt that they no longer governed the policy of the Board and of the Management, it would be unfair to myself and to the other Directors if I were to continue as a Member of the Board.[2]

By 1948, the bank had 94 Indian and 72 European officers. It was estimated that about half of the European officers would seek retirement by 1950 and all but six of the remainder between 1950 and 1955.

Coming back to the issue of branch expansion, with such a large number of branches to be managed, a post of Manager, Northern India Branches, was created to supervise and control all branches in northern India, north of a line drawn from Mussoorie to Bahawalpur via Meerut and Delhi. A salary of ₹3,500 was fixed with furnished accommodation and a house allowance of ₹250 per month. Later, in 1933, the post was abolished with the appointment of district managers at Calcutta, Lahore and Cawnpore.

The bank's branch network increased from 70 in 1921 to 162 by 1925. With this expansion, the bank now accounted for more than 25 per cent of the total bank branches in India. The total cash deposits of Imperial Bank of India accounted for about 40 per cent of the total deposits of all banks. The authorised and paid-up share capital of the bank stood at ₹11.25 crores.

In a rare instance, the Government of India stepped in when the Alliance Bank of Simla Ltd. went into liquidation in 1923, and asked the Imperial Bank of India to protect the interest of the depositors. Before this, in the aftermath of the First World War, a total of 57 banks had failed across the United Provinces, Madras, the North West Frontier Province, Delhi, Bangalore and Baluchistan had failed. This also included the People's Bank of India in the Punjab region. The Alliance Bank of Simla Ltd. was registered on 14 May 1874 and commenced operations in Shimla. To cut a long story short, the fall was a direct result of greed on part of the directors, who had allowed Boulton Bros and Co., an issuing house in London, to milch the bank.*

When the news of the failure of the Alliance Bank spread, there was panic for three days and a virtual run on the banks in Calcutta. But the importance of the Imperial Bank of India as a pivotal institution was seen when people withdrew money from many banks to deposit it there.

The Imperial Bank of India decided to pay 50 per cent of the deposits of the Alliance Bank. The total deposits of the bank amounted to ₹8.5 crores. Payments to the depositors were suspended for a while when S.R. Bomanji,

---

* In 1914, R.G.H. Boulton, a senior partner of Boulton Bros and Co., had managed to convince Alliance Bank to issue capital of ₹10 lakhs at 100 per cent premium. After gaining the confidence of the bank, Boulton Bros. and Co. set about exploiting the bank's resources more and more and many companies floated between 1916 and 1918 had the directors of the Alliance Bank as directors in those companies through acquisition of shares. The bank was induced to grant loans to these companies. At one time the shares purchased by Alliance Bank of Simla Ltd. in the Boulton group of companies aggregated to ₹88.25 lakh while loans were in excess of ₹4 crores. The auditor was complicit in the affairs and eventually it led to the ruin of the bank when Boulton Bros and Co. failed to repay the loans. The directors of the bank met for the last time on 27 April 1923.

a shareholder of the Imperial Bank, served a notice on the governors asking them not to pay the depositors of the Alliance Bank as it was in contravention of the Imperial Bank of India Act and stating that the shareholders of the bank were not benefitting in any manner. The advocate general defended the bank's action stating it was entitled to take up any business of the government and in this case was merely paying out money from government balances of the bank. A demand was placed in the Legislative Assembly for the Imperial Bank of India Act to be amended to permit direct intervention by the Imperial Bank in times of financial crisis. The bill received the assent of the viceroy on 24 September 1924.

While most of the staff, including officers, of the Alliance Bank were absorbed by the Imperial Bank of India, the case of Charles Henry Stuart, the secretary of the Alliance Bank, was not approved by the central board committee for continuing his job in the bank. Stuart had rich experience in banking but the directors of the Imperial Bank quite evidently did not wish to recruit a person who could well have been associated with many of the misdeeds of the liquidated bank. This is not very different from what we see today when one company is taken over by another—the axe falls on the one heading the ill-fated institution.

The issue of a bank taking over or bailing out an ailing institution, be it a company or a bank, appears as a recurring theme over the past many decades. There is an ongoing debate with many views on it and the jury is still out.

In 1925, the Imperial Bank of India was clearly ahead of other joint-stock banks with 162 branches while the PNB had 39 branches, the Bank of Baroda had five and the Canara Bank had just one branch. The branches of the Imperial Bank covered the whole of the British empire of India, Ceylon and Burma. It had also cornered a sizable share of the banking business with nearly 40 per cent of the total deposits of all banks.

The practice of requiring current accounts to have a minimum balance was not seen as being in favour of private enterprise and in 1923, the Imperial Bank of India did away with this requirement. Private deposits were accepted as fixed deposits and the minimum amount for fixed deposits was ₹500 while the minimum sum required to open a savings account was ₹5. The maximum balance accepted in a savings bank deposit account was ₹50,000 and the maximum savings bank account balance on which interest would be paid was ₹10,000. The rate of interest on savings bank deposit account was 3.5 per cent in May 1926.

The concept of safe deposit lockers was introduced in 1937. They were first installed in the Bombay circle and the Bengal and Madras circle authorities were asked to investigate the possibility of introducing the concept there as well. Two hundred and fifty lockers made by Allwyn Steel Equipment Co. Ltd were placed in the branch at Ahmedabad. In 1940, the annual rent of a locker varied from ₹14 to ₹72, depending on the size of the receptacle. The safe deposit locker scheme continues to be popular even today with millions seeking the comfort of a locker where valuables can be deposited without any worry of theft or damage.

The Imperial Bank of India was not the State Bank of India as envisaged by John Maynard Keynes. It was more of a bank functioning as a commercial bank and a bankers' bank. While it was the sole banker to the government and was given the task to manage public debt, the Imperial Bank was not responsible for regulating note issue or managing foreign exchange.

When the London office of the Imperial Bank of India was opened, there was a proposal to 'marry' the Imperial Bank with the Bank of England. There was a strong feeling that the proposal would be strongly objected to in India. The managing governors of the Bank of England made a rather interesting comment on the proposed relationship, in a letter to Bernard Hunter, manager of the bank's London office dated 6 May 1921:

> The Imperial Bank is young and pretty and (we) do not think should marry an old and rich man like the Bank of England in haste. Old and rich men are apt to treat their young and pretty wives with harshness once they have them in their clutches.[3]

The Formation of the Reserve Bank of India

On the recommendations of the Royal Commission on Indian Currency or the Hilton Young Commission, the Reserve Bank of India Bill was introduced in the Indian legislature in 1927 but it was soon dropped 'after acrimonious and kaleidoscopic discussions'.[4]

The real reason for the delay in the formation of the Reserve Bank of India (RBI) was the efforts of the India Office and the Bank of England to ensure that the control over critical Indian matters like money and finance continue to be retained in their hands. Even Montagu Norman, the longest-serving Governor of the Bank of England, was wary of an Indian central bank with large investible funds at its command, which could eventually pose a threat to the London market. He wanted to delay the formation of a central bank in India as much as possible. But the creation of the RBI was inevitable as a precondition for any 'transfer of financial responsibility from the agents of the Parliament to a minister answerable to the Indian Legislature'.[5] The Hilton Young Commission had opined that the Imperial Bank, once the central bank was formed, 'should be freed altogether from the restrictions which its present charter imposes upon it. ... there is no reason why the Imperial Bank should not be as free and unencumbered in its sphere of activity as any other of the commercial banks. Its important task of giving the widespread banking facilities which it needs will thereby be facilitated.'[6]

The Hilton Young Commission had emphasised the need for both a central bank and a great commercial bank which had the government backing to 'inspire confidence' amongst an 'uninstructed public' and 'to perform the function of the initiator of banking facilities'.[7] While the recommendation of a central bank was being made, it was clear to everyone that converting the existing Imperial Bank of India into the central bank was not in the best interest of the country, though there were certain advantages to utilise its existing organisation as a central bank. There was a clear need for a bank like the Imperial Bank of India to continue to assist in fostering, among the people as a whole, the habit of banking and investment.

The RBI was finally set up on the basis of the recommendations of the Hilton Young Commission. The Reserve Bank of India Act, 1934 provides the statutory basis of the functioning of the bank, which commenced operations on 1 April 1935. The central bank was constituted to regulate the issue of bank notes, to maintain reserves with a view to securing monetary stability and to operate the credit and currency system of India to its advantage. The RBI began its operations by taking over from the government the functions so far being performed by the Controller of Currency and from the Imperial Bank of India, the management of government accounts and public debt. The existing currency offices at Calcutta, Bombay, Madras, Rangoon, Karachi, Lahore and Cawnpore became branches of the Issue Department of the RBI. Offices of the Banking Department were established in Calcutta, Bombay, Madras, Delhi and Rangoon. Burma was separated from the Indian Union in 1937 but the RBI continued to act as the Central Bank for Burma till the Japanese occupation of Burma during the Second World War and later post the Second World War up to April 1947. After the partition of India, the RBI served as the central bank of Pakistan up to June 1948, when the State Bank of Pakistan commenced its operations. The RBI, which was originally set up as a shareholders' bank, was nationalised on 1 January 1949. The appointment of Osborne Arkell Smith, one of the managing governors of the Imperial Bank of India since 31 October 1926, as the first governor of the RBI was yet another recognition of the importance of the Imperial Bank of India.

With the formation of the RBI, the restriction on foreign exchange business was removed and the Imperial Bank of India was authorised to open branches and undertake banking business of any kind inclusive of borrowings abroad. *The Evening Standard*, London, on 17 August 1933, commented that 'the other exchange banks in India and are not expected to benefit by this legislation since the Imperial Bank with its 170 branches will now prove serious competition in the Exchange markets, both internally and for foreign financing'.

The Great Depression of 1930

Meanwhile, the Great Depression of 1930 had affected both agriculture and industries, the impact on the latter being positive. Prices of agricultural commodities fell substantially. For example, raw jute prices fell from ₹9 per maund to ₹3.75 per maund* and the prices of pulses, oilseeds and many other items produced in eastern India fell by as much as nearly 45 per cent.

There was a lurking threat of unrest among the Indian peasantry as they were likely to lose their occupancy rights as tenants and the menace of forced sale of land by authorities in case of loan default. However, the Gandhi–Irwin Pact of 1931 stalled the possibilities of a widespread peasant uprising

---

*After 1947, the definition formed the basis for metrication, one maund becoming exactly 37.3242 kg.

all over India.* The pact was significant in terms of the demands accepted; the government agreed to withdraw all ordinances against the activities of the Indian National Congress. They also agreed to withdraw trials relating to several offences, except ones involving violence, and agreed to release all political prisoners arrested for participating in the civil disobedience movement. The ban on the Indian National Congress was revoked while the confiscated properties of the satyagrahis were restored. Salt was allowed to be collected near sea coasts. Unfortunately, the death sentence of Bhagat Singh and his associates was not commuted to life sentence.[†]

Unlike the impact on agricultural commodities, industry fared quite well. The second half of the 1930s saw a remarkable recovery. The number of sugar-cane-crushing mills shot up from 29 in 1931 to 137 in 1936–37 after the introduction of tariff protection to the industry in 1932. Sugar production went up from 3.5 lakh tons in 1930 to nearly 13.7 lakh tons by 1940. Cotton mills showed a substantial rise in production. This was also the time we see a significant rise in business houses who had amassed immense wealth in 'wartime speculation' diverting their energies and resources to the development of industries—Walchand Hirachand, Ambalal Sarabhai and Kasturbhai Lalbhai from Gujarat, the Tatas and other Parsis in Bombay, Lala Shri Ram and Karamchand Thapar in the North. We see the emergence of a large number of Marwaris—the Birlas, Dalmias, Singhanias, Seth Sarup Chand (his son Sir Hukam Chand was called the 'Cotton Prince of India' and such was his reputation that the New York Cotton Exchange was closed for two days on his death), Surajmull Nagarmull, Jaipurias, Bangurs, Goenkas and others. These business

---

* The Great Depression of 1930 caused a considerable fall in import of cotton piece goods from Britain. The collapse of agricultural prices in India was equally catastrophic. The rapid fall in agricultural prices coupled with the heavy burden of revenue, rent and debt service inevitably led to unrest among the Indian peasantry. The lurking threat of the loss of their occupancy rights as tenants on the one hand and the menace of forced sale of land by the concerned authorities in case of default on the other worsened the plight of the peasantry. The regional differences in revenue administration and agrarian relations, however, prevented the outbreak of a general rebellion and the peasants chose to flock to the Congress to provide a stable base to the organisation. With the signing of the Gandhi–Irwin pact, the civil disobedience movement was stalled.

† Contrary to recent popular perception, Bhagat Singh, Sukhdev and Rajguru were not hanged on Valentine's Day (14 February) but on 23 March 1931.

groups were initially focused on jute and cotton but in the 1930s they diversified into other areas. The Hirachand group forayed into shipping while the Tatas began their airlines. Shri Ram set up a sewing machine factory (the iconic Usha brand) while the Birlas started manufacturing textile machinery. By 1937, nearly 60 per cent of the total employment in large-scale industry was provided by Indian firms, which increased to 80 per cent in another seven years.

Banking for the Masses

While the Imperial Bank of India had increased its branches considerably, it still remained out of reach for a large majority of Indians who continued to depend on the shroffs, moneylenders, Chetties, Multanis, Nidhis, chit funds and the like. It is surprising that even today we find vast majority of Indians underbanked, despite the penetration and sincere efforts of microfinance organisations and self-help groups. Chit funds continue in the southern part of the country and scams by such funds are still rampant, leading to poor people often losing all their hard-earned money. More on this later. (The recent Pradhan Mantri Jan Dhan Yojana is an effort at financial inclusion that aims to expand affordable access of all banking and other facilities to all Indians.)

The Imperial Bank of India was aware of the immense potential of engaging with the masses. In March 1926, we find evidence of this, when W.R.T. Mackay, the chief inspector of the bank, in a detailed memorandum to the managing governors recommended the 'extension of banking facilities to one and all where it could be done on sound lines'.[8] The managing governors were in favour of allowing agricultural advances against produce and such advances were given to small traders. The loan limit was reduced to ₹2,500.

A lengthy discussion on the government's desire to institute an enquiry into the banking organisation of the country took place in Indian Legislative Assembly. The discussion was based on a resolution moved by Sarabhhai Nemchand Haji on 10 February 1927 for such an investigation. Lala Lajpat Rai, in the legislative debate, emphasised the need for an enquiry to understand the economic progress of the country and to investigate the position of the banking institutions and the facilities and conditions in India as well as to make recommendations for their improvement and expansion. He added:

> ... I know from personal experience that during the Indian banks' failures in 1913, several banks failed for want of sympathy and help on the part of the Government. I was at that time concerned with the management of the Punjab National Bank, one of the biggest banks of the country, which has as many as 34 branches scattered all over the country. It was with great difficulty and in the absence of any sympathetic help from the Government and the Government Bank at the time—I considered the then Bengal Bank the Government Bank—that we tided over a crisis at that time. It is that knowledge which deters many investors, particularly small investors, from giving their money over to the Indian Bank. No amount of branches opened by the Imperial Bank will solve that problem for them. The small investor is not likely to go and invest his money in the Imperial Bank or in any of these European-managed banks. I know that the European-managed banks have not been looking at the Indian banks, even the joint-stock banks, with a favourable eye. They have been trying to discredit them and to say to people that they should not trust these Indian banks. An inquiry of this kind will help the small investors as well as the big investor to know how the Indian banks stand.... What we want is a committee of experts and non-experts to inquire into the condition at present existing in the Indian banking and to provide such facilities and checks as will encourage small investors and those who have money to invest, to go and invest their money in these banks under certain guarantees.[9]

As R.K. Shanmukham Chetty pointed out to his fellow legislators, the recommendation of the External Capital Committee in 1925 had mentioned that India had huge dormant capital awaiting development. He mentioned that the creation of the Indian Institute of Bankers (it was established on 30 April 1928) was to promote banking education in the country. Another Legislative Assembly member, N.C. Kelkar expressed that the Imperial Bank was not in touch with small investors and small-savings man in the mofussil and up-country. He urged the bank to give interest on current and small deposits to attract the common man.

Against the backdrop of the need for the banks to engage more extensively in the development of the nation, the first Indian Central Banking Enquiry

Committee was set up on 22 July 1929 under Bhupendra Nath Mitra, who till then was a member of the executive council of the governor general.

It was clear, the committee found, that the Europeans enjoyed more credit than the deposits held by them. The tea gardens and collieries owned by Indians had suffered on account of lack of finance from the Imperial Bank of India and other joint-stock banks. The Imperial Bank had not played any role in financing industries in Bihar and Orissa.

One of the most damaging criticisms made against the Imperial Bank of India by the committee was in respect of the financing of cotton mills in the Bombay Presidency. It was alleged that the bank had practically tried to discourage and paralyse the textile industry by demanding money when there was a crisis and strike in Bombay and had the Nizam of Hyderabad not invested a crore of rupees, the Bombay textile industry would have been doomed. The committee went on to observe that the bank had financed the English racers at Calcutta with very large capital, even as it did not accommodate the textile industry's demand for money at an inopportune and critical time. The central committee expressed its opinion in favour of close ties between industry and commercial banking. In order to ensure the supply of financial assistance to industries, it recommended the creation of industrial credit corporations in the provinces and an all-India institution for industries of national importance. Unfortunately, it was only as late as 1948 that the Industrial Finance Corporation of India (IFCI) was established.

Multiple witnesses deposed before the provincial and central-banking enquiry committees and the Imperial Bank of India received criticism on several counts. The aspects which attracted the harshest criticism were: failure to train Indians for responsible positions in the bank, unhealthy competition posed to Indian joint-stock banks, curtailment of facilities to co-operative banks, poor financing of Indian industries and agriculture and the exclusive privileges conferred on the bank.*

Further, to facilitate lending to agricultural sectors, Sardar Buta Singh moved a motion in the Council of States in March 1933 for amending the

---

* The Bengal provincial committee mentioned the case of a firm in Dhaka, which had been doing business with the Imperial Bank for decades, yet its cheque for a large amount was dishonoured because it exceeded the amount lying in the credit of the firm by a paltry sum. This was despite the cheque being drawn by a firm which deals with the bank in lakhs of rupees a year.

Imperial Bank of India Act, to empower the bank to lend on mortgages of agricultural estates. The resolution, however, was not passed.

In order to facilitate the Imperial Bank for business, the Imperial Bank of India (Amendment) Bill was introduced in 1934. With the introduction of the Reserve Bank of India Act, 1934 and the Imperial Bank of India (Amendment) Act, 1934, there were notable changes in the position of the powers of the Imperial Bank. The bank ceased to be the sole banker to the government of India. Moreover, at places where the banking department of the RBI had no branch but the Imperial Bank had a branch, the Imperial Bank became the sole agent of the RBI. The restriction on the foreign exchange business was removed and the Imperial Bank was allowed to open branches and undertake business of any kind, including borrowings abroad. The bank could also give loans based on movable and immovable properties. The Imperial Bank was now truly poised to play a key role–and a dynamic one at that—in the Indian commercial banking business.

In order to facilitate the opening of the RBI, the premises of the Imperial Bank of India in Calcutta (8, Council House Street), Bombay (the ground and first floors of the old Bank of Bombay building and the first floor of the old Bank of Bengal building), Madras, Delhi and Rangoon were leased out to the new bank in August 1934. Officers and staff of the Imperial Bank were transferred to the RBI from the three circles and its London office. They would continue to enjoy the same terms and conditions as far as their remuneration was concerned.

❧

Meanwhile, things were heating up on the political front in India. The call for independence was gaining ground. In its 1929 convention at Lahore, the Indian National Congress had already adopted the demand for Purna Swaraj and the Dandi march (12 March to 6 April 1930) had marked the beginning of the civil disobedience movement. In 1935, a federal scheme was proposed by Samuel Hoare, the secretary of the state for India. The bill was introduced in the House of Commons for the establishment of a federation of the governor's provinces and Indian states. The bill for the Government of India Act, 1935, had deliberately kept the RBI and Railways outside the ambit of the Legislative Assembly and viceregal permission was made obligatory for all legislation on currency and finance. Hoare believed that the RBI and the Railway Board, if they were to fulfil their purpose, must be kept as independent as possible and free of any interference from politics.

Nehru was exasperated at Hoare's proposal and wrote:

India was to be converted into a glorified Indian State, with a dominating influence of the states' feudal representatives in the Federation. But in the states themselves no outside interference would be tolerated and undiluted autocracy would continue to prevail there. The real imperial links, the chains of debt, would bind us forever to the city of London and the currency and monetary policy would also be controlled, through a Reserve Bank by the Bank of England. ... There was going to be Provincial Autonomy, but with the Governor as the benevolent and all powerful dictator and high above all would sit the supreme Dictator, the Viceroy, with complete powers to do what he will and check what he desires. Truly, the genius of the British ruling class for colonial government was never more in evidence, and well, maybe Hitlers and Mussolinis admire them and look with envy on the Viceroy of India.[10]

With opposition from both Congress and the Muslim League, the proposal of a federal scheme was dropped and it was planned to introduce only a provincial scheme on 1 April 1937. Burma had been annexed in 1886. In 1921, the British Parliament had extended the dyarchical form of constitution to Burma and it had been placed under a governor in 1923. Now with the introduction of the bill for the Government of India Act, demands were made by the Burmese Legislative Council for a full responsible government lest it became a vassal state of India. With the passing of Burma Monetary Arrangements Order, 1937, the RBI was appointed to manage the currency of Burma and continue to carry out the business of banking in Burma.*

Rapid changes were taking place in Europe, which resulted in the Second World War. It created an initial demand in industrial activity and a widespread boom appeared to be a possibility, but that was not to be. Assuming that demand for cotton would go up, there were many speculative deals in Bombay.

---

* With Burma becoming independent in 1947, the Union Bank of Burma was created under an Act in October 1947 and was made banker to the government. However, the Rangoon branch of the Imperial Bank continued even after formation of the SBI in 1955, till its assets and liabilities were taken over by the Peoples' Bank No. 8 of Burma on 23 February 1963 after the nationalisation of banks in Burma.

The jute industry too benefited in the latter half of 1939 with increased demand for sand bags in Europe, but this too did not last for long.

One industry which did very well in those circumstances was the iron and steel industry. Its performance was primarily on account of demand for the production of armaments. Cement too saw a good offtake. The banks too did well by providing finances for many such businesses.

The most serious problem which affected India was the distribution of food grains. India saw a tragedy of great magnitude in the form of the Bengal Famine in 1943. Various studies put the number of people who perished because of the famine between 22 lakhs and 30 lakhs. The food shortage, unfortunately, was not because of lack of production of food grains, but the inability of distribution of the same owing to pressure on the transportation system and the overall callousness of the government. Recent studies clearly blame the Churchill administration which ordered the diversion of food from India to British soldiers fighting in Europe. Such was his disdain for Indians that Churchill has been famously quoted as blaming the famine on the fact that Indians were 'breeding like rabbits', and of asking how, if the shortages were so bad, Mahatma Gandhi was still alive.*

The war also intensified the demand of the Indians for freedom. In 1940, Viceroy Linlithgow had proposed to set up a new constitution for India and to add Indian members to the Viceroy's executive council. The Congress rejected the proposal and began a movement of civil disobedience. But the threat posed by the advancing Japanese army forced the Congress to offer their cooperation, albeit only for the time being.

In 1942, the Stafford Cripps Mission arrived to secure full cooperation and support of India for the Second World War. It was headed by Sir Stafford, who was sympathetic to the cause of Indian self-rule but was also a member of Churchill's war cabinet. The mission failed as the proposals for an 'earliest possible realisation of self-government in India' was rejected by all. The Muslim League rejected the proposal on the grounds that it favoured an Indian Union while they were demanding a separate nation for the Muslims.

The Quit India movement began in 1942. Churchill, adamant as ever, was in no mood to compromise and declared, 'I have not become the King's First Minister to preside over the liquidation of the British Empire.'

---

* This is a popular notion attributed to Churchill.

It was becoming increasingly clear that the British could not hold on for long and that independence was in the offing.

The effects of the war on Indian banking, however, were far-reaching. India was a supply base for Allied forces and the expenditure on defence and supplies increased considerably, which resulted in the expansion of currency and the total money income of the community. This, combined with other factors like import shortages, diversion of internal supplies to war needs and so on, led to a rapid increase in the 'unspent margin' in the higher income groups and the reserves of trade and industry. The net result was a rapid rise in bank deposits. Of the 147 new banks floated between 1 July 1939 and 30 June 1945, as many as 82 banks were created between July 1942 and June 1945. The total number of scheduled banks in India increased from 91 at the end of 1945–46 to 97 at the end of 1946–47.

The net profit of the bank was just under ₹107 lakhs in the year ending June 1946.

The war led to an increasing need for laying a foundation for a new world order and a sound structure of international economic relations. The Bretton Woods Conference in July 1944 endorsed the creation of an international monetary fund and a bank for reconstruction and development. There was a need for reconstruction and development of economies of member countries. By early 1946, both the International Monetary Fund and the World Bank (officially, the International Bank for Reconstruction and Development) were in place.

Much before the increase in the number of new banks in the 1940s, the government of the day had attempted banking legislation in 1937 based on the recommendation of the Indian Central Banking Committee. In 1939, the RBI drew up proposal for an Indian Bank Act, which was designed to bring the entire joint-stock banking under the control of the central bank. The managing director of the Imperial Bank of India believed that appropriate amendments to the Indian Companies Act would suffice and there was no need for a Bank Act. (The RBI's proposal was put off and re-introduced only in 1949, when the Banking Companies Act was enacted.)[*]

---

[*] One of the systems adopted by the Imperial Bank of India, that of compilation of a weekly statement of affairs, was made part of the Banking Companies Act, 1949. Scottish banking practices had formed the backbone of the rules and regulations framed for the presidency banks.

The Imperial Bank's branch expansion continued at a very slow pace—only 15 more branches and sub-branches were opened between 1931 and Independence. Limited business opportunities coupled with the need to economise on establishment costs were factors which prompted the bank to opt for pay offices in place of branches. As mentioned earlier, with the Amendment Act coming into play, the Imperial Bank was allowed to take up other businesses. The bank then entered into agreements with American Express Company and Thomas Cook and Sons for undertaking business in travellers' cheques and travel services.

The bank also started handling income tax business for its constituents. Some of the largest constituents in Bombay were E.D. Sassoon & Co. and Tatas Sons Ltd. E.D. Sassoon enjoyed a credit limit of ₹175 lakhs in 1938 while TISCO enjoyed a total cash credit and demand loan limit of ₹300 lakhs. Not just TISCO, the bank had close associations with the fortunes of a number of companies in the Tata group, including Tata Aircraft Ltd., Tata Chemicals Ltd., Tata Locomotive & Engg. Co. Ltd., Tata Oil Mills Ltd. and many others. Binny & Co. enjoyed a limit of ₹100 lakhs in 1924, which was raised to ₹350 lakhs by 1951.

Independence and Thereafter

On 15 August 1947, India became an independent nation. However, this hard-earned independence brought with it the partition and violent communal clashes. To add to this, India found itself reduced to an agrarian appendage and a subordinate trading partner to Britain. As discussed earlier, the Britishers had not left India as an industrially developed nation. Owing to the extensive transfer of surplus to Britain over the centuries, India was clearly very impoverished when the Britishers left.

During 1911–41, per capita agricultural production and per capita food grain output declined by 0.72 per cent and 1.14 per cent per year, respectively. Nearly 70 per cent of cultivated land in British India came to be owned by zamindars and landlords thanks to usury—the practice of lending at high rates—making many peasants work as bonded labourers. Out of a population of nearly 40 crores in 1939, not more than 15 lakh people were employed in factories.

Luckily, many local Indian businessmen had emerged as a capitalist class and India was nearly self-sufficient in consumer goods. The share of Indian joint-stocks banks in total bank deposits had increased from 25 per cent in 1913 to nearly 64 per cent by 1946. By the end of 1947, the Imperial Bank of India had a market share of a little over 30 per cent of the advances of all scheduled banks in India. A sprawling network of 437 offices (including sub-offices) out of a total of 3,462 offices of all scheduled banks ensured the Imperial Bank's presence in practically every important trading centre of the subcontinent. The bank was ready to take up a more enterprising role in a country which had just been freed from the shackles of imperial rule.

The government of India announced two important measures immediately after Independence—the laying down of the industrial policy and the formation of the Industrial Finance Corporation of India (IFCI), whose charter was to provide medium- and long-term finance to public limited companies and cooperative societies engaged in manufacture or processing of goods, mining, or generation or distribution of electricity.

The year 1948 also witnessed the unfortunate wrangle between India and Pakistan on the splitting of the financial assets, which included the cash and sterling balances of undivided India. Pakistan was to get its share of ₹75 crores, of which ₹20 crores was given on the day of the partition. Gandhi's insistence on paying the remaining share by dictating a statement to his secretary on the third day of his last fast in January 1948 forced the government's hand and they reluctantly agreed to release the amount. It was to become one of the reasons for his assassination a few days later.*

The year also marked the nationalisation of the RBI in September 1948, which was to be effective from 1 January 1949. It was a legal recognition of the well-accepted principle that the policies pursued by a central bank were

---

* When Mahatma Gandhi was assassinated on 30 January 1948, his ashes were sent in small urns to different provincial capitals of India for immersion in the rivers there. For some reason, the urn sent to Cuttack in Orissa was not immersed. The urn was placed in a sealed wooden box and deposited with the safe deposit custody of the Imperial Bank of India's branch in Cuttack. It remained there, unknown to most, for the next 46 years! It was only when Tushar Gandhi, great-grandson of the Mahatma, requested the bank to take possession of the urn that it became public. On the 49th anniversary of Gandhi's martyrdom, in 1997, the urn was immersed in the Triveni Sangam at Allahabad. The wooden casket now is at display at the SBI Museum at Kolkata and is a prized possession.

to subserve the social and economic objectives of the government. The RBI retained its autonomy but the government assumed the power to direct the policies of the central bank appropriate to public interest. Recalling the issue later, C.D. Deshmukh, the then governor of RBI wrote, '... After all, it is not the theoretical constitution of the Institution that matters, but the spirit in which the partnership between the Ministry of Finance and the Bank is worked. The success of the partnership will, in the ultimate analysis, depend on the manner in which the Government desires to be served and provides opportunities accordingly. No country can have better public institutions that it deserves."

The major step in the nationalisation of the RBI was completed and put to work and the smooth working of the partnership was ensured, according to Deshmukh, by his subsequent and perhaps 'fortuitous' appointment as union finance minister in 1950.

How much autonomy have successive governments allowed to the RBI is a matter of another debate!

In the meantime, with India having gained independence, the clamour for the nationalisation of the Imperial Bank of India began as early as in 1948. But it would be a few more years before the bank was nationalised. S.K. Handoo was the first Indian to be appointed as the Managing Director on 12 January 1953, for a period of five years, when Roderick Chisholm retired. Handoo was appointed on generous terms with a salary of ₹7,500 per month, a house each in Calcutta and Bombay or a house allowance of ₹500 per month in lieu thereof, a first-class return 'A' P&O passage to

---

* C.D. Deshmukh, *The Course of My Life* (New Delhi, Orient Longman, 1974), Part III, Section 5, p. 169. Sir Chitaman Dwarkanath (C.D.) Deshmukh was the first Indian Governor of the RBI. After matriculation, he went to England for higher studies. He topped the Indian Civil Services (ICS) exam in 1918 and was posted to India. He worked in the province of Central Provinces and Berar before being made the governor of the RBI. He was later the union finance minister. Even after moving away from politics, Deshmukh played an important role in education and social work as Chairman of University Grants Commission, Vice-Chancellor of Delhi University and in various other such posts. The only post which he aspired to, but did not hold, was that of the President of India! Both Deshmukh and his wife, Durgabai, were awarded the Padma Vibhushan, the second highest civilian honour, making them the only couple to have received this honour. A matter of personal pride for Deshmukh was that he had the unique distinction of having a personal current account with the RBI.

London, or air passage, to be given when leave was to be taken out of India. Additional return passage was to be given if he was accompanied by his wife, and travelling expenses to and from the place where he would spend his leave was to be paid by the bank, together with his wife's expenses, if accompanied by her, in case leave was to be availed of in India, Pakistan or Ceylon. The new managing director was also to be provided with a car at a cost not exceeding ₹25,000 or was to be given a conveyance allowance of ₹200 per month in lieu thereof. The car was to remain the property of the bank but the expenses for maintenance of the car and a driver, together with the cost of petrol up to ₹200 per month, were to be borne by the bank.*

Another Indian, T.S. Ragavachary, till then an inspector at the central office, was appointed as the deputy managing director, for a period of three years, on a monthly salary of ₹5,500 per month. He too got a house allowance of ₹500 per month, till a house was made available to him, while other terms and conditions were the same as for the post of the managing director.

As we saw earlier, many banks had opened in India. The uncontrolled expansion, coupled with lack of adequate regulations, inevitably led to several banks collapsing—between 1939 and 1949, as many as 647 banks failed and savings of around ₹26 crores were lost. It was a situation we would see repeated many times in the years to come and the reasons wouldn't be different either—unsound policy in investments and branch expansion without any proper study. The maximum number of failures took place in West Bengal (51 of 145 banks failed between 1948 and 1950). The common man would continue to lose his hard-earned savings in ponzi and other schemes in Bengal much later too.

One of the banks to fail was Nath Bank, which was established in 1926 and with 38 offices in 1948. When Nath Bank was not able to honour cheques, there was a run on other banks as well and the RBI amended the act of 1949 to allow amalgamation of principal banks. This was the beginning of bank mergers and in December 1950, four scheduled banks in West Bengal—the Bengal Central Bank, the Comilla Union Bank, the

---

* Another important event took place around the same time. On 29 May 1953, Edmund Hillary and Sherpa Tenzing Norgay became the first people to stand atop Mount Everest. The SBI archives have the letter written by Tenzing in August 1965, wherein he talks of his association with the SBI Darjeeling branch since 1953.

Comilla Banking Corporation and the Hooghly Bank—were merged to form the United Bank of India, as it was known till 1 April 2020, when it was amalgamated with PNB. The next year, PNB took over Bharat Bank.

One of the major failures in banks was that of the fourth largest bank in India, the Travancore and Quilon Bank (TNQ Bank). The Travancore Bank was established in 1912 by K.C. Mammen Mappillai in the town of Thiruvalla. Mappillai was a member of the prominent Kandathil Christian community which had been responsible for floating 15 banks. Mappillai is best known as the founder of the *Malayala Manorama* media group. Among the bank's founders was a priest who had experience with running chits. The Quilon Bank was established by another Christian, C. Mathen. In 1937, both these banks merged to form TNQ. Interestingly, Mappillai's and Mathen's fathers had earlier partnered in a bank named Thayyil Bank. The merged entity, TNQ, had 75 branches spread over the country with its central office at Madras and the registered office in Travancore State. The local press hailed it as the 'greatest banking amalgamation in South Indian history'.[11] Within a year the bank collapsed. The family alleged the role of the then Dewan of Travancore State, Sir C.P. Ramaswamy Iyer. The Dewan was against the bank's founders, but that is a story for another day.

On an interesting aside, in April 1942, the Nizam's government decided to launch of the Hyderabad State Bank (HSB) with an authorised capital of ₹1.5 crore. All department accounts were shifted from the Imperial Bank of India to HSB. Once Hyderabad State was merged with the Union of India, Indian rupees became legal tender alongside HS currency, which continued to be legal tender till April 1955.

Soon, the passing of the Banking Companies Act in 1949 allowed the RBI to have regulatory and supervisory powers which were essential for Indian banking. The central bank was to give directions to banking companies with regard to their lending policies and could stipulate the maintenance of sufficient liquid assets, rates of interest to be charged on advances, margins to maintained, etc. It had the powers to inspect any bank either on its own initiative or on being directed to do so by the government. Prior permission was required from the RBI to open a new branch or transfer existing ones. The RBI, in turn, was required to prepare an annual report for the central government on the trends in and the progress of banking in the country, with suggestions, if any, for strengthening the banking system.

The Imperial Bank of India began to be pushed for opening more branches due to the need for expansion of banking into rural and semi-urban areas. The report of the Rural Banking Enquiry Committee in 1953 stressed the need for such an expansion. After discussions with the RBI, the bank agreed to open 75 branches during a three-year period ending June 1956, but it managed to open only six branches in the first 12 months. The justification was lack of business opportunities, which would result in the branches being loss-making, if they were to be opened. Later, in 1956, John Matthai, the first chairman of the SBI, echoed the same views saying, 'One of the chief reasons which prevented the Imperial Bank from pursuing a more vigorous policy of expansion was that, as a private shareholders' bank, it could not afford the heavy expenditure involved in opening new branches which were likely to prove unremunerative.'[12] Profit was a key motivating factor for the continuance of an Imperial Bank branch and the days of mass banking and priority sector lending were still in the distant future. But there is no denying that the Imperial Bank was playing a key role in the gradual industrialisation and economic progress of India.

(The real thrust for branch expansion, mass banking and rural focus happened only after the formation of the SBI.)

As mentioned oftentimes earlier, while HR policies for European officers were very liberal and beneficial to the employees, Indians continued to suffer. In its feature titled 'Bank Clerks' Plight' that appeared in February 1940, *The Hindustan Standard*, a daily newspaper, described the plight of bank clerks as: '... there is no time limit of the working hours in the Banks. The poor clerks have to attend office at 10 a.m. and they do not know when they will be able to leave the office because they are not allowed to leave until and unless the day's accounts, the cash balances, are found correct and ... this can go on

John Matthai

till 10 p.m. or even midnight. The clerks are therefore compelled to work 12 to 14 hours a day. They are poor (*sic*) paid on the other hand. They are made to work like beasts of burden at the sweet will for their masters ... is there nobody in the land to prevent such cruelty to human beings, although there exists law punishing cruelty to animals?'

A few years earlier, in 1930, B. Das had brought up a similar issue in the Indian Legislative Assembly about the failure of the 'Indianisation' of the Imperial Bank. He had observed:

I am sorry I have not yet seen any list to show how rapid Indianisation of the superior staff of the Imperial bank has been going on. But this much I know, that when the Presidency Banks were amalgamated, they had 89 European officers, and at present they have much more than 250 European officers. Every year bank clerks from England are imported as Agents; and I also have definite information that Indians born of high families and trained in banking and commercial institutes in India have been taken as probationers and they have been allowed to drudge as clerks till 10 p.m. at night, while these young clerks who come from England, go away at 4 o'clock to play tennis or anything they like, and the Indian probationer rots in the second grade almost as a clerk. That is the tradition which the authorities of the Imperial Bank of India have developed.[13]

Das had drawn the attention of the House to reports published in the *Bombay Chronicle* and *Forward* (Calcutta), both appearing on 12 February 1926. *The Bombay Chronicle* commented: 'The Imperial Bank is a hot bed of racial nepotism: Indianisation of the staff is a mockery if we compare the appointments made in its development with the proportion obtaining before the programme of 100 branches was instituted.'

The *Forward* observed, 'The State has therefore every right to press for Indianisation of the Bank; but there is a more urgent reason in the addition to this. It is a matter of common knowledge, which has also been publicly expressed on more than one occasion; that the Imperial Bank makes racial discriminations in the matter of credit. Unless the Bank is Indianised more effectively the evil will continue.'

※

Going back a few years, after the Second World War, industrial disputes in Bengal had taken a serious turn and there were many strikes in the jute and tea industries. The post and telegraph workers went on strike in 1946. The first-ever strike was to take place in the Imperial Bank in Bengal. The strike lasted 46 days and was called off on the intervention of Jawaharlal Nehru. The workers had been demanding a 40 per cent increase in the salary of all clerical staff in the cash department and subordinate and menial staff, apart from other demands related to medical aid, payment of medical bills and other things. But the bank authorities were firm about not giving a raise beyond 25 per cent. The agents also threatened retrenchment. The effect of the strike was felt elsewhere. Leaflets showing the disparity in basic pay between the RBI and Bank of India employees were circulated. The revised pay scale in 1946 for the lowest paid clerk in RBI was ₹145 (basic pay of ₹75, dearness allowance of ₹30, local allowance of ₹10, and a combined allowance of ₹30 for three children) whereas the clerk in Bank of India started on a total salary of ₹102. A clerk of the Imperial Bank in Calcutta drew a salary of ₹49-8-0 on confirmation. Clerks in mofussil towns were paid even lesser. Many changes were implemented. A tribunal proposed fixing the working hours from 10 a.m. to 5 p.m. with an interval of half an hour for lunch on weekdays and from 10 a.m. to 2 p.m. on Saturdays. The matter related to the dearness allowance remained unresolved though. The issue was discussed by a few commissions. It was finally in 1954 that the Bank Award Commission agreed to the decisions given by a labour appellate tribunal.* On dearness allowance, the tribunal opted for a rate which was linked to the cost-of-living index. Linkage was provided with the cost-of-living index of the place where the bank was located or the nearest place for which the index was available. The year 1944 was adopted as the base year.

The cry for nationalising the Imperial Bank of India was getting louder by the day. Many parliamentarians wanted to see it getting nationalised. They all grudgingly agreed that the bank carried a status of its own and that its share of ₹500 had been well over ₹2,000 in 1948. As A.M. Thomas, an MP from Ernakulam said, when the move of nationalisation was first

---

* Bank holidays have not changed much over the past century. The year 1949's list of bank holidays for the Delhi branch of the Imperial Bank shows 23 holidays. Some of those holidays no longer exist today, such as the King's birthday on 9 June and Salono (celebrated in Haryana on Raksha Bandhan day) on 8 August in that particular year.

announced in 1948, that an Imperial Bank cheque book was 'considered to be a coveted possession.'[14] But the new political class did not take kindly to the reputation the bank carried. The same Thomas referred to the bank as an 'unapproachable, aristocratic, patrician institution, which thrived on a colonial economy as well as on State patronage'.[15] To most parliamentarians the bank was a bete noire and deserved no mercy. Thomas referred to an incident wherein a distinguished member of the Cabinet, despite being a successful businessman, was not given accommodation in the Imperial Bank and had to invest a small amount simply for the purpose of possessing a cheque book.

The clamour for the nationalisation continued to increase. Multiple debates took place across the country. In the course of the debate on the Reserve Bank of India (Transfer to Public Ownership) Bill on 2 September 1948, demands were once again raised for the nationalisation of the Imperial Bank. Seth Govind Das, a parliamentarian, demanded that the government should stop treating the Imperial Bank as its 'pet child' and added that as the RBI and the Imperial Bank were 'very closely associated with each other', the nationalisation of the Imperial Bank should follow without any delay. The debate was yet another opportunity for Das to chastise the Imperial Bank, which he had indulged in ever since he became a legislator in 1924. Referring to the RBI as 'the maid of the Old Lady of the Thread Needle Street (as the Bank of England was called) ... throughout the British rule,' Das observed: 'There were two enemies before 15 August 1947—the British Civil Service was Enemy No. 1 and the Imperial Bank of India was Enemy No. 2. If the Imperial Bank would have helped India, India's industries and trade would not have been in the sorry plight that it is in today. It helped every other Tom, Dick and Harry and every Britisher that came to Indian with 50 pounds in his pocket and had 50,000 pounds credited to him in the Imperial Bank.'[16]

T.T. Krishnamachari also opined that while the legislators were not very particular about the immediate nationalisation of the RBI as the government control over it was adequate and complete, the primary object, he said, was to have a 'State Bank' which would cover the 'entire country'.[17] Quite obviously, he believed, the RBI could not perform that role. When the issue of nationalisation was raised in the Constituent Assembly on 1 February 1949, John Matthai, the then finance minister, announced that the nationalisation was 'not feasible' because of 'possible repercussions in the investment market' and the 'existing unsettled economic conditions in the country'. The finance minister confessed that he was a believer in the doctrine of the State as a positive instrument of social and economic progress but expressed doubts whether the management of commercial banks was a suitable sphere of nationalisation. He did propose, though, to look into the Imperial Bank Act.

Many were in favour of nationalisation and the hostility towards the Imperial Bank was evident and undeniable. But many in the government were not fully convinced that the time was ripe for the Imperial Bank to be nationalised. C.D. Deshmukh, then governor of RBI, wrote in a memorandum for his central board committee that 'I am more than ever convinced that the proposed nationalisation of the Bank would be a serious mistake... Nothing is to be gained and much is likely to be lost by nationalising the Imperial Bank at any rate at this stage.'[18] Some other senior officials too agreed with Deshmukh saying the formation of a State Bank was neither necessary nor advisable. It was supported by leaders like Vallabhbhai Patel, then deputy prime minister, saying, 'Government had neither the capacity nor the means to undertake nationalisation of any industry at present.' He further added that 'in order to restore confidence, a categorical statement of this nature is long overdue and it is a matter for deep satisfaction that the Bank may now be considered free to function as a Commercial Institution and that the danger of its being sacrificed at the altar of socialistic ideologies has meanwhile receded.'[19]

In the meanwhile, various committees had been set up which were evaluating the proposal to nationalise. A Rural Baking Enquiry Committee (RBEC) was set up under the chairmanship of Purshottamdas Thakurdas, who had not only served on the board of the Imperial Bank but had also played a significant role in the deliberations of the Hilton Young Commission. After the devaluation of the Indian rupee in 1949, the necessity of pooling the savings of the rural areas to make them available for increasing production had become crucial and this had led the Indian finance minister to announce that the stimulation of investment through the extension of banking facilities in the rural areas would be one of the measures of the government to deal with the situation. It was in pursuance of this undertaking that the RBEC was appointed. The committee was also to suggest measures for streamlining rural credit, mobilising rural savings and improving the treasury arrangements in the states. The distribution of banking offices in the provinces and states in the country were lopsided with heavy concentration in larger town and cities, while smaller semi-urban towns had lesser branches. T.T. Krishnamachari was critical of the RBEC's report and some of its recommendations. Referring to the recommendations, he said, 'It suggests that the imperial Bank should act as an auxiliary to the Reserve Bank and for that purpose it suggest[s] that certain sections of the Imperial Bank Act, which have been more of less repealed, should be restored to provide for government control of that bank.'[20]

T.T. Krishnamachari demanded an assurance from the finance minister that the government would undertake a survey of the banking conditions in the country and put forward proposals for a comprehensive banking enactment. The creation of the All India Rural Credit Survey (AIRCS) Committee in August 1951 under A.D. Gorwala* was perhaps influenced by this demand.

The RBI, under the said survey, had conducted field enquiries which covered more 1,27,343 families in 600 villages selected from 75 districts across the country. One of the startling revelations of the survey was the magnitude of the inadequacy of the governments and the cooperatives as sources of rural credit. It was clear from the survey that the private creditor, mostly money-lenders, reigned supreme in the field of rural credit, supplying 70 per cent or more of the total need.

Not many were aware that the AIRCS was working on a plan to nationalise the Imperial Bank. In a speech of Badridas Goenka, who chaired the Imperial Bank's 34th annual general meeting on 27 August 1954, it was clear the bank had in fact already accepted the need to absorb losses in the country's interest with branch expansion into other areas.

But the day of the reckoning arrived soon, much to the consternation of the country's business circle. The recommendations of the Committee of Direction of the AIRCS for nationalisation of the Imperial Bank of India and the government's acceptance of the proposal were first made public by the finance minister, C.D. Deshmukh, during his speech on economic policy in the Lok Sabha on 20 December 1954.

---

* Gorwala was an Indian Civil Services (ICS) officer.

One important recommendation that had emerged from the nationalisation committees was a scheme in which the SBI would be formed by amalgamating the Imperial Bank of India and ten 'State-associated banks', namely the State Bank of Saurashtra, Bank of Patiala, State Bank of Hyderabad, Bank of Bikaner, Bank of Jaipur, Bank of Rajasthan, Bank of Baroda, Bank of Indore, the Bank of Mysore and the Travancore Bank.

The most significant recommendation, however, was to move towards the establishment of a SBI with the objective of extending the concept of state partnership to the important sector of commercial banking. The government envisioned the proposed SBI to be a strong, integrated, state-sponsored institution, which would be able to provide vastly extended remittance facilities for cooperative and other banks and stimulate the further development of those banks. Moreover, in its loan operations, in so far as these have a bearing on rural credit, the SBI would follow a policy which, while not deviating from the cannons of sound business, would be in effective consonance with national policies.

To constitute SBI and to transfer to it the undertaking of the Imperial Bank of India, a Bill was moved on 22 April 1955.

The directors of the Imperial Bank, however, were miffed. They were taken by surprise as they had not been consulted in the process. The management of the Imperial Bank had not been taken into confidence on such crucial a matter, particularly when both the government of India and the RBI had confided in the bank in practically every issue in the past. It had been a similar situation when the central bank's apex governing body was denied prior intimation of the government's decision to nationalise the bank in 1948.

The Bill was placed in the Lok Sabha on 22 April 1955 by A.C. Guha, minister of revenue and defence expenditure, in place of Deshmukh, who was indisposed. Referring to the speech at the special meeting of the shareholders of the Imperial Bank which had been ridiculed as a 'swan song' or 'funeral oration' by an MP, the minister observed that 'the Imperial Bank by itself is a big institution and it has served the interests of the country, but I think, as at present constituted, it has outlived its utility. Instead of the unusual tune which the chairman of the board uttered in the meeting, I think he should have remembered the legendary bird phoenix which used to burn itself after every hundred years to be reborn in a new shape and a new form, and will serve the real interests of the country.' The minister concluded by reminding the House that the purpose of the bill was 'not merely to take over' the Imperial Bank of India but 'to recreate our rural life, to vitalise and strengthen our peasanty, and to rejuvenate our rural lives.'[21]

Many MPs also demanded the nationalisation of all insurance companies and banks. This too happened later, as mentioned earlier, with the passing of the LIC Act in 1956. The merger and nationalisation of general insurance companies happened much later with the passing of General Insurance Business (Nationalisation) Act, 1972 (GIBNA).

The State Bank of India Act, 1955 was passed and it was to come into effect from 1 July 1955. This was published in *The Gazette of India Extraordinary* on 11 May 1955.

The Imperial Bank of India had a rich legacy and was a launching pad for the new SBI. It would be fair to conclude that the Imperial Bank was taken over not because it was mismanaged but because the priorities of a newly independent India required a different approach, which a financial institution in the private sector would not probably best address. India had just acquired freedom and there was a commitment to create a welfare state. Against the backdrop of such emotions, it is easy to imagine the opportunity to seize a fine instrument of banking, despite the opposition from shareholders. It was, nevertheless, a new chapter for India and it was for the newly formed SBI to ensure that the dream was fulfilled.

5

DAWN OF A NEW AVATAR

Among the first decisions that the SBI had to take was one regarding the location of its head office. Predictably, a debate ensued over this. Although the Imperial Bank's central board was in favour of continuing the system of mobile central office, the framers of the State Bank of India Act, 1955 chose Bombay as the fixed location of the new bank's central office. However, Dr B.C. Roy, the then chief minister of West Bengal, in a letter dated 7 July 1955 to C.D. Deshmukh, the finance minister, objected to the decision to have the central office in Bombay. He cited the pre-eminence of the Bengal circle, which outpaced both the Bombay and Madras circles in terms of deposits, advances and branches. Stressing on the overwhelming importance of the Bengal circle, he argued in favour of having the central office in Calcutta. The RBI advanced several arguments in defence of the decision favouring Bombay—an important one being that having the central offices of both the RBI and the SBI in Bombay would ensure proper coordination between the two banks. Moreover, it was also felt that a mobile office was not conducive to expeditious dispatch of business and that with Bombay being a financial centre, it made sense to have the SBI central office there.

Dr John Matthai, the former finance minister of India, was appointed as the first chairman of the SBI. S.K. Handoo, the managing director of the Imperial Bank of India, was retained in the same capacity in the SBI. One of the prime objectives for the SBI was to open 400 new branches within the first five years. The Act also vested the ownership of eight state-owned or state-associated banks in the SBI and enabled the latter to take them over as its subsidiaries. The banks were the State Bank of Hyderabad, State Bank of Jaipur, State Bank of Indore, State Bank of Patiala, State Bank of Mysore, State Bank of Travancore. State Bank of Bikaner and State Bank of Saurashtra. Later, on 1 January 1963, the State Bank of Bikaner and State Bank of Jaipur were amalgamated to form State Bank of Bikaner and Jaipur. Thus, there were seven associate banks.

A new SBI with a sense of social purpose was being formed.*

With a new identity, it was important to change the logo of the bank. The logo of the Imperial Bank of India had two lions and a British symbol. This was replaced with a round-shaped logo depicting a banyan tree. The banyan tree, with its roots and branches growing in all directions, was considered symbolic of growth, safety, security and solidity. Moreover, the motif of the banyan tree was typically Indian. In ancient times, merchants would gather under the banyan tree. The tree represented shade and thus comfort to a common man. Historical events were centred on it and the tree was considered a symbol of strength and usefulness to others. It was also decided that the existing telegraphic addresses of the Imperial Bank of India, namely the Thistle (a Scottish national emblem) in India and 'Hondee' in foreign countries would be retained by the SBI for the time being. All letterheads and bank advices were to be imprinted with these lines:

State Bank of India
(Successors to the Imperial Bank of India)
Incorporated in India under the State Bank of India Act 1955
The liability of the members is limited.

Many years later, in 1971, the SBI adopted its new logo, the one which is recognised all over India as the 'keyhole' logo. The logo, designed by Shekhar Kamat of the National Institute of Design, Ahmedabad, was a blue circle with a small cut running from the bottom to the centre of the circle. Some believe it is a keyhole which represents security, stability and strength while others see the white circle in the centre as a branch with the narrow lane leading to the larger circle representing the presence of SBI across India.

---

* When SBI was born, it inherited deposits of about ₹213 crores, advances of ₹116 crores and a total business of ₹327 crores. It had 477 branches and eight overseas offices and a staff strength of 14,388.

It is a bank to serve you, wherever you go. While it isn't true, it is commonly believed that the logo was inspired by the Kankaria lake in Ahmedabad.

The logo in circular form was to represent unity, completeness, the fullness of man's being and his growing consciousness and continual expansion of the bank, like concentric rings in water, to cover the entire country. The small circle in the centre connoted that despite the bank's size, it was the small man—or the common man—who held the centre of the stage in the SBI. Announcing the adoption of the new logo,[*] chairman R.K. Talwar wrote in the quarterly house magazine of the bank:

> More important is what people will think of instinctively when they see it.... The symbol will be what we make of it. What they think of us all, is what they will think of the symbol. And that is the meaning the symbol will ultimately acquire.

The SBI was formed when the socialist policies of the government were in force. The first Five Year Plan (1951–56) was still in operation when the government announced the takeover of the Imperial Bank of India. The plan bore the imprint of Jawaharlal Nehru, the first prime minister of independent India. The focus for investment in the Plan was on two areas—infrastructure and agriculture. The Plan aimed to use public-sector outlays to stimulate increasing savings and investment in the economy as a whole with special emphasis on agriculture and community development. The First Five Year Plan thus prepared the ground for more ambitious planning in the future. The second half of the 1950s thus saw the rapid development of heavy and capital goods industries, mainly in the public sector. Steel plants were set up at Bhilai, Durgapur and Rourkela and there were investments made in sectors like oil refining.[†]

––––––––––

[*] Even the RBI logo, though inspired from the logo of the East India company as seen on the coins, was tweaked a little to show its unique identity. The original seal and mohur of the Company had a palm tree with a lion in the centre. In order to incorporate 'Indian-ness' in its design, the lion was replaced with a tiger which was considered more Indian. By the time the RBI was formed, the lion had been killed across India by Maharajas and East India officers and was found only in parts of Gujarat, unlike the tiger. The tiger also represented an independence that the RBI wanted to emphasise.

[†] Moving away from Nehru's focus on public-sector industrial investment, in the late 1960s, the government set out to increase agricultural production by following a new agricultural strategy pioneered by the Ford Foundation. The result of disseminating high-

The Imperial Bank had left behind some rich legacies like its discipline in weekly reporting. It was incumbent on the newly formed SBI to carry on this discipline. One of the important traditions of the Imperial Bank, which was adopted by many banks later, was the hiring of probationary assistants, the forerunners of present-day management trainees, which ensured the continuation of the legacy. On-the-job training provided to young recruits laid the foundation for developing a rich source of future managers. Eminent bankers like R.K. Talwar and B. Gupta, the former chairman and deputy managing director of the SBI, respectively, joined the Imperial Bank as probationary assistants and rose to the highest levels of office. While the Imperial Bank had been hailed as a 'fine instrument of banking', newly independent India required a bank which was able to reach the vast majority of the rural masses who continued to remain indebted to the local zamindar or the local moneylender. The takeover of the Imperial Bank was necessitated by the need to focus on the new priorities of India which needed a different approach. A financial institution in the private sector was unlikely to address the concerns.

A New Agenda for a New Nation

The SBI had now clearly broken from its colonial past and was expected to herald a new future representing a resurgent India. Development banking, geared to the needs of the artisan and the farmer, was an unchartered territory. There was an urgent need for expansion of branches into all parts of India. Quite clearly, the role of the leader would come into play as the bank expanded into new areas to fulfil the needs of an aspirational India. Apart from banking, the SBI was to contribute to nation-building as part of its mandate.

Apprehensions due to nationalisation remained for a while. There were many who felt that the nationalisation would achieve nothing while many

---

yielding varieties of seeds developed in Mexico and the Philippines was combined with the use of chemical fertilisers and enhanced irrigation. The result was what is now called the Green Revolution. (A little on that later, though it is beyond the scope of the current work to discuss the benefits and long-term effects of the same.) Quite naturally, with the Green Revolution, the SBI, being the government-sponsored bank, had the mandate to develop rural banking and support agriculture.

others felt that it would create a pathway for future development and that an institution like SBI would play a significant role in disbursement of credit and growth of India as a whole. The Times of India carried views both in favour and against nationalisation. H.T. Parekh, who would later go on to head institutions like ICICI and HDFC, found little justification in the formation of a new entity for a function like providing cheaper remittances that could well have been accomplished by the existing set up, that is, the Imperial Bank of India. What perhaps rankled him the most was the routing of loans to agriculturists and craftsmen through cooperatives. He said, '… it is unreasonable that in an agriculture-dominated economy the State Bank should keep out of its purview direct loans to the rural community for whose advancement the State Bank is brought into being. Only then will there be some hope of weaning away the cultivator from the village banker who is regarded as beyond redemption.' He reiterated that 'the formation of the State Bank cannot be the end but the beginning of a new chapter.'[1]

He further added that 'more than the mere opening of branches it involves a basic change in the outlook and approach. It means readiness to take risks by lending to sub-marginal borrowers who by present standards are not considered credit-worthy but who through state assistance are to be brought up to a condition of credit-worthiness. The attainment of this end will call for much initiative and ingenuity on the part of the new management of the State Bank. The formation of the State Bank cannot be the end but the beginning of a new chapter.'[2] (emphasis added)

There was anxiety in all quarters and the Annual General Body Meeting of the Indian Merchants' Chamber in 1955 expressed severe concerns about the move. Ghanshyamdas Birla, a prominent businessman and founder-chairman of the United Commercial Bank, was apprehensive that the control of the Imperial Bank and the incorporation of other state banks into it would enable the government to corner a major part of the bank deposits.

Among the first to comment on the Imperial Bank's nationalisation was A.D. Shroff, director, Tata Sons Ltd, who had chaired the Committee on Finance for the Private Sector appointed by the RBI in 1953. Addressing the Rotarians of Ahmedabad in January 1955, Shroff observed that the proposal of nationalisation was provoked by the 'unresponsive attitude of bankers to the nation's requirements' and should serve as an 'eye-opener' to private enterprise.[3]

J.R.D. Tata, who championed free enterprise, criticised the nationalisation decision. In his letter dated 20 January 1955 addressed to Rama Rau, the RBI governor, he expressed 'unrelieved dismay' and said 'that the decision to nationalise the bank, a great national asset', despite earlier declarations to the contrary, could not but 'create nervousness and serious misgivings regarding the future of free enterprise' in the country.[4]

JRD had already suffered the nationalisation of Air India. While he had opposed it on several platforms, he was never invited by the government to express his views. The communications minister, Jagjivan Ram, who supervised the modalities of nationalisation consulted him only about the compensation to be given to companies being nationalised. The decision to nationalise Air India was a fait accompli.

A disheartened JRD expressed his anguish to Nehru about the way the government had intentionally treated the Tatas shabbily, and how it was a planned conspiracy to suppress private civil aviation, particularly the Tata group's air services. Nehru reassured him of no such intentions. In fact, in a personal letter to JRD, he placed on record the high appreciation he had for the Tatas, who had pioneered several projects, and the excellent services rendered by Air India International. JRD's contention was that the new government of India had no experience in running an airline company, and nationalisation would mean bureaucracy and lethargy, decline in employee morale and fall in passenger services.

Piqued by a speech by the communications minister, Rafi Ahmed Kidwai, in the Constituent Assembly in 1949, JRD had written to Prime Minister Jawaharlal Nehru that 'by resorting to incorrect and unfair statements and allegations, he [Kidwai] has convinced the majority of the members of the Assembly ... that the airlines in general, and Air-India in particular, are dishonest and greedy, cannot be trusted, and fully deserve their present plight.' It was a battle which JRD could not fight though the government tried to save face by requesting him to head the airlines.[*]

---

[*] Life came a full circle when in 2019 the government announced the decision to privatise Air India. Among the bidders was the Tata group, which had already made an entry into the sector by floating Vistara. If the bid comes through for the Tatas, it will bring Air India back into the Tata fold once again. According to latest reports at the time of going to press, the Tatas have won the bid.

Notwithstanding the battle regarding airlines, JRD would have to fight later with the Indira Gandhi government to prevent nationalisation of the Tata Iron & Steel Co. (TISCO), but fortunately, the intentions of Indira Gandhi and her government did not work out the way they wanted and Tata Steel, as it is called now, remains outside government ownership.

Coming back to the nationalisation of the Imperial Bank of India, concerns were raised by many that if the Imperial Bank under state control could open branches regardless of cost, the government would control most of the deposit money. As we have seen over the decades since, many banks, including private ones, have flourished and the apprehensions raised at that point did not turn out to be real.

The government on its part had done well in constituting the SBI board. The board, with eminent businessmen and financiers as directors, was hailed as one of the most outstanding boards associated with any corporation in the country. Dr John Matthai was the chairman and Vaikunth L. Mehta was the vice-chairman, both of whom were considered experts in the field. Matthai had insisted on a 'no fanfare' opening of the bank though the *Times of India* brought out a special supplement on 1 July 1955.

In time, the concerns that the government or the RBI would interfere in the matters of the SBI were laid to rest. In 1957, H.V.R. Iengar, the then chairman of the SBI, admitted that he had earlier believed nationalisation to be unnecessary and provocative but 'all doubts and apprehensions raised at one time had been largely dissipated within five years.'[5]

The SBI was now in place with its administrative issues sorted out to some extent. On 21 February 1957, H.M. Patel, finance secretary, wrote to Iengar, to see that 'no further time should be lost in formulating a broad programme of action for the State Bank, both as a commercial bank in its own right and as an instrument of national

H.V.R. Iengar

policy'.[6] He was keen to see the bank spearhead development banking across the country. As far as the commercial bank aspect was concerned, there had been complaints about 'undue delay' in encashing cheques of customers 'who were not particularly important in the eyes of the bank'. Many steps were taken to see that the common man received the services which he expected from the bank.

Ownership Issues

In 1954, before the SBI had been formed, the issue of ownership had not been fully sorted out. In March 1955, the central board of the RBI recommended the vesting of the major ownership solely with the RBI and not jointly between the RBI and the government of India. In a letter written to Rama Rau on 20 January 1955, J.R.D. Tata, who was member of the RBI board, observed, 'The less Government is brought directly into the picture as the owner of the shares of Imperial Bank, the better this will be for maintaining the continuity of the Imperial Bank's commercial and other activities.' Eventually, the government would accept the RBI's proposal.

We divert a little to talk of the shareholding pattern of the SBI. The AIRCS committee had proposed expansion of the share capital of the SBI in such a manner that the new shares, non-transferable and eligible only for 'statutorily limited' dividends, would be allotted at part to the RBI and the government of India so that 'a voting power of not less than 51 per cent' would be ensured for them.[7] The raison d'être was to not only ensure effective state control but also safeguard the essentially autonomous and commercial character of the institution. When the SBI Bill came up for discussion in the Lok Sabha in April 1955, there were questions regarding the proposed 55 per cent allotment instead of 100 per cent to the RBI.[8] Sadhan Gupta, member of parliament, argued that the private shareholding should be restricted to 20 per cent instead of the proposed 45 per cent. The minister of state for finance pointed out that the bill was aimed at gaining 'control' of the Imperial Bank of India and using it as machinery for rural banking. The amendment was ultimate rejected when put to vote. Eventually, a small proportion of the Imperial Bank's shareholders opted in favour of the SBI shares within the deadline of 1 October 1955. A month later, only about 8 per cent of the shareholding thus rested in private hands, including public institutions. Of this 8 per cent, about 1.7 per cent of shares were held by PSUs like LIC (formed in 1956) and banks, while the remaining 6.3 per cent rested with about 1,300 private shareholders. Transactions in the SBI shares were mainly confined to individuals elected as directors or members of local boards to enable them to hold the minimum number of shares (50 in case of directors and ten in case of members of local boards). It was understood that on relinquishing the charge, the person would sell the shares back to the RBI.

But trading in the SBI shares was happening even in those days. In 1956, Matthai, while reporting a growing demand in the market for the SBI shares priced slightly above the official price of ₹350, sought clarification from the RBI regarding whether it would have any objection on grounds of policy to the bank's shares being listed on the stock exchanges of Calcutta, Bombay and Madras. Rama Rau promptly wrote back saying that since the RBI had no intention of reducing its 92 per cent holding, it would not make the listing worthwhile. The matter was taken up again later and finally, it was in 1959 that the shares were listed on the Bombay Stock Exchange.

A decade later, in 1969, Morarji Desai as deputy prime minster revived the issue as he wanted the RBI to acquire all the private shares. Senior officials of the RBI, however, quick to dismiss the remarks as 'merely meant to choke off' someone interested in giving a higher dividend 'to satisfy' private shareholders.[9] The issue of private shareholding again cropped up in 1972. While looking through proposals for filling up vacancies in the central and local boards of the SBI in which some representation was given for the 8 per cent private shareholders, the finance minister Y.B. Chavan observed, 'I am not aware of the rationale for keeping this small private shareholding in the State Bank of India, but in any case, in the changed context, there is hardly any justification to continue the private shareholding of the issue.'[10]

Private shareholding was to remain more or less same till 1993, when in an effort to increase its capital base, the SBI made the largest ever public cum rights issue of equity and bonds in the Indian capital markets. With the mobilisation of ₹3,206 crores, including share premium, the bank's capital base as of 31 March 1994 went up from ₹200 crores to ₹473.83 crores. The number of shareholders increased from 29,681 to 19,31,075. The RBI holding, by the end of March 1997, came down to 60 per cent. It was much later that the government promulgated the SBI Amendment Ordinance, 2007 on 21 June by amending the SBI Act, 1955, for buying the entire RBI stake of 59.7 per cent.

Since the very beginning, the SBI was known for its corporate governance. It followed the best practices of other banks to set up committees and hold regular meetings to discuss business decisions. At Barclays Bank, for example, the general managers met the chairman, his deputy and the vice-chairman at regular intervals since the mid-1930s. Similarly, Midland Bank had introduced a management committee in the UK. Many banks in the United States, like the Chase Manhattan Bank, had a weekly meeting of the top policy-making body. The SBI too followed similar practices and time and again set up committees to look into various aspects, like the salary structure of officers (1955), coordination of policies of the SBI and cooperative banking and credit structure (1956), branch expansion (1960), management audit (1979) and so on.

While Matthai and Iengar were responsible for ensuring the bank's smooth transition from a shareholders' bank to a nationalised institution, it was people like Venkatappaiah, a far-sighted civil servant, who made far-reaching contributions to the success and welfare of SBI. There were other civil servants like B.C. Bhattacharya and V.T. Dehejia who, too, played a role.

The Term of R.K. Talwar

In March 1969, fourteen years after the formation of the SBI, the government appointed Raj Kumar Talwar as the managing director of the bank. He was the first non-civil servant to hold the position. Talwar's appointment was in line with the new government policy of not having men from the administrative service heading PSUs. Talwar had joined the Imperial Bank of India as a probationary assistant in 1943 and became its youngest chairman at the age of 46.* He was a highly principled banker known for

---

* D.N. Ghosh writes about the appointment of R.K. Talwar in his memoir, *No Regrets* (Rupa, 2015). He says, 'It was late February 1969. I was then in the banking division of the Department of Economic Affairs. I.G. Patel sent for me and told me that Morarji Desai, then finance minister and deputy prime minister, had decided to appoint Talwar (one of the two managing directors, the other being Ramanand Rao) as the successor to Dehejia. He showed me a half-page note on which he had obtained Morarji's approval. This was final; in those

his values, integrity, dynamism and professionalism. He created a culture of open and frank discussions and transparency in all decision making. He helped rehabilitate many sick industries and created credit plans for rural development. He initiated the first-ever organisational restructuring exercise in 1971 which withstood the test of time for nearly two decades. He launched new schemes for the benefit of smaller entrepreneurs. The keen intellect and judgement of people like Talwar placed the SBI in an unassailable position as the premier bank of the country.

Even before the RBI came up with prescribed norms for credit analysis of large advances, Talwar had put in place systems to ensure the end use of bank funds besides comprehensive analysis of corporate balance sheets. In one such case he even locked horns with the government, in particular, with Sanjay Gandhi.

In his book, *R.K. Talwar: Values in Leadership*, Narayanan Vaghul, who had joined SBI as an officer and later rose to be the chairman of ICICI, writes about how Talwar was treated for his upright stand. It was a simple case of a cement company wanting a restructuring assistance. The SBI had put some conditions, which included removal of the promoter for gross mismanagement. The promoter, being close to Sanjay Gandhi, approached the politician and requested him to intervene.

Vaghul writes that on being summoned by Sanjay Gandhi,

Talwar refused to come and see him on the ground that he held no constitutional authority and he was accountable only to the Finance Minister.' Sanjay Gandhi's response was swift and clear. He told the Finance Minister (FM), C. Subramaniam, to 'sack Talwar'. The FM could not sack Talwar as the post of the Chairman was created by an act of parliament and the FM did not have the authority to remove him. Also, removing him for a trivial reason would send shock waves in the industry.

The FM tried to persuade Talwar to take up the chairmanship of a banking commission which Talwar happily agreed to take up along with

---

days, the minister had the prerogative of appointing the chiefs of public undertakings and no approval of the Appointments Committee of the Cabinet was required. Talwar was four years younger to Ramanand Rao but Morarji stuck to his decision. The finance minister had never met Talwar, and it had always remained a mystery as to who could have suggested his name.'

his job! The FM was in trouble now. When the FM looked somewhat uncomfortable with this suggestion, Talwar very calmly looked the Finance Minister in his eyes and told him, 'Mr. Minister, you seem to be very particular that I should not continue as the Chairman of the State Bank of India, is that correct?'

The FM replied, 'Yes, Mr. Talwar, you know what the problem is. We all have the highest regard for your abilities but unfortunately you do not seem to be very flexible on this one issue which is of great importance to the highest authority in the country. If you do not want to accept any other position, I may have no option but to seek your resignation or in the alternative, to dismiss you from service. This would be extremely painful to me but I would be left with no other option.'

Talwar replied, 'Mr. Minister, I have no intention of resigning from my position. It is entirely up to you to decide whether you want to dismiss me. In any case, I have just about a little more than a year left in my second term and I see no reason why you should not allow me to complete it.'

The Finance Minister looked pained and miserable. He terminated the interview and hoped that some solution would be found. He reported the matter to Sanjay Gandhi who was infuriated and asked the CBI to investigate Talwar to find out whether there were any grounds on which he could be dismissed. Talwar's personal reputation for honesty and integrity was quite well known and in the normal course it would have been virtually impossible for any investigating agency to charge him with any misconduct. He, however, had a few chinks in his armour. One was his almost monthly visits to Pondicherry which attracted widespread attention both within the Bank and in the political circles. His attachment to the Mother and the Aurobindo Ashram was well-known and he made it clear to the Government when this issue once came up for discussion that he needed these visits for what he called 'recharging his batteries' and that if as a condition of his employment he were to stop these visits, he would as well step down from the Bank. In any case, this could not be construed as a sufficient cause for his dismissal in terms of the Act.

The second one was a little more serious. Talwar had sent appeals on behalf of the Ashram to a large number of industrialists, many of whom were clients of the Bank, seeking donations for the Auroville project. Those who were close to him, feared that the CBI could focus on this issue and charge him with abuse of authority. While Talwar himself was completely unperturbed by the reported investigation, Vaghul and his colleagues came to know from several sources that the CBI was meeting several industrialists who had given donation to the project with a view to taking from them a statement that they were coerced into giving this donation at the instance of Talwar. At the end of the investigation, two things became very clear to the CBI. One was that not a single industrialist was willing to say that Talwar either spoke to them or in any way tried to persuade them to make the donation. The second was that all Talwar had done was to forward to these clients an appeal signed by Prime Minister, Ms. Gandhi, and the Secretary General of the United Nations, U. Thant, commending the Auroville project for support. The CBI also tried, unsuccessfully, to audit the expenditure of Talwar's office which was a 'stately dome'.

Under these circumstances, there was no way in which the CBI could charge Talwar with abuse of his position. While the CBI closed the case, as far as the FM was concerned, it was back to square one and he faced the unpleasant task of reporting back to his political master his failure to carry out his diktat. Sanjay Gandhi now lost his patience. He directed the FM to amend the State Bank of India Act to provide for a summary dismissal of the Chairman. The Legislation amending the State Bank of India Act was passed in record time and received the assent of the President without any delay.

Armed with the new provision in the Act, the FM summoned Talwar once again and told him that if he did not resign from the service, there was no alternative but to remove him in terms of the new provision. But Talwar was defiant. He told the FM that he had no intention of resigning and that the FM could take whatever action he deemed appropriate. On the evening of 4 August 1976 Talwar received a message from the FM sanctioning him thirteen months leave and asking him to hand over charge to the Managing Director. It is amazing that with all the powers in its hands, the government could not summon up enough courage to dismiss Talwar, but instead gave him leave preparatory to retirement for as long as thirteen months, which he did not ask for!! This was the respect he commanded in the industry. Nani Palkhiwala advised Talwar not to challenge the government. As expected, Indira Gandhi refused to entertain Talwar's request for a meeting.[11]

Vaghul further shares,

> Talwar left the Bank promptly at 5.30 p.m. which was his usual time of departure. There was hardly anybody to see him off. Everyone was scared even to be seen to be associated with him. I had by then left the Bank service and joined the National Institute of Bank Management.
>
> The residence of the Chairman of the State Bank was just across the road and as soon as I received intimation that he had reached his home, I walked across to meet him. I found him smiling and cheerful. Extending his hand to greet me on my birthday (which by a curious coincidence happened to be 4 August) he said, 'Vaghul, look at the Divine will. What a pleasure it is to be gifted with His blessings.'
>
> I did not know what to say. I mumbled something to the effect that the Divine always tested His true bhaktas and every such test would only serve to reinforce the faith. He looked me at my eyes and said, 'How can you call this a test? As far as I am concerned, I am only an instrument of the Divine and His Will is the only thing that is important to me. If you see this as a suffering, it only shows your ignorance. We cannot sit in judgment over the Divine Will.' I then said, 'I agree, Sir that we have to accept the Divine Will with humility.' But he was not finished with his lesson. 'Where is the question of accepting or not accepting? You have to learn to enjoy all the time the Divine play. The work in the Bank is over. What the Divine has in store for me I do not know. Whatever it is, I will serve the Divine with devotion and always enjoy being His instrument.' I could only think of one example when I looked at him—the picture of Rama when he was told by Kaikeyi that he was not to be crowned as the King but had to go to the forest for 14 years. The Tamil poet Kamban says that when he heard this pronouncement from Kaikeyi, Rama's face resembled that of a lotus with a full bloom. He was happy to carry out the behest of his father. In the case of Talwar, it was the behest of the Divine. That was the only difference.[12]

In 1976, within three years of his second term as chairman, Talwar resigned. He spent the next few decades in the tranquility of Aurobindo Ashram until his death in 2002. There were attempts made in between to get a suitable position for Talwar but the Janata government under Morarji Desai was in no mood to entertain such proposals. In 1979, during Charan Singh's tenure as prime minister, Talwar was made chairman of IDBI, but as soon as Indira Gandhi returned to power in 1980, Talwar knew it was best for him to step down. For a man of integrity like Talwar, his independence and his views were far more important than any position. Years later, one of Talwar's successors, who had known him for many years, would recall that those like him 'who were privy to the resignation could unequivocally assert, without a moment's hesitation, he grew taller on the day he resigned. This, to my mind, was his finest hour.'[13]

It is a different matter that the said cement company, which had been refused the loan, was later granted the same by the Central Board of Directors, after T.R. Varadachary, a batchmate of Talwar and then the managing director of SBI, was made the Chairman of the bank. The 'Talwar Hatao Act', as it was popularly called, had done its job in the removing someone who would be known for decades to come as one of the best leaders of the SBI.

Another interesting episode that had taken place during Talwar's tenure was the famous Nagarwala case. India was then in a state of tension with the imminent Bangladesh war brewing. In the midst of all this, on 24 May 1971, an ex-serviceman, Rustom Sohrab Nagarwala, conned the Parliament Street branch of SBI in New Delhi to the tune of ₹60 lakhs. R.K. Talwar, the chairman, recalled this incident later:

> One afternoon, I was shocked to receive a telephone message from the Secretary and Treasurer, New Delhi that a high-value fraud has been perpetrated during the day. Cash, amounting to ₹60 lakh was fraudulently withdrawn from the Currency Chest at New Delhi Branch.
>
> The sequence of the events was something like this. At that time a public telephone booth had been installed inside the branch premises for the convenience of customers. The cubicle of the Chief Cashier (CC) of the branch had transparent glass walls. One Mr. Nagarwala decided to play a confidence trick on the CC. He went to the booth and telephoned him, 'I am speaking from the Prime Minister's office and she would like to speak to you. I am connecting you to her.' He then mimicked the prime minister's voice and told him that for a secret mission in national interest, he was required to take out a sum of ₹60 lakh in cash immediately and deliver it as early as possible in accordance with the directions of her Assistant. He was asked to bring the cash in ₹100 denomination notes to a point close to a certain church. He was also given a password for identification. (The password was to be as follows:

when the person asks '*Aap kis desh ka babuji?*' you will reply '*Bharat ka*' and he will say, '*Mai Bangladesh ka babuji.*' This was the confirmation that the person was the right one).

It was the time of the Bangladesh war.

I knew the CC very well, a very upright officer, hard-working but overbearing. Immediately, he went to the Branch Accountant and requested him to open the strong room to withdraw ₹60 lakh urgently. When the Accountant enquired about the purpose, he told him, 'I will let you know later but please do not delay.' Overbearing as he was, the Accountant withdrew the amount after making appropriate entries in the register. The CC went to the payment cashier, asked him to show the amount as having been received by him for some urgent payment. The payment cashier asked for the document against which the payment was being made. He told him, 'I will give you the cheque later.' He then carried the amount in a vehicle all alone to the specified place. The password was exchanged, money changed hands and was carried away in a different taxi. He was asked to go to the prime minister's office to collect the cheque.

Our CC proceeded to meet the PM. But all his efforts proved futile. He then approached Mr. P.N. Haksar, Secretary to PM and requested him for the cheque. Mr. Haksar told him that no such telephone call had been made and obviously he had been duped. Luckily, our CC had remembered the number of the taxi in which the cash was taken away. He reported to the police and immediately action was initiated. Investigation revealed that the money moved from place to place until it landed with Nagarwala in a dharamsala in the outskirts of the city. Luckily, for the bank, the entire amount except around ₹4000 was recovered the same day.

This incident very soon became a matter of serious inquiry by the government. It was also raised in the Parliament. We supplied a full report to the Finance Minister. Soon thereafter, I appeared before him. He put this question to me: 'Talwar, how could such a thing have happened in SBI, where you have well laid-out systems and procedures?' I answered, 'Sir, everybody puts this question to me but nobody has asked me how the money came back to the Bank, the very same night. I will tell you how that had happened. The State Bank is very lucky that it is under the protection of the Divine to whom I had made a fervent prayer for help. The answer has come in form of recovery of the money. You are aware of my devotion to the Mother of Sri Aurobindo Ashram and SHE is the one under whose guidance I believe I have been working in the discharge of my responsibilities. I pray that this kind of protection be continued for the Bank for all time to come.[14]

The P. Jaganmohan Reddy Commission of Inquiry, which investigated the fraud, concluded that the money belonged to the bank. It, however, found no evidence to show who actually requisitioned the money and for what purpose. In less than a year, Nagarwala and the senior inspecting police officer were dead: one after a cardiac arrest and the other in a mysterious car accident.

One of Talwar's many important contributions was hiring the services of the Indian Institute of Management Ahmedabad (IIMA), under Prof. Ishwar Dayal, to suggest organisational changes to make the SBI more efficient and productive and to ensure better controls. McKinsey had demanded an exorbitant fee of US$ 1 million for the same, which had prompted Talwar to approach IIMA.

One of the important pillars of restructuring suggested by the study was the introduction of performance budgeting as an important tool for management control. The idea behind this was to facilitate interpretation of financial, operating and economic information at every level, so that it becomes an effective tool for management control. This needed providing information not through multiple channels but as a consolidated whole. A planning department was created to monitor the entire process of performance budgeting at various levels. It was Talwar's idea to engage with IIMA so that he may make the bank stronger, at the same time agile and responsive to changes.

Raj Kumar Talwar surely left a lasting legacy.

The SBI: A Rich Heritage of Leadership

Even before Talwar, SBI had a rich tradition of exemplary leaders, whose allegiance was nonpareil. S.K. Handoo, the first managing director of the bank, was one such leader. His resignation is reported to have been occasioned by his resentment over the questions and answers in the Rajya Sabha regarding his emoluments. He felt that B.R. Bhagat, deputy minister of finance, had failed to recognise the gesture of senior Imperial Bank of India executives in agreeing to continue with the reincarnated bank despite dilution in emoluments and less favourable service conditions. The inference drawn from Bhagat's answer was that the government consented to 'maintain' Handoo and his senior colleagues in employment for no better reason than to ensure 'continuity' in the policy of the credit institution. Loyalty to the institution and individual brilliance had obviously been given a go by. The drastic curtailment of remuneration and the discussion of its constituent parts in carping terms in Parliament were perhaps too much for any self-respecting person to put up with. Handoo promptly decided to quit. Such was his allegiance to the institution that when questioned by his London manager about the reports of his resignation in the London press, Handoo replied, '... that I am unable to detail (my) reasons without running the risk of being in breach of my Declaration of Fidelity and Secrecy. I realise that this does not take you very far in answering queries but my anxiety is that nothing should be said or done which could cause any harm to the institution that we have all served for so many years. After giving the matter very careful consideration, I would suggest that if enquiries are made, you might adopt the line that the Managing Director is leaving the Bank as he is getting on in years, has done over 31 years' service and is now desirous of retiring.'[15]

The board decided to grant him a retiring gratuity of ₹50,000 free of all taxes, a monthly pension of ₹1,000 plus dearness allowance of ₹200 per month. The government expressed its unhappiness about the special gratuity sanctioned to Handoo and observed that 'they were definitely opposed to grant of special gratuity to retiring officers, as the normal retirement benefits of the Bank were quite generous and there was no valid reason for supplementing them.'[16] It was eventually left to the chairman to settle the issue (of asking for the appropriate relief under Section 60[2] of the Income Tax Act as he been promised earlier) with the government.

Matthai, the first chairman, had faced the same problems in Parliament over salaries and perquisites being paid to senior officials of the Imperial Bank. The enormous disparity in the salary of an ICS secretary in the government (₹4,000) and the managing director of the Imperial Bank (₹7,500) in the early 1950s obviously irked politicians and bureaucrats alike. The prime minister admitted that the salaries of the senior officers in the Imperial Bank were 'preposterously high' and 'could not be continued'.

S.K. Handoo, we may recall, was earlier given a salary of ₹7,500 per month. After the creation of the SBI, his salary was fixed at ₹4,500 per month plus house rent together with a personal allowance of ₹2,000 per month in the first year, starting from 1 July 1955, ₹1,000 per year in the following year; the allowance was to be discontinued thereafter. Moreover, he was made ineligible to receive bonus and entertainment allowance in future. But when it was found that he was actually receiving a salary lower than some of the officers of the bank, the central board decided to restore the entertainment allowance to Handoo on the firm understanding that it would not be extended to his successor.

The central board was not content with mere reduction in salary of top officials. Even perquisites connected with free accommodation, such as free electricity, servants and maintenance, extended in the days of the Imperial Bank were put under scrutiny. From 1 January 1958, free supply of water, electricity (including power consumed by air-conditioner) and gas was discontinued in all cases. Installation of separate electricity meters and a common cleaning and scavenging service for all office-cum-residences was introduced to curtail expenditure. Only senior officers, not below the rank of deputy secretary, were provided with house peons and watchmen. In all other cases, the provision of separate servants for home and office was dispensed with and common servants provided instead. Senior officials like Saradindu Gupta, secretary and treasurer, Bengal circle, quit immediately.

Matthai also faced a major issue with the government regarding payment of bonus. All categories of staff, including the managing director of the Imperial Bank, had been drawing bonus every year since 1942. The bonuses were paid on 1955 by the central board to all staff and in January 1956 the same terms were proposed with only the chairman and the managing director along with the entire London staff, except the manager there, excluded from the payment. Matthai was in favour of continuing the practice of paying bonus to all the supervising staff, which was called 'non award'. He believed they had done exceptional work and deserved to be paid. The finance minister was against the proposal of bonuses to non-award staff. Matthai argued that the question was not about quantum but the very principle of paying bonus to higher paid staff in an institution largely owned by the state. Quite clearly, Matthai was irked. He had earlier stated his view of nationalisation of life insurance being unnecessary. Matthai could not silently tolerate being overruled by the finance minister. He could not forget that Deshmukh in the Lok Sabha in the not-too-distant past had assured of 'no interference in the day-to-day operations of the bank'. Finally, he resigned as chairman on 19 June 1956 expressing 'various reasons' and sought release. He had expressed to the board while reporting the episode, on 20 July 1956, 'Though owned by Government, the bank must work primarily as a business institution; in doing so, it should pay regard to public policy; and—this is important—it is a matter for the Central Board of the Bank, and its Chairman to decided where the line should be drawn between the business aspect on the one hand and that of public interest on the other. Bonus pertains to the business aspect of the bank, not to that which attracts consideration of public policy. On a matter like this, it is wholly wrong for Government to interfere. In seeking to do so, Government is being unfair not only to the chairman, but also to many of the other directors, notably those who had been with the Imperial Bank.'[17]

Ministers, then and now, are known not to get influenced by such comments and C.D. Deshmukh was extremely prompt in conveying—in less than a week—the government's acceptance of Matthai's resignation. The first chairman of the SBI thus made an unceremonious exit much before the expiry of his term. We have already seen how, much later, another chairman, R.K. Talwar, had to demit office under similar circumstances.

A week before Matthai, S.K. Handoo too submitted his resignation. It was not a coincidence that Sir Vithal C. Chandravarkar, a director of the Imperial Bank since 1945 and later a central-board director of the SBI since inception, also resigned on 2 August 1956 without giving any reason.

In an article on the SBI that appeared on 29 June 1956, *Eastern Economist* commented, '... if nationalisation means the incursion of petty interferences into the highest reaches of nationalised institutions, it will not be very long before the dire prophecies of the critics of nationalisation will be fulfilled.'[18] By end of September 1956, the first central board of the bank had lost three of its key members, many months before their terms were to end.

The SBI would seldom see the likes of Matthai, Handoo or Talwar within its fold. There were other eminent men who worked for the love of their job and not money. The first vice-chairman of the SBI was Vaikunth Lal Mehta who worked in an honorary capacity. His successors—N.V. Gadgil, Mangaldas Pakvasa, D.G. Karve, H.M. Seevai, Kantilal Desai and

B.D. Garware—all eminent men also worked in an honorary capacity without drawing any emoluments. Since Garware's departure in 1975, the bank has had no vice-chairman.

As mentioned earlier, it was Iengar who succeeded Matthai, but his term was short. He was succeeded by P.C. Bhattacharya under whom we see the rapid branch expansion of the SBI. He was followed by Bora Venkatappaiah and then by V.T. Dehejia before Talwar, the first career banker, was made the chairman.

⚯

Talwar was succeeded by T.R. Varadachary, who was the managing director when Talwar was chairman. Varadachary was appointed chairman for the balance of the term that Talwar would have served in normal circumstances. It was during his tenure that a perspective plan was prepared for opening 44 offices of the bank at important financial centres in the world in three years. These offices, operating in different time zones, would serve as nuclei for development of exports, help Indian joint ventures overseas, recycle some of the petro-funds for use by Indian projects and promote remittances to India by NRIs.

In 1977, Varadachary left abruptly. His exit was not without drama and he was succeeded by P.C.D. Nambiar. In his memoir, *No Regrets*, D.N. Ghosh talks of the rumour that it was Varadachary who had raised objections to Talwar's visit to Pondicherry. Now it was P.C.D. Nambiar who apparently accused Varadachary of visiting a distant village in West Bengal during election time to meet the then finance minister, C. Subramaniam. Varadachary had been chairman for seven months and had an ignominious exit at the age of fifty-two. Many also accused Varadachary of allowing the bank to be used by many politicians for their personal gains. Life had come a full circle.

Life at the top post of the biggest bank in the country is not easy, as we have seen earlier. Nambiar and Varadachary were best of friends but fell out and after Varadachary's exit, Nambiar was made the chairman.

There is a light-hearted anecdote relating to P.C.D. Nambiar, who was a perceptive and, as it appears, caustic observer. He was the deputy managing director (personnel) when an officer from the audit department had applied for being reverted to the normal station duty from his mobile audit duty as he was suffering from spondylitis. Nambiar knew the officer well, having worked with him at a branch earlier. The officer too was banking on this association to get his request approved. Nambiar felt that he had no difficulty in approving the request on medical grounds. But he made an interesting noting in the margin: 'Request granted. But this is the first evidence of spine in that man.'[19]

Humour often makes an unexpected appearance in a mundane communication. It so happened that a senior agent of the bank once travelled on official work by train from Ahmedabad to the seaside port of Okha, also in Gujarat. In those days, it was a tortuous journey and one had to change trains to reach Okha. When he submitted his travel allowance bill, the same was passed 'as a special case', taking into consideration his seniority. But still the head office made a query by way of a branch memo as to why he had travelled by a circuitous route and not by a 'direct' route as laid down in the service rules. The agent had the briefest of replies: 'Reference reverse— Because I am not a crow!'

One other example is that of a branch manager at Bilaspur who had an annoying habit of writing in long sentences using numerous clauses, commas and other punctuations like semi-colons. He also liked to used difficult-to-pronounce and tongue-twisting words to show off his vocabulary. He once wrote a letter to his head office which was somewhat like this: 'what with the recrudescence of communal violence in the vicinity of the Branch ....' and the first sentence ran to about eighteen lines. The head office, quite likely miffed with such liberties, replied with a snub: 'We have brought it to your notice on umpteen occasions in the past and we reiterate again that your letters to this office should be couched in simple English!'[20]

6

THE GROWTH YEARS

As stated earlier, the SBI had been given a target to open 400 branches between 1956 and 1960. It was the second bank, after the Imperial Bank of India, in the history of Indian banking with a statutory obligation to open a specified number of branches within a given timeframe. The objectives of this unprecedented expansion was to extend remittance facilities to cooperative and other commercial banks in rural and semi-urban areas, to take over cash work at non-banking treasuries and sub-treasuries in those areas and to also provide suitable banking services to cooperative marketing and processing societies. There was one other objective—to mobilise savings in underbanked and non-banked areas. The problems faced by the bank were no different from what many businesses face even today—finding the right personnel, the right infrastructure and the right location for the premises. Accommodation for staff was also a cause of worry.

Many financial dailies raised their concern about the rapid expansion of the bank. One leading daily wrote: 'If the State Bank of India does incur needless and fruitless losses, it will not be because it does something very different from what the Imperial Bank did but because it tries to the same thing on a bigger scale.... Ultimately it would be the Government that is subsidising the vast network of bank offices, if the losses involved outturn the profits on Imperial's normal business.'[1]

Optimism, however, was not altogether missing. A daily from Bombay hailed the bank's expansion as a 'practical necessity' for reaching out to rural and semi-urban areas. The daily reported, 'The leeway that India has to make up in the sphere of banking, more especially in branch expansion, can be gauged broadly from the fact that Midland Bank alone has in the U.K. more or less the same number of branches that Indian scheduled banks put together have in India.'[2]

In order for the bank to meet its expansion target, it needed the support of various state governments. B.P. Patel , the then bank's managing director, felt that there was lack of awareness about the branch expansion programme not only among the officials of the various state government but even among bank officials connected with the implementation of the scheme. While the government of Bombay agreed to provide accommodation to branches in the local treasury buildings wherever possible at a standard rate fixed by the government, free armed guards were also provided for three years instead of five. But rent-free accommodation for employees was denied. The Uttar Pradesh government, on the other hand, expressed its inability to find any space in the treasury buildings and denied any provision for armed guards free of cost. Some governments like those of Madhya Pradesh and Madras State (later Tamil Nadu) extended full support. The secretary and treasurer of Calcutta was not in favour of opening a branch in Port Blair citing reasons like absence of reasonable postal services to and from the Indian mainland, as well as the time of three to four weeks that it took for a steamer to arrive from Port Blair to Calcutta.

The SBI thus had no option but to purchase private buildings or to construct new buildings in many places. Those were the days of restrictions on imports and availability of basic materials. As an example, the bank purchased and stored, in 1958, 200 tonnes of steel at import prices for meeting its requirements for another two years. This was necessitated by the fact that many portable strong rooms were required where the private landlord was not inclined to allow construction of permanent ones!

In 1957, the second year of branch expansion, 75 branches were opened while another 115 were added in the third year and 94 in the penultimate year. The bank was confident of achieving or surpassing the target of 400 branches within the stipulated time.

The inauguration of the 400th branch at Kairana in Muzaffarnagar district of Uttar Pradesh by the then finance minister, Morarji Desai, on 1 June 1960 marked the fulfilment of the statutory obligation well ahead of the deadline. In his welcome address, chairman P.C. Bhattacharya described it 'as an event which had no parallel in the history of Indian banking and perhaps ... no parallel in the banking history of any other country in the world.'[3]

Competition, even in those days, was not far behind. Notwithstanding the limited business potential of the new branches, there was also competition from the branches of other banks. Within six months of the SBI opening a branch in Hindupur, Andhra Pradesh, the Bank of Mysore too set up a branch there. Sardar Patel objected to it with a letter to the RBI in February 1957 demanding a time lag for opening of a branch by the any other bank. The RBI declined to entertain the request. The deputy governor of the RBI, B. Venkatappaiah, said, 'Our policy of allowing banks to open offices at places where the State Bank of India has opened or is due to open its offices is based on the principle that the role which an office of the State Bank plays is different from that of an office of any other commercial bank. We treat the branch expansion of State Bank as in a somewhat special category ... each application from a commercial bank for the opening of a branch at a particular place is considered by the RBI on its own merits and it will not be quite in consistence with our policy if our licences are not granted to other branks of opening offices at places included in the expansion programme of the State Bank of India solely on the ground of such inclusion.'[4]

Patel was not convinced and expressed fear of 'unhealthy competition' but Venkatappaiah did not agree. Meanwhile, Canara Bank decided to open a branch at Palghat (Kerala) where the SBI had opened a branch on 27 May 1957. The RBI did not agree to the 'time lag' as proposed by Patel. The precise impact of the competition from other banks on the performance of the SBI branches in question is not known, but it does appear that notwithstanding its majority ownership in the SBI, the RBI took an independent view as a regulator while deciding on the matters related to the SBI and other banks.

The branch expansion continued as planned, and the bank opened its 1,000th branch on 5 September 1962. Morarji Desai opened the branch in South Extension in New Delhi. The minister in his address on the occasion mentioned that the number of branches were still 'inadequate' for a country with more than 5 lakh villages. He urged the bank authorities to continue the branch expansion.

While the bank wanted the pace to be slowed down, the government wanted the opposite. There were 29 treasuries and 1,061 sub-treasuries yet to be covered by the bank. The bank tried to explain the difficulty in opening so many branches in five years but the RBI refused to give in. The SBI insisted on the government providing additional finance apart from reimbursement of losses of branches.

From Goa to NEFA

In 1961, the Portuguese colony of Goa finally came under Indian control. The armed action was code named Operation Vijay by the Indian Armed Forces. In less than two days, the combined efforts of the air force, navy and army ended 451 years of Portuguese rule. The brief conflict drew a mixture of worldwide praise and condemnation. In India, the action was seen as liberation of what was historically Indian territory, while Portugal viewed it as an act of aggression against its national soil and citizens.

The SBI was called upon to fill, on an urgent basis, the vacuum created by the closure of the Portuguese bank, Banco Nacional Ultramarino, following the liberation of Goa, Daman and Diu. The first branch of the SBI was opened at Panjim on 2 January 1962 and soon four more branches were opened at Vasco da Gama, Margaon, Mapusa and Daman by February of that year.

From Goa, the SBI then had to focus on the North East. Even before the formation of the state of Nagaland in 1963, the government had proposed a branch at Kohima. The North-East Frontier Agency (NEFA, now primarily Arunachal Pradesh, with some parts in present-day Assam) was yet another region that needed coverage. Residential accommodation was an acute problem but the bank ensured that its staff got the accommodation it needed at Pasighat, Ziro, Along, Bomdila, Tezu and Khonsa. In Along the problem was so acute that even the offices of the deputy commissioner and executive engineer were housed in ordinary temporary buildings with mud floor and bamboo walls with a thatched roof. Later, the NEFA administration agreed for 'Assam type' quarters, which meant a wooden floor, half wall and a cast-iron-sheet roof!

By the end of 1965, the SBI had as many as 72 per cent of its branches at centres with a population of less than 50,000. The presence of other scheduled banks at such centres was 40 per cent. In rural and semi-urban areas, one of every two offices of scheduled banks belonged to the SBI or its subsidiaries, said the chairman V.T. Dehejia in the eleventh

Annual General Body Meeting of the shareholders, held at Bombay on 18 March 1966.

From 1967, the RBI introduced a condition that one of every three branches licensed must be in underbanked states like Assam, Bihar, Madhya Pradesh, Uttar Pradesh, West Bengal, Orissa and Jammu & Kashmir. The expectations from commercial banks were heightened when the government began to emphasise the pivotal role they could play in the economic development of the country. The then deputy prime minister and finance minister, Morarji Desai, wrote in the *Economic Times* on 25 May 1968: 'With the economies of the rural areas linked to the broader framework of the national economy, their dependence would be retarded and their potential unexploited, if commercial banks are not able to cover these areas more efficiently and more quickly.'

Two events took place on 19 and 20 July 1969. Blasting off on 16 July, the Apollo 11 space shuttle's destination was the moon. Commander Neil Armstrong and lunar module pilot Buzz Aldrin landed the Apollo Lunar Module Eagle on the moon on 20 July. Armstrong became the first person to step onto the lunar surface six hours and 39 minutes later. When he put his left foot on the lunar surface and famously declared, 'That's one small step for man, one giant leap for mankind,' his words would reverberate across the world and be remembered forever.

While America and the world at large were busy following the path of Apollo 11 and the moon landing, another chain of events were taking place in India which culminated on 19 July 1969.

The RBI termed the event as the 'single most important economic decision taken by any government since 1947. Not even the reforms of 1991 are comparable in their consequences—political, social and, of course, economic.'[5] This event was the nationalisation of the 14 largest private banks of the country by the then prime minister, Indira Gandhi, who also held the portfolio of finance minister.

This event was considered so important that All India Radio decided to forgo the live broadcast of the moon landing which was heard in India through the Radio Ceylon broadcast!

A Brief Background to Nationalisation

India had had a disastrous war with China in 1962 followed by Jawaharlal Nehru's death in 1964. Lal Bahadur Shastri served a short stint as prime minister (June 1964–January 1966) before his sudden death. The Indian National Congress was left weakened by these events. The clamour for nationalisation had been going on since Independence. While the Imperial Bank of India had been nationalised in 1955 and the LIC created after nationalising life insurance companies in 1956, the other banks had been left untouched. The rupee had been devalued from ₹4.76 to ₹7.5 per dollar in 1966. It was termed as a 'sell out to the Americans' by the then Congress president, K. Kamaraj, who had a difficult relationship with Indira Gandhi.

Nationalisation was an instrument in the hands of Indira Gandhi to reposition herself as a reformer and signal change. A major reason given for the step was the fact that the share of agriculture in credit was 2 per cent and had not changed since 1951 while the share of industry had increased from 34 per cent to 64 per cent.

The deputy prime minister, Morarji Desai had tried to find an amicable solution in the form of National Credit Council (NCC) under the Banking Laws Amendment Act, 1968, which mandated change of directors and prevented loans to be given to directors and their firms. Under the new terms of the Banking Regulation Act, the number of industrialists on the board of directors of banks was reduced to under 50 per cent of the total. Simultaneously, more representation was given to persons with specialised knowledge of agriculture, cooperatives, small-scale industry, economics, accountancy, law and other related subjects. The idea was to snap the traditional link between industrial houses and banks so that any particular client or group of clients was not favoured while approving loans. Thus, Naval Tata, for instance, resigned from the board of the Bank of Baroda. Although the terms of the Act did not apply to the SBI and its subsidiaries, V.T. Dehejia, the then chairman of the bank, wanted the central and local boards of the bank to comply with the revised legislation. By December 1968, industrialists like J.D. Choksi, Pratpsinh Mathuradas and K.K. Birla resigned from the central board of the SBI after having served as directors for many years. Choksi, who incidentally was a director of Tata Sons and also the company's legal advisor, had been a director of the Imperial Bank's local board at Bombay since 1949, its central board since 1951 and the central board of the SBI since its inception.

The NCC was to direct lending to sectors such as agriculture and small-scale industry and had proposed doubling credit to these sectors. T.A. Pai, chairman of Syndicate Bank, and Homi Mody, chairman of the Central Bank of India, had strongly objected to the move for nationalisation stating how their banks were making progress towards opening branches for rural credit.

One of the main targets of Indira Gandhi, as mentioned by some political analysts, was the Swatantra Party started by stalwarts like C. Rajagopalachari, K.M. Munshi and others who were not in favour of Nehru's socialist ideas.[*]

D.N. Ghosh, then deputy secretary in the Ministry of Finance, has written in great detail about the chain of events leading to bank nationalisation in his memoir, *No Regrets*.[6] He spoke about how the banks to be nationalised were selected based on the deposits they held as on the last Friday of June of that year. He had been called on the night of 17 July 1969 by P.N. Haksar, the principal secretary to the prime minister, for drafting the note on the proposed bank nationalisation before sending it to the prime minister. Two days later, on 19 July 1969, 14 commercial banks were nationalised.

In the discussion that ensued, it was suggested that banks with deposits worth more than ₹50 crores were to be considered. The National & Grindlays Bank, being a foreign bank, was left out as it would send a wrong signal to the industry at large. The ordinance for bank nationalisation was to be drafted within 24 hours so that V.V. Giri (acting as president after the death of Dr Zakir Hussain) could sign it the day before demitting office (he had resigned to run for the office of president) and before Parliament met the day after. Andhra Bank missed the list as its deposits were ₹42 crores though many people from that state were keen to see it getting nationalised too. (It was nationalised much later in 1980.)

Two days later when Parliament came in session, it enacted the Banking Companies (Acquisition & Transfer of Undertaking) Act, 1969 with the same provisions as in the Ordinance. The banks which had been nationalised were Allahabad Bank, Bank of India, Canara Bank, Dena Bank, Indian Overseas Bank, Syndicate Bank, Union Bank of India, Bank of Baroda,

---

[*] Indira Gandhi later targeted the erstwhile rulers of independent princely kingdoms who supported the Swatantra Party by abolishing the privy purses in 1971.

Bank of Maharashtra, Central Bank of India, Indian Bank, PNB, UCO Bank and United Bank of India.

In the course of time, more banks would be nationalised and several mergers would take place. The latest case in point being the amalgamation of Dena Bank and Vijaya Bank into the Bank of Baroda in 2019. Oddly, none of the banks in 1969 challenged the Act in court. One Rustom Cavasjee Cooper, a shareholder of the Central Bank of India and the Bank of Baroda, filed a writ petition in the Supreme Court of India challenging the Act. Another person named T.M. Gurubaxani too filed a separate petition. Cooper was also a director on the board of Central Bank of India and had engaged the services of the eminent lawyer Nani A. Palkhiwala, who was willing to fight the case on a pro bono basis. The main challenge was the lack of any clear legal principles in determining compensation. The Act did not value the entire bank in any systematic way, but valued only some components. Important assets like goodwill were left out of the valuation, and land, rents, interest payable, etc. were undervalued. The most outrageous provision of the Act was that once the total compensation was determined, it was not paid in cash, but in government of India securities maturing in ten years.

In a landmark judgement, the court ruled in favour of the government stating that since the Ordinance was already replaced by an Act of Parliament, deciding the validity of the said impugned Ordinance was fruitless. The issue had been raised by Atal Bihari Vajpayee of Jana Sangh, who had questioned the promulgation of an ordinance only a couple of days before the Parliament was scheduled to begin. As president Dr Zakir Hussain had died while in office and the vice-president, V.V. Giri, had resigned as acting president to run for the office of president, the chief justice of the Supreme Court, Mohammad Hidayatullah had been made the acting president. An eleven-judge bench, led by Justice J.C. Shah, heard the case. Shah (joined by ten justices) wrote in the majority opinion that the Act violated the principles for compensation guaranteed under Article 31(2). The majority also held that the ordinance amounted to an act of hostile discrimination, preventing the fourteen banks from carrying on their business under Article 19 of the Constitution, whereas other Indian and foreign banks could carry on with their business. The lone dissent came from Justice A.N. Ray, who upheld the constitutionality of the legislation.

The Supreme Court delivered its judgement on 10 February 1970, striking down the Act while upholding the legislative competence of the Parliament. A fresh ordinance was issued on 14 February 1970. Palkhivala had won the battle but lost the war against nationalisation. The offending portions of the Act were removed. The schedule of compensation was replaced by another schedule that fixed the specific amount of compensation. In March 1970, soon after the judgement, the government redrafted the Banking Companies Act. The main difference was an additional ₹58 crores paid out to bank owners. The ordinance was taken to the acting president, M. Hidayatullah. The bill replacing the ordinance was passed in the Parliament by the end of March and it received the president's assent on 31 March 1970. As expected, the Left and other parties hailed the nationalisation of banks while industry captains warned of doom in the future. Looking back, D.N. Ghosh says that those were days of social control and that nationalisation was an inevitable outcome.[7] One consequence of the Act was that a separate department of banking was created in the Ministry of Finance.

Many missed an important point in the process of nationalisation. Morarji Desai had been advocating the cause for nationalisation. The collapse of Palai Central Bank based in Ernakulam and Laxmi Commercial Bank of Akola, both of which had to be liquidated, further highlighted the need for consolidation which allowed compulsory merger to protect the interests of depositors. The genesis of the Deposit Insurance Corporation (DIC) was due to these issues. India was the second country in the world, after the USA, to introduce a scheme to protect depositors. Through mergers and consolidations, by the mid-1960s, Morarji Desai had managed to reduce the number of banks from about 328 in 1960 to 94 by 1965. While a lot of credit goes to Morarji Desai, the point missed by many is that Indira Gandhi in one stroke had managed to control more than 80 per cent of the resources of banks!

When the DIC commenced operations in the early 1960s, 287 banks registered with it as insured banks. By the end of 1967, this number was reduced to less than 100, largely as a result of the RBI's policy of the reconstruction and amalgamation of small and financially weak banks so as to make the banking sector more viable. In 1968, the Deposit Insurance

Corporation Act was amended to extend deposit insurance to 'eligible cooperative banks'. The process of extension to cooperative banks, however, took a while as it was necessary for state governments to amend their cooperative laws. The amended laws would enable the RBI to order the Registrar of Co-operative Societies of a state to wind up a cooperative bank or to supersede its committee of management and to require the registrar not to take any action for winding up, amalgamation or reconstruction of a cooperative bank without prior sanction in writing from the RBI. Enfolding the cooperative banks had implications for the DIC. In 1968, there were over 1,000 cooperative banks as against the 83 commercial banks that were in its fold.

Now, many decades later, we can analyse the events better. D.N. Ghosh calls it the 'original sin' and wonders whether the event had 'bad economic reasons but [was] good politics'.[8] For a growing economy, the banks needed to serve a wider set of borrowers while in reality, the number of borrower accounts had shrunk in the period between 1961 and 1967. Ghosh says, 'Clearly, the public savings mobilised by the banking system were being cornered by a select few. This is what was at the root of the strident demand for bank nationalisation that the government then had to confront, both within Parliament and outside. The government, however, consistently maintained that change in ownership, by itself, would not redirect the flow of bank credit from trade to industry. The RBI already had adequate statutory powers to bring about the directional change over time, the government argued, refusing to succumb to ideological pressures for the nationalisation of banks.'[9]

But it was the demand from the agricultural sector that urged the government to look into the matter. One of the effects of the Green Revolution was an increasing demand for credit. This demand was being fulfilled by the self-sufficient and self-financing institutions covering all agriculture and allied activities, such as production, processing, credit provision and marketing. Commercial banks had been kept out of this sector. The Green Revolution brought about a tectonic shift in agricultural productivity, which in turn called for a surge in credit that the cooperative system was simply unable to come up with. While the RBI and the government wanted the commercial banks to take up this task, the banks were simply not geared up. They had no reach and little infrastructure.

Quite naturally, they were averse to getting involved in agricultural credit. Questions were asked, writes Ghosh, such as,

> Would commercial banks actually be able to achieve the massive geographical and functional diversification required? Would they be able to raise the kind of resources needed to meet the galloping increase in credit demand? Would short-term profit considerations, as are inherent in private ownership, deflect their attention from the larger national interest?
>
> The doubts festered even as it was becoming increasingly evident that without a credit thrust, agriculture and even industry would not be able to shift to a higher growth trajectory. With evidence on the need for institutional credit piling up, gradually the government came around to the view that it had to shed its earlier inhibitions against nationalisation of private commercial banks.[10]

When to do it was a political call, as per Ghosh. He says, 'That Mrs Gandhi used the occasion to consolidate her political power, should not depreciate the economic rationale behind what indeed was a historic step. Perhaps the worst that can be said, if it must be said, about the whole saga of bank nationalisation is that a virtue was made out of a necessity.'[11]

To come back to nationalisation, while it was intended to make the banks focus on rural and other sectors, the SBI had already taken upon itself to address the issue several years ago. The risk involved in financing the agriculture sector had made banks shy away from lending to farmers. In keeping with the recommendations of the AIRCS committee, the SBI was mandated to 'generate facilities for rural credit, to take banking to villages where India mainly resided'.[12]

The Imperial Bank of India had funded agriculture indirectly through merchants and cooperatives, so it was not a new idea for the SBI. Surety against goods and personal surety had been used to give advances for agriculture. At the instance of R.G. Saraiya, a member of the bank's central board, in March 1956 the SBI adopted several measures for assisting cooperative banks who were tasked with helping those involved in agriculture. In 1957, an informal ad hoc committee of the RBI examined the SBI's role in agricultural finance to formulate a programme of action for the bank vis-à-vis cooperative banks. The committee suggested that the advisory, developmental and coordinating functions relating to agricultural credit continue to be the responsibility of the RBI, while the SBI should endeavour to meet the growing credit requirements of agricultural marketing and processing societies (other than sugar cooperative societies). The bank took up the role assigned to it and financing was in the form of advances against government securities, pledge of goods, land mortgage, bank debentures and state government guarantee. The bank supported Primary Agricultural Cooperative Societies (PACS) and also financed agriculture through State Agro Industries Corporations. The corporations were set up to distribute tractors and agricultural machinery for modernisation. The bank provided letters of credit for import and cash credit for storage and hire purchase. The bank also initially funded state electricity boards for energisation of wells in rural areas, thus enabling agriculture indirectly. Later, when the Rural Electrification Corporation was set up in 1969, the scope of commercial banks, including the SBI, became narrower and assistance came to be provided more by way of investments in bonds of the corporation.

The nationalisation of the 14 leading commercial banks in 1969 not only brought these banks within the fold of public-sector banking but also ensured that the government's mandate of developing the national economy would be fulfilled jointly by these banks. Clearly, the banks had failed to open branches in rural and semi-urban areas and what had perhaps been lacking was a sense of urgency.

As stated previously, it was also the time when the impact of the Green Revolution was being seen in rural agriculture and economy. The Green Revolution grew from an initiative by Normal Borlaug, an American agricultural scientist and plant pathologist, who had leveraged agricultural research and technology to increase the productivity of agriculture, especially in the developing world. Scientist M.S. Swaminathan proposed the same in India with modern technology, high-yielding seeds, irrigation facilities and extensive use of pesticides and fertilisers. Lal Bahadur Shastri promoted the Green Revolution in 1965 and it was extensively carried out in the states of Punjab, Haryana and Uttar Pradesh. While use of high-yielding seeds resulted in India becoming self-reliant, especially in wheat, the extensive use of pesticides and fertilisers had a tremendous negative impact by way of land degradation, though this wasn't evident in the initial years. The Green Revolution brought in tremendous prosperity. Punjab increased its production by nearly six times and by 1970, the state was producing more than 70 per cent of the food grains for the national pool even as farmers improved their lifestyles owing to better incomes. Punjab became a model for many states to follow.

Normal Borlaug was given the Nobel Peace Prize in 1970 for his contribution. According to the Nobel Prize Committee, 'the kinds of grain which are the result of Dr Borlaug's work speed economic growth in general in the developing countries'. The 'miracle seeds' that Borlaug had created were seen as a source of new abundance and peace. Science seemed to have the magical ability to solve problems of material scarcity.[*]

Against the backdrop of focus on rural areas, the NCC had already appointed a study group, popularly called the Gadgil group, in October 1968, to study the organisation framework for the banking system to meet the problems of credit gaps in the country. The group found, not surprisingly, that the growth in banking facilities had been uneven, with 617 towns out of 2,700 in the country not having a single branch of a commercial bank. In August 1969, the RBI had appointed a committee on branch expansion programmes of public sector banks under F.K.F. Nariman, custodian of the Union Bank of India, to evolve a coordinated programme for setting up adequate banking facilities in under-banked districts. The committee recommended that banks be allotted specific districts where they could take the lead in surveying the potential of banking developments in extending branch banking and expanding credit facilities. The RBI accepted the recommendation[†] and evolved the 'Lead Bank Scheme' in 1970, under which various districts in virtually the entire country were allotted to the State Bank group, the 14 nationalised banks and two other Indian banks. The State Bank group was allotted 89 districts, almost all in backward areas.

---

[*] There is a lot of criticism of the Green Revolution for its impact on soil fertility, soil contamination, water shortage, soil erosion, reduction on genetic variety, greater vulnerability to pests and reduced availability of local food crops. Due to its demand for investment in agricultural production, the Green Revolution was in fact loaded against the small and marginal farmer who suffered in the process. There has also been a lot of criticism against the use of high-yielding genetically modified (GM) crops and against companies like Monsanto who produce the seeds.

[†] Regarding expansion in unbanked centres, the committee not only wanted that priority be accorded to cover unbanked towns but also that the programme be completed by 31 December 1970 in three phases.

The Travails of Relentless Expansion

The public sector banks needed a sort of ballast to absorb losses arising from branch expansion and this was done in the form of additional offices in cities and urban areas where the scope of a profitable operation was much higher. The RBI allowed one urban office for every two opened in rural or semi-urban areas in the case of banks which had 60 per cent of their offices in rural or semi-urban areas. But finding space in cities continued to be a problem. The minimum requirement for a branch office was a space of 4,000 sq. ft. and the demand for high rents coupled with reluctance of local bodies like Metropolitan Development Authority in New Delhi to permit opening of offices in industrial and residential areas proved to a problem. Elsewhere, there were issues like delays in sanctioning plans for alteration to selected buildings by entities such as the Calcutta Municipal Corporation. There was also acute scarcity of building materials like cement and steel.

Nevertheless, despite such problems, the SBI continued its branch expansion and the 2,000th office of the bank was opened in Kanjhawala near Delhi on 3 November 1970. Y.B. Chavan inaugurated the branch and commended the SBI for its 'pioneering work in the field of banking' and 'keeping pace' with the changes taking place in the economic and other spheres.[13] Chairman Talwar observed, '… the banking system today seeks to touch the lives of millions and to subserve the priorities and objectives, as it had never dreamt of doing before. In this process we regard the opening of the 2000th office, appropriately enough in the rural setting of Kanjhawala, as but a milestone from which to review the past and contemplate the future.'[14]

In 1970, the bank introduced on an experimental basis a scheme of opening satellite offices for conducting and developing business, particularly mobilisation of deposits. Such offices were set up at places which did not warrant the opening of a full-fledged office but where deposits could be mobilised. In two years, the bank had opened 46 such satellite offices in rural areas. While bank expansion continued (in 1971 alone, another 365 branches were opened, of which 229 were in unbanked centres), the difficulty of obtaining a suitable location and non-availability of accommodation, coupled with the onerous task of moving staff to backward areas which lacked housing facilities, continued to plague the bank.

Even against the backdrop of the Bangladesh War of 1971, the SBI continued with rapid expansion. In 1973, the bank crossed another milestone by opening its 3,000th branch on 3 December at Rayagada in the Koraput district of Orissa (now Odisha).

In 1978, with a view to facilitating branch expansion in the short run and also to enable banks to consolidate their existing position, the RBI directed banks to draw up perspective plans only for that year. This was necessary, it explained, as the future plan of expansion was dependent on the findings of several committees—the James Raj committee, the Dantwala committee and the Kamath Working Group—appointed by the RBI to look into specific areas of banking.[*]

The RBI policy for the period 1979–81 saw a major orientation of branch licensing towards bringing down the population covered per office in rural and semi-urban areas to the significantly lower national average of 20,000. An additional dimension of the policy was to open offices at all unbanked block headquarters by the end of June 1979.[15]

This was additional burden for the SBI as it had a large number of unbanked block headquarters. The bank had volunteered, when the concept of lead bank was introduced, to take the responsibility for most of the backward areas of the country. The RBI's allotment of centres in deficit states placed the SBI at a double disadvantage in that while in other banks' lead districts, the better centres were being allotted to the lead banks concerned, hardly any centres were expected to be taken up by other banks in the lead districts of the SBI since most of them were in the backward areas.

Of the 147 unbanked blocks allotted to it, as many as 25 still remained to be covered by the end of 1979. All these blocks were in the north-eastern hill areas. Though not inaccessible, they posed problems of accommodation and security. The efforts nevertheless continued. By then, the bank had reached the most backward and difficult regions of the country. It was a matter of pride for the SBI that it had reached places like Leh and Drass in Ladakh, the coldest and remotest region in the north, Chazouba in Nagaland in the north-east, the Andaman and Nicobar Islands and the remote tribal belts of

---

* The James Raj committee was set up to study the functioning of the public sector banks, the Dantwala committee for conducting a study on RRBs and the Kamath Working Group to study problems arising out of the adoption of the multi-agency approach in agricultural financing.

Madhya Pradesh and Orissa. All this was against heavy odds of inadequate communication facilities, insufficient security, absence of minimum basic facilities, problems of accommodation and difficulties of moving personnel to inaccessible places. Even today, one would shudder to imagine the plight of the bank staff posted to these branches. The bank staff did the bank proud by serving in such remote areas. It was surely a useful start in the SBI's contribution to the development of the backward regions of the country.

Work in rural branches was not easy. In 1976, the bank started a concept of village branches, where the branch was manned by an 'energetic young officer', a cashier-cum-clerk and a messenger. Such an arrangement helped the bank to run at a low cost without putting administrative strain for finding large number of staff members. The job of the bank staff was to help build the banking habit in those areas and meet the credit needs at such places where the population was often less than 5,000. It also served as an implementation agency for rural development plans drawn by the lead bank or the SBI. Since the branch offered limited bank business, they were asked not to maintain currency chests or small coin deposits and developmental work was possible as the working hours were reduced.

On 21 August 1976, the SBI opened its 4,000th office at Mon in Nagaland, one of the most difficult areas of the country. Today, the SBI has three branches there. This extract from the Nagaland Tourism website give us a glimpse of life there: 'Mon is the land of the captivating Konyak Naga. Konyaks are known for their tattooed faces, blackened teeth and head-hunting prowess, the last thankfully being in the past. When they appear in the markets to sell their agricultural produce, the Konyaks cut an impressive figure among the uninitiated. The village head, Angh, enjoys considerable power over his people—his house is a reflection of tribal power and glory and flashes both human and animal skulls alike on the porch.' One can imagine the life and experience of a young probationary officer posted there!

Soon, another landmark was achieved when the bank opened its 5,000th office at Satbarwa in Palamu district of Bihar (now Jharkhand) on 13 February 1979. Instead of a large city 'with its pomp and splendour', the bank chose to opt for a small tribal village in one of the most backward regions of the country to bring on the banking map of India and give it pride of place on this special occasion. As the then bank's managing director explained, 'Having opened hundreds of offices in unbanked rural areas with the primary focus on economic development, we wanted our 5000th office to epitomise the Bank's commitment to rural development, in all humility, the largest bank was looking for a small place for a big mission.'[16]

By the end of 1980, the bank had 5,569 offices, excluding administrative ones, of which 77 per cent were situated in rural and semi-urban areas. Many claimed that it had the largest commercial banking branch network of its kind in the world!

Financing Agriculture and Non-banking Programmes

With continued focus on providing credit to the agricultural sector, especially small farmers who were not benefiting from the Green Revolution, the SBI designed a liberalised scheme of agricultural finance in 1969. But the bank could not cover farmers who were below subsistence level and did not own any land. The assistance provided to others was mainly in the form of working capital for purchase of fertilisers, pesticides, seeds and short-term loans for marketing. Medium-term loans were given for land development as well as for setting up irrigation facilities. Loans were given to individuals but they were secured by the guarantee of all the farmers in the group. Today we see a lot of self-help groups (SHGs) operating under similar arrangements but the SBI's efforts were pioneering, to say the least.

The bank came up with various methods to finance agriculture. Under the crop loan scheme, finance was provided according to the size of the land holding for purchasing seeds and other activities. An instalment credit scheme was created for purchase of tractors, pump-sets, etc. The bank also introduced a farm graduate scheme wherein technically qualified personnel like graduates in agriculture, dairy and veterinary science were given loans. The bank adopted villages under its innovative village adoption scheme. In the first year, it adopted nearly 200 villages throughout the country and by September 1970, the number had risen to 880.

Ultimately, the bank's vision of achieving the most efficient coverage of rural areas, including the financing of all credit needs of eligible households through village adoption scheme, could not be realised due to pressures of populism. In a communication dated 3 December 1980 sent to all public sector banks, the RBI stated that 'adoption of a village by a bank should only mean that it had declared its intention to do intensive lending in the area but does not mean that other banks are excluded from financing in that area.'[17] The letter further warned that the 'non-adopted' villages may feel ignored. This stymied the scheme to a great extent.

P.C.D. Nambiar, chairman of the SBI, would later lament the RBI's decision to discontinue the village-adoption scheme. He said, 'It would appear that every bank branch is now expected to finance agriculture in all the villages falling within its area of operation, irrespective of the number of such villages and the ability of that branch to service them all. This policy change would set the clock back by more than a decade in that banks would again face all the problems they had almost tided over. In fact, the circumstances which impelled banks to adopt the area approach not only still exist but have assumed greater consequence in view of the mounting overdues ... It is true that that area approach may appear inequitable to farmers in non-adopted villages; this, however, is the result of the credit gap in the rural markets [which] ... would take years for banks to bridge.... I do not see how a return to scattered lending in the meantime will improve the position.[18]

The bank used a market-segmentation approach, which led to the creation of an agricultural banking division at large branches. Branch performance was designed to be controlled and monitored through a system of budgets whereby, in keeping with the policies laid down by the central office, targets were fixed for each branch and corrective action was required to be initiated, wherever warranted.

The bank was the first to create a training course in agricultural financing which was organised at U.P. Agricultural University, Pantnagar, in 1967. Later many other universities were added to the programme. An Agricultural Development Bank (ADB) was created, which differed from a conventional branch in that it identified bankable propositions of a defined area consisting of a group of at least 100 to 150 contiguous villages and provided 4,000 to 5,000 farmers with loans aggregating to a crore over a period of four to five years. The ADBs were also to cover the financing of cottage and small agro-based industries like rice mills and oil-processing units and to support artisans and small rural traders.

P.C.D. Nambiar clarified, '... if the Bank ... chooses to strengthen its network of ADBs, it is not for commercial aspirations; our purpose is none other than spurring the process of rural development in whichever area we are permitted, regardless of whose lead responsibility it is.'[19] The bank also introduced the Integrated Rural Development Programme (IRDP) as a pilot in 1977 with the belief that only an integrated approach to problems in villages could lead to perceptible improvements. Later, when a similar programme with an identical name was introduced by the government, the IRDP was renamed as State Bank Gramodaya Project.*

Today, we see a large number of corporates adopting villages under their corporate social responsibility (CSR) schemes. It is admirable that the SBI had thought of social welfare several decades ago, when CSR was not a mandatory requirement as it is for large corporations today.

Under the non-banking programme, a wide range of activities, such as provision of drinking-water facilities, running of adult-literacy classes, construction of school buildings, providing financial assistance to poor students for purchase of books, awarding prizes to meritorious students, building and repair of roads, bridges and village lanes, electrification of villages and provision of street lighting, organising medical camps, family-welfare programmes, thrift weeks and audio-visual shows on various social problems, assisting in low-cost housing for Scheduled Castes and rehabilitation of tribals, etc. were undertaken in coordination with government officials and voluntary agencies.

It was clear that while the SBI and other banks were trying to serve the needs of the rural community, there was a clear need for formation of credit institutions which would combine the advantages of both cooperative banks and commercial banks.

Regional Rural Banks

The regional rural banks (RRBs) were thus formed on the recommendation of the Narasimhan committee in 1976. It was decided that the banks would be set up, to start with, in comparatively backward or in tribal areas where coverage by commercial banks and cooperatives was relatively poor and which had a real potential for development though not at the expense of

---

* A noteworthy feature of the project was that agriculturists started switching over to more remunerative cropping patterns using large quantities of fertilisers and seeds of better quality leading to higher productivity.

cooperatives. The RRBs would be sponsored by commercial banks and were, in fact, to supplement the efforts of commercial and cooperative banks. By June 1977, as many as 48 RRBs, including 8 by the SBI, had been set up across the country.

The RBI also set up the Dantwala committee to get feedback from all sponsoring banks on their experience in organising and running RRBs. Based on the feedback, one of the principal recommendations made by the committee was that RRBs should form an integral part of the rural credit structure wherein all commercial banks—not only the sponsor banks alone— would hand over, in a phased manner, such of their rural credit business to the local RRB as fell within its jurisdiction or which it would handle effectively. The reasons for preferring RRBs over commercial banks included lower cost of operations, local involvement through appropriate staffing pattern and composition of share capital. The RRB was recommended to be confined to one district so that it could be in close contact with the development programmes of the district as well as the operations of the local cooperative and commercial banks.

Over the years, the RRBs, which are often viewed as the small man's bank, have taken deep roots and have become an inseparable part of the rural credit structure. They have played a key role in rural institutional financing in terms of geographical coverage, clientele outreach and business volume as also contribution to development of the rural economy. Over the next few decades, many committees were set up to investigate not only the impact of the RRBs but also their financial viability. There have been debates on the lack of a single owner with clear ownership and control, and no prospects for profits, diffused accountability and weakened oversight of the RRBs, but we shall not attempt to analyse it here.

Banking on Societal Development

Unemployment continues to be a problem discussed with each successive government, ever since India gained independence in 1947. In Indira Gandhi's twenty-point programme (1975), the twentieth point referred to creating apprentices so that they could get employed! But it never saw the light of the day. In 2014, the Modi government took various steps for skilling, including setting up a skills ministry to create personnel who could be 'job ready'. However, the problem of unemployment continues even today. Getting jobs to people rather than people to jobs is a problem that has not been solved for more than 70 years. The problem was even more acute in the late 1960s and the 1970s. As per one estimate, in the beginning of the 1970s, about 16 million people were without jobs. The figure may have been even higher as we tend to assume that the self-employed are in a job while it might actually be 'disguised unemployment'. The state and central government's Half-a-Million Jobs Programme (HAMJP) initiated in 1973 was one endeavour to overcome unemployment.

Realising the gravity of the situation, the RBI appointed a committee in July 1970 under the chairmanship of V.D. Thakkar* to review the role played by commercial banks in generating employment in the country. According to the committee, financial intermediaries like banks were effective instruments of economic growth and had an important role to play in stimulating employment. For this, the banks needed to consider how best integrated financial and management assistance could be arranged considering the totality of the requirement of the borrowers.

The committee found that banks were lending to small industries and small businesses but their lending policies were not responsive to social needs. Many self-employed persons were asked to provide personal guarantees or that of third parties, which was not possible. There were no facilities for a bridge loan which a businessman may require for urgent need for raw material or otherwise. As loans repayment started immediately, it was not possible to take loans for machinery as there would be a lag time before production started. Loans to transport operators did not cover spares and repair cost. Educational loans then did not have a waiting period and repayment started immediately, making them unviable. The chairman of the SBI, R.K. Talwar was of the view that the bank could not play the role of both a coordination and a developmental agency. He felt that bank was not in a position to take a total view of the economy and formulate multifaceted schemes to help entrepreneurs. He stressed the role of the government in total planning and felt that the bank could play a significant role but not assume full responsibility of employment-oriented lending.

---

* At that time, he was the joint general manager of the Bank of Baroda.

Over the years, the SBI played many lead roles in employment-oriented lending. Lending to unemployed graduates to set up bookstalls on railway platforms is one such example.

With the draft Sixth Five-Year Plan (1980–85) envisaging the creation of employment opportunities of the order of 49.26 million person-years, banks were assigned an even bigger role for providing credit to bankable schemes. Remaining fully alive to this vital problem, the SBI and other commercial banks took a number of measures to improve their lending under employment-oriented schemes.

Even P.C.D. Nambiar opined that the credit support from the bank was just one of the ways to tackle the problem of unemployment. He believed that the solution to the problem of rural unemployment was to focus on promotion of minor irrigation, allied agricultural activities and to promote rural industries.[20]

As we saw earlier, the improvisations and innovations introduced in small-scale industries, small business and in the agricultural sector were part of the SBI's response to development banking.

Continuing the focus on social banking, the SBI came up with an innovative banking philosophy in August 1973, which gradually became part of its corporate philosophy. The genesis of this philosophy lay in making the bank a useful and effective 'corporate' citizen whereby 'greater sensitivity' to pressing community problems could be developed.[21] The efforts were to be primarily focused on ameliorating poverty, improving the quality of life, bringing or restoring dignity to human life and winning the acceptance and recognition of the community. While announcing the adoption of this corporate philosophy, Talwar also added that while the post-1969 period saw the banking industry earmarking a larger portion of loanable funds for the priority sectors, including employment-oriented and differential rate of interest schemes, the bank had also initiated 'creative and innovative' projects which 'may or may not be regular banking propositions' but were essential for the development of the community. These were not, he said, 'normal banking innovations, but something more.'*[22]

---

* It was around this time that Talwar in a letter to the circle chief general managers urged that, to start with, the bank must adopt small and compact localities of metropolitan or large urban centres and try to finance the downtrodden and weak for some productive economic activity.

The SBI was the first commercial bank in India to take such a step. Referring to the new culture as 'at best a humble beginning', Talwar did not hesitate in admitting that 'whatever little may so far have been achieved is qualitative in nature though quantitatively not altogether insignificant. Far more important is the promise that the effort holds for the future effort being made by our numerous branch managers and other employees, and in fact, even by their families. I owe them a word of praise.'[23]

Under the bank's innovative programmes, the neglected and downtrodden were covered. Those included tribals, Dalits, prisoners, ex-prisoners, physically handicapped, disabled, mobile barbers, lepers, slum dwellers, butchers and bone collectors, itinerant vendors and many such. Financing of prisoners was especially lauded at it helped the prisoners to take up work and help their families. The SBI provided assistance for self-employment and resettlement of ex-convicts, who were shunned by the society. These are shining examples of how the bank was leading the way in social banking.*

Any pioneer in its field has to take on an evangelical role and we find the bank playing that role multiple times. One such example was the 'State Bank comes to classroom' programme which was introduced in November 1973. As the name suggests, the aim was to encourage the idea of thrift from childhood. While encouraging good habits, the bank was targeting the large population of teenagers, who could become the bank's customers in future. By June 1980, the State Bank group had opened more than 15 lakh accounts in the name of children throughout the country with deposits of nearly ₹15 crores in 13,116 schools adopted by the SBI. The author recalls having his first bank account opened with the SBI when the bank authorities had visited his school in Begusarai, Bihar.

The SBI continued its tradition of social banking with the right intent and earnestness. Medical camps and free medical advice were part of activities for many bank branches. So were initiatives like tree-planting programmes, collection of used magazines and their distribution among patients in hospitals, donation drives for calamities and 'shramdaan' for

---

* Tribals, prisoners, physically handicapped and disabled, orphans, lepers, slum dwellers, butchers and bone collectors, hawkers, mobile barbers, itinerant vendors, middle-class householders, barter traders, self-employed and underemployed women and industrial workers were all brought under the purview of the scheme.

construction of roads in adopted villages. The bank staff played a stellar role in building India without clamouring for visibility.

Efforts were also made to constantly get newer areas into innovative banking. Offices in urban areas were encouraged to adopt slums. School-going children were provided with support for purchase of books and bridge loans to poor students till they received their scholarships. In 1979, the International Year of the Child, the bank created a State Bank Children's Welfare Fund with voluntary contributions from members of staff and matching contribution of ₹5 lakhs from the bank. Contribution to the Prime Minister's Relief Fund during natural calamities were regularly done but what was admirable was that the bank introduced a Social Service Leave Scheme in 1977 to enable staff to volunteer at relief centres in areas devastated by natural calamities. In cyclone-affected areas, volunteer bank employees were granted a special leave on full pay for not more than 15 days. The employees were also reimbursed actual railway or bus fare apart from travel time for him or her to contribute to local relief centres or social-service organisations and provide help. To ensure smooth running of the said area, not more than 25 employees from each circle and ten from all central office establishments were allowed at one time. The bank also allowed employees to take leave up to six days every six months, in addition to their usual leave, for implementing meaningful projects in rural areas.

The culture of innovative banking initiated and developed by the SBI eventually brought the bank and the community closer to each other. Today, this philosophy is known as CSR and has caught on with most corporate entities.

Forays in Core Banking Areas

The SBI continued to play an important role in the lead bank scheme which had helped rapid expansion of banking services in the rural and underbanked and unbanked areas of India. It also helped to institutionalise the concept of planning of banking services for rural development at the district level. Similarly, the bank also played a major role in the implementation of the twenty-point programme. 'A bank is a community-based organisation and it should take steps, on an ongoing basis to blend its business goals with social obligations. It should strive to serve the community in more ways than only financial. It has to win the co-operation of the community in which it operates in visualising and devising plans on a broader social canvas, and, what is equally important, in ensuring their successful implementation,' says Talwar, explaining the role of the SBI.[24]

When the government gave a target of 5 million hectares of land to be brought under irrigation, the SBI managers were given discretionary powers for grant of term loans to farmers for minor irrigation schemes. Water development corporations of Haryana, Bihar, Gujarat, Orissa and Maharashtra were financed by the SBI. The bank also participated in the command area development projects of Rajasthan, Chambal and Gandak. The SBI had taken the words of its chairman, R.K. Talwar, seriously!

When in 1975, by an Act of Parliament, the system of bonded labour was done away with, the bank issued instructions to all local head offices to obtain list of such persons from the district administrative authorities concerned, identify rehabilitation possibilities for them and commence lending financial support. The activities to be financed included basket weaving, purchase of milch animals, cycle-rickshaws, bullock-carts, sheep-rearing and such. Even financing handloom weavers was taken up with renewed vigour to promote the handloom industry. Besides financing the food procurement operations of the central and state procurement agencies on a massive scale, the bank, as a matter of deliberate policy, provided financial assistance to fair price shops, consumer cooperative stores, super bazaars, etc., which were effective instruments for ensuring equitable distribution of essential commodities at fair prices. The bank played a crucial role in helping people who were allotted land under government's programme of distributing surplus land by giving them loans for animal husbandry like dairy, poultry, goat and sheep farming, and piggeries.

It was also the time when many institutions were set up for long-term finance. Formed in 1956, LIC was an important player in providing long-term finance to private companies. The Unit Trust of India (UTI) helped small investors who were looking at a less risky instrument for investing in shares. It helped in bridging of long-term credit gaps in industrial sector. The Industrial Credit and Investment Corporation of India (ICICI) and Industrial Development Bank of India (IDBI) too were focused on long-term financing for projects. A lot of consortium lending was led by the SBI and by 1980, it had participated in more than 100 such projects acting as the lead bank in most of them.

By the mid-1970s, the SBI had started playing a key role in foreign financing as well. In 1976, it assisted in a town project in Kuwait and a power station and airport complex in Libya. Infrastructure projects in Saudi Arabia, Libya, Kuwait and UAE were being financed by the bank. Oil and Natural Gas Commission (ONGC) raised a US$ 50 million loan where SBI played the role of a co-manager. Similarly, with Midland Bank, the SBI helped in syndicating a loan of US$ 50 million for Air India for the purchase of three Boeing aircrafts. In 1978, the SBI became the sole canalising agency[*] for import of gold for sale, to exporters of gold jewellery. In 1979, the bank assisted two large turnkey projects: one for laying a railway line in Nigeria with an outlay of ₹520 crores and the other for setting up a power plant in Doha with an outlay of ₹500 crores. These are some examples of overseas financing by the SBI in those years. During the 1990s, loans to joint ventures amounted to US$ 20 million. The bank successfully took the lead in managing a syndicated Euro-dollar loan of US$ 35 million for an Indian company for setting up a viscose staple fibre plant in Indonesia.

In 1980, the bank lead managed a consortium formed for the purpose of adding confirmation to letter of credit (LC) aggregating to ₹16.5 crores received from Uganda for the export of a variety of Indian goods. This type of risk participation was the first of its kind in India.

It was during T.R. Varadhachary's time[†] that the SBI looked at a plan for 44 offices in important financial centres across time zones in three years from 1977 onwards. The offices would help in development of exports while providing help to Indian joint ventures overseas and also recycle some of the petro-funds for use by Indian projects. Remittances from NRIs was also expected.

As we have seen, the Imperial Bank of India had insisted on an office in London to ensure close proximity to power and share in some business from there. When the SBI was created, it had 11 offices, of which eight were in Pakistan and one each in UK, Burma and Ceylon. During the 1965 war,

---

[*] Canalised items, which can be imported using only specific procedures or methods of transport, can be brought through canalising agencies appointed by the government.

[†] He was the chairman between August 1976 and April 1977.

Pakistan took over the SBI branches as enemy property while in Burma, the Rangoon branch was taken over by the Peoples' Bank in 1963 following nationalisation. To ensure remittances of NRI funds, the bank conducted a survey of states of Mauritius and Fiji, which had a large Indian ethnic population, but initial reports were not very encouraging. However, while allowing branches to be opened abroad and for foreign banks to operate in India, the RBI and the government had to look at the policies to ensure that the laws of the country in which the foreign bank was incorporated did not discriminate against Indian banks. American banks were already functional in India but the proposals by PNB and Bank of India in the early 1960s for opening branches in the US were not approved. There was a fear of outflow of foreign exchange as compared to earnings.

In 1969, the RBI reviewed the overseas network of Indian commercial banks and of foreign banks in India. The review revealed that 13 foreign banks with head offices in six different countries were operating in India while Indian banks had branches only in three of those countries, namely the UK, Hong Kong and Japan. Indian commercial banks had branches in 11 countries in Asia, Africa and the West Indies, which had a sizeable Indian immigrant population, many of whom were successful professionals or businessmen. The countries were South Yemen, Ceylon, Fiji Islands, Guyana, Kenya, Malaysia, Mauritius, Singapore, Thailand and Uganda.[*] After nationalisation, the RBI and government started having periodic meetings with all banks for setting up of foreign offices.

The SBI's New York branch was very successful. From 1979, the International Division (ID) was treated as a market segment and a full-fledged planning department was set up in the Division to give the required focus. By 1980, the number of foreign offices had gone to 36 and branches to 22. The representative office in Tokyo was made into a full-fledged branch. Moreover, by 1980, branches in Paris, Antwerp, Jakarta, Moscow, Sao Paolo, Seoul, Dubai, Zurich and many other places were under progress

---

[*] The six countries with 13 banks in India in 1969 were the UK (National and Grindlays Bank, Chartered Bank, Eastern Bank, Mercantile Bank and British Bank of the Middle East), the US (First National City Bank, Bank of America, American Express International Banking Corporation), Japan (Bank of Tokyo and Mitsui Bank), the Netherlands (General Bank of Netherlands), France (Banque Nationale de Paris) and Hong Kong, then a British colony (Hong Kong and Shanghai Banking Corporation).

or awaiting government clearance. A survey was also being carried out for evaluating business prospects in countries as diverse as Channel Islands, Luxembourg, Surinam, Mexico, Australia, North Yemen and Thailand.

In the US, the ubiquitous motels are colloquially called 'Patel motels' as many of them are owned by Gujaratis.* The prosperous Napa Valley and Yuba City has Punjabi settlers who own orchards of anywhere between 10 acres to 2,000 acres where they harvest grapes. These became the target segment for business in the US.†

As we see in most of the Indian forays into banking, the SBI has led the charge. The case for merchant banking was no different, though the services for merchant banking were started first by National Grindlays Bank in 1967. With Foreign Exchange Regulation Act (FERA) promulgated in 1973, many foreign companies were required to dilute their shareholding and merchant banking activity in India got a boost.

While commercial banks were in the business of lending and raising deposits, the merchant banker specialised in areas of raising capital or advisory services. Merchant bankers, worldwide, had been in vogue since the thirteenth century. This was done through family-owned firms with Amsterdam as the centre of such activities till the eighteenth century and later taken over by London when it became a centre of international trade. Many of the bankers were of Jewish origin. One of the earliest activities of merchant banking was acceptance credit, which involved the merchant banker accepting a bill and guaranteeing payment to the holder. Bill discounting helped to promote trade. The merchant banker soon became an advisor and started helping in raising capital, syndication of loans and promoting joint ventures in other countries.

---

* In his book, *Life Behind the Lobby: Indian American Motel Owners and the American Dream* (Stanford University Press, 2012), Pawan Dhingra reckons that one out of two motels in the US is now owned by Indian Americans. Of this, 70 per cent are owned by Gujaratis—and among them, three-fourths share the last name Patel. There are some 22,000 hotels and motels owned by Indians across the US, together valued at US$ 128 billion.

† https://www.sikhpionners.org. In Yuba-Sutter County, Sikh farmers account for 95 per cent of the peach farming, 60 per cent prune farming, 20 per cent almonds and walnuts. In the Bakersfield and Freson area, 20 per cent of the table grapes are grown by Sikh farmers.

Merchant banking per se was not new to India. In India, the managing houses had played the role of the merchant banker.[*] Most of these houses were owned by businessmen like the Tatas, Birlas, Dalmias, Singhanias, Thapars, Poddars and the Ruias. The managing agency system was eventually abolished in 1970. Then institutions like ICICI, IFCI, LIC, IDBI, and UTI helped in assisting the industry. It was not till the late 1960s that the commercial banks stepped into the merchant banking arena, though the Act did not prevent it. The banks were far too tied up with traditional commercial banking and development banking priorities as we saw earlier.

The SBI got into the merchant banking field in 1972 under the leadership of R.S. Bhatt, who was earlier the (first) chairman of UTI (1964–72). R.S. Bhatt was the consultant and a senior official of the bank was appointed as officer on special duty under him.[†]

One hurdle in setting up of the merchant-banking division was the inability of the SBI to underwrite share issues. But as other bankers were offering advice as part of their services, it was decided to allow advisory services and the risk associated thereof as part of the business offering.

The first issue managed by the merchant banking division was public issue of 3,43,000 shares of ₹10 each on behalf of Excel Glass. The next one was Eddy Current Control. The experience of the two issues was not very satisfactory but the bank managed two more issues in 1973 as part of earlier commitments. The issues were of Karnataka Steel and Wire Products and Bundy Tubing of India. A total of 53,000 share applications were received and the bank was not adequately staffed to handle the volume. Due to delays, the division had to send letters of apology to those who had applied for Bundy Tubing.

---

[*] The managing agency or house was a peculiar corporate structure that allowed the few partners who set it up to control a number of public-limited and joint-stock companies, despite a very small shareholding in the latter. It allowed men with great entrepreneurial drive and organisational abilities to get involved in a number of businesses and promote others, but it was also a system prone to abuse. The managing agency essentially managed these firms through long-term management contracts that gave them total control and big returns while the investors of the firm got the short shrift.

[†] His engagement, initially for a period of two years from March 1973, was renewed on several occasions as his guidance was invaluable.

Soon more proposals started flowing in and the division would evaluate the same based on technical and economic viability of the projects as well as the promoter's antecedents and business experience. As business picked up, the division was decentralised with bureaus being set up in Bombay, Calcutta, Madras and New Delhi. For advisory assistance, C.J. Khanna, the ex-chairman of IFCI, was taken on as a consultant in 1975.

As underwriting of issues was a crucial part of the offering, the State Bank of India Act was amended in 1975 to allow the same. The activity was taken up not to just earn commission or profits on appreciation of share value but for those projects which were of national priority and to prevent delays.

Soon, the merchant banking division was making rapid progress. Successful management of seven public issues, all of which were oversubscribed, in the very first year of its operations indicated the division's preparedness for taking up challenges in this field. Two large clients—a tobacco company and a tyre manufacturer—switched over to the bank from two large foreign banks in India, the only ones engaged in merchant banking business at that time. The merchant banking division handled 24 projects in 1975 and 40 the next year. The rapid progress of the division saw it managing the 100th issue in 1979—the bank managed 25 issues of shares/bonds/debentures aggregating ₹40.35 crores in the year. These included clients like SAE (India), Bombay Tyres International (Firestone), Tea Estates India and Malayalam Plantations (India). Other clients included Garware Nylons, Atlas Cycle Industries, Raasi Cement, Mico Products, etc. The bank had established its expertise in helping foreign companies in their strategies of Indianisation involving restructuring of capital and raising of equity in Indian markets. Three multinational companies—Cadbury, Davy Ashmore and Indian Duplicator Co.—brought out issues aggregating ₹2.66 crores. The division also helped companies to prepare documents for term loans.

Having managed more than 150 assignments and over 100 public issues, the bank decided in early 1980 to enter the realm of portfolio management as well. A very minuscule percentage of the Indian population participated in shares and the government was keen to develop the capital market. The immediate objective was to help customers with large shared holdings and investible surplus to manage their portfolios.

While the above activities were going on, the bank management took steps to groom internal talent rather than hire expensive talent from outside. Many managers were sent to IIM Ahmedabad and the Jamnalal Bajaj Institute of Management at the bank's cost for training.

By the end of 1980, the bank had managed 122 capital issues aggregating ₹130 crores and accomplished syndication of term loans to the tune of ₹337 crores in 62 projects with an aggregate capital outlay of ₹921 crores. The high ethical and professional standards of the division were one of the key reasons for the success of the merchant banking division despite stiff competition. Within seven years, the division had earned a name for itself in underwriting, corporate counselling and portfolio management. In August 1986, a subsidiary in form of SBI Capital Markets Limited (SBICAP)* was formed. Today, many leaders in the industry owe their success in careers to the initial training with SBI Caps, as it is sometimes called. Today, SBICAP offers the entire gamut of investment banking and corporate advisory services. These services encompass project advisory, structured debt placement, capital markets, mergers and acquisitions, private equity and stressed assets resolution.

The company is a complete solutions provider offering diversified financial advisory and investment banking services, innovative ideas and unparalleled execution to its client base across all stages of the business cycle. Its services range from venture-capital advisory, project advisory, buy and sell-side advisory, accessing financial markets to raise capital and even restructuring advisory in their turnaround phases.

If commercial banking involves mainly raising deposits and providing loans, the merchant banker specialises in facilitating the promotion and consolidation of enterprises through offering specialised services in areas like raising capital or other advisory services. In the SBI, with its subsidiary SBICAP, the two are seamlessly combined, thereby offering unique value to the customer.

---

* SBICAP was set up as a wholly owned subsidiary of the SBI. In 1997, Asian Development Bank (ADB) picked up a 13.84 per cent stake in SBICAP. The ADB's stake was purchased by the SBI in March 2010 and SBICAP is once again a wholly owned subsidiary of the bank.

Keeping in mind regulatory concerns which may arise on account of the bank having lent to its customer, SBICAP in 2018 ceased to offer debt resolution and other advisory services, bringing them into the fold of the bank. It thus avoids a conflict of interest situation where SBICAP pitches for advisory business where the parent is the lender. Another jewel in the bank's portfolio, SBICAP continues to win numerous domestic and international awards consistently.

7

FOCUS ON THE 'AAM AADMI'

The common thread we see in every sphere of business undertaken by the SBI is the focus on the common man. Millions of pensioners, government servants and farmers would remember having a fixed deposit account with the nearby SBI branch at some point in their lives. The bank also served princely states and large corporates. In the days of presidency banks, the banks held only public deposits, which were primarily government funds lodged with them. They did not have to attract deposits from retail customers as they had access to government funds on which they didn't have to pay interest. This ended with the passing of the Presidency Bank Act of 1876, and this is when the banks turned to private deposits. Fixed deposits were introduced in the 1880s and savings bank schemes in the early twentieth century.

Till 1935, the Imperial Bank of India held not only government funds but also funds belonging to other semi-government bodies and even individuals who seemed to have more trust in government-associated institutions. At that time, the interest paid on fixed deposits was 1.5 per cent for a period of 12 months while that on savings accounts was 1 per cent per annum.

In 1955, the deposits of the Imperial Bank of India (later SBI) declined. This was in the aftermath of the announcement made on 20 December 1954 about the government's decision to assume effective control of the Imperial Bank. Matthai, the first chairman of the SBI, attributed the decline to the 'initial apprehension' in the minds of the public regarding the future policy of the bank and 'continuance of its commercial character in its altered status'.[1] It took a while—six months or so—for the fears (like those about undue interference by the government or a sudden fall in service) to be allayed.

The deposit rates had not changed since 1936–37. The RBI was in favour of the SBI increasing its deposit rates as that would be an incentive for people in smaller places to keep their savings with the bank. It also suggested that the rates offered should be such that that it did not lead to a shift of deposits from other banks to the SBI but rather be aimed generally at attracting money held outside the banking system. H.V.R Iengar, the chairman of the SBI, dismissed the criticism that the SBI had certain 'inherent advantages' over other scheduled banks and that it used 'its privileged position to attract business to itself'. He explained, 'If it were indeed to be the policy of the State Bank to operate flat out as a commercial institution irrespective of the consequences to other Scheduled Banks, it would have been quite easy to increase its interest rates further [the bank had increased savings bank account rates from 1 per cent to 1.5 per cent] and I have little doubt that thereby a much larger volume of deposits would have accrued to us, some of it perhaps in the form of fresh deposits but a larger proportion as diversion from other banks.... It is not our intention to enter into a race, as we could easily do if we were merely concerned with swelling our profits. On the contrary, it is our hope that by pursuing a policy of moderation in our rates both for deposits and advances, we may act as a steadying influence, more particularly during a period stringency when runaway conditions are so easy.'[2]

There were many in the banking industry who were critical of the SBI. C.H. Bhabha, chairman of Indian Banks Association (IBA), for instance, pointed out that since only eight of the 66 branches opened since inception till the end of 1956 were in places where no branch of a commercial or cooperative bank existed, it did not 'say much for the pioneering spirit' of the bank.[3]

It was in 1960 that the bank undertook an intensive drive using visual publicity at bank branches to promote deposits. Films were made enumerating the advantages of fixed deposits, similar to the publicity being done by the newly formed LIC which was spreading the habit of insurance and savings through its schemes.

The bank also liberalised its savings-bank rules reducing the minimum balance for bank accounts with cheque book facility from ₹200 to ₹100 and increasing the limit for maximum deposits during a calendar year from ₹10,000 to ₹25,000. The maximum balance in a savings-bank account was raised from ₹50,000 to ₹75,000. Withdrawal facilities were increased from once to twice a week. Defence personnel were given special privileges with waiver of charges for maintenance of accounts, free remittance for settlement of education fees or maintenance of deposits, and free collection of outstation cheques, including immediate credit for outstation cheque on any bank.

All banks, foreign and Indian, with deposits of ₹5 crores or more for the first time entered into a voluntary All India Inter Bank Agreement effective from 1 October 1958, fixing ceilings on interest paid on deposits. Hailing the scheme of voluntary regulation as the 'hard-earned fruit of a campaign' conducted by leading bankers, the Eastern Economist (12 September 1958) hoped that the bank managements 'as much in their enlightened self-interest as in the interest of the country's banking system' would extend 'unflinching support' to its implementation.

Many innovative schemes were evolved but in keeping with its ethics and values, the SBI did not pay brokerage in any form for securing deposits. In a spurt of advertisements released in 1975, several banks had adopted questionable tactics in deposit schemes showing fabulous rates of interests, by juggling figures and basically fooling the ordinary customer. People like R.K. Talwar were totally against such ideas and hoped that banks would not resort to such practices. Later, IBA would frame rules to ensure that all advertisements for deposits, deposit receipts and publicity literature were to state the exact rate of interest as simple rate of interest per year and not mislead the depositor. The exact nature of the benefits and facilities had to be truthfully revealed in advertisements and all prizes, gifts, etc. given to depositors in cash or kind were to be from the interest amount and not in addition to it.

During this time, non-banking finance companies emerged, which were not bound by these rules. Seeing the huge deposits being garnered by banks, state governments too got into the act and many states passed orders directing all corporations owned by the state to keep their surplus funds with the state treasury only. Some states paid a rate of interest higher than what the RBI had prescribed for commercial banks.

In continuation of the trust the SBI enjoyed, customers were also happy to use the services of both safe deposits and safe custody services. In the case of safe custody services, customers were required to put in securely sealed envelopes or parcels, with the receipt explicitly stating 'contents unknown'. Many old safe deposit items, some well over a century old, continued to remain with the bank. Safe deposit lockers continue to be a very popular service even today. Most bank branches may indirectly ask for a fixed deposit amount as a bargaining tool, but the service in itself is a huge relief to an individual who can safely put her jewellery, important documents and other things in the bank's safe deposit vault.

Earlier, many safe deposit lockers would remain unopened for years together. Now the rules have changed. 'In case the locker remains unoperated for more than one year, the bank would have the right to cancel the allotment of the locker and open the locker, even if the rent is paid regularly,' said the RBI guidelines, issued in 2007 in the wake of an incident in which explosives and weapons were found in a locker!

Trust continues to be a recurrent theme on which the SBI is built and 'serving the customer' has been priority. While in the days of the Imperial Bank, the common man may have hesitated to venture into the portals of the bank, with the SBI he felt encouraged to become a successful businessman with assistance of credit from the bank.

In 1962, the bank introduced a facility of a special credit transfer for personal accounts. The constituent could use the services of any office of the bank in India for transferring funds tendered by him in person in cash. Only one instance of such a transfer was allowed free of charge per day and the amount could not exceed ₹1,000 (the limit was increased to ₹2,500 in 1965). The scheme helped the needs of lower- and middle-income groups. The facility was considered a landmark in the history of Indian banking and, as expected, others copied it quickly. In 1967, a cheque transfer scheme was introduced. Under this scheme, any customer of the bank maintaining a personal current account or a savings bank account with chequebook facility could transfer funds up to ₹2,500 to any other customer's account in the bank or its subsidiaries by cheque. While the cheque could be collected or negotiated at the bank's discretion at par, it had to be drawn on a personal account and not on an account in the name of a firm, association or a company. This helped to popularise use of cheques and promote banking habits in the common man.*

The most remarkable facility devised by the bank for improving customer service was the teller system introduced in April 1966, which helped to provide cash up to ₹1,000 without signature verification of the cheque. By 1973, it was extended to all large- and medium-sized branches. The tellers were also issuing drafts up to ₹1,000 and gift cheques; in addition, they were also signing cash receipts up to ₹1,000 relating to recurring deposits and Janata Deposit accounts. By 1980, the system was extended to nearly 1,800 branches and the teller could encash cheques up to ₹2,000. With today's technology and money transfer through apps and the proliferation of ATMs, these initiatives might sound irrelevant, but they were significant improvements in the banking system spearheaded by the SBI then.

Concern for the customer was a prime focus of the bank. Even as early as in September 1957, in a special letter to the branches, the bank strongly impressed upon its officials the necessity for showing the utmost consideration and courtesy to constituents in all matters without, of course, sacrificing the bank's interests or impairing its efficiency.

Commercial bank deposits were a big potential and the SBI focused on it. A working group was formed to look into it. The group suggested that all personal accounts, particularly of those associated with corporate customers, needed to be handled with special care. It also added that marginal overdrafts, extending concessions for remittances and giving immediate credit for cheques tendered by them on their personal accounts would go a long way in retaining important commercial deposits. This had been highlighted by an incident wherein the bank had returned a cheque drawn on the personal current account of a chairman of a prestigious corporation owing to a shortfall of a few hundred rupees, which triggered a chain reaction and led to the withdrawal of large deposits of the corporation immediately thereafter. Readers will recall how more than a century ago,

---

* The scheme was not a novel one for the Indian banking industry as Dena Bank had introduced such a scheme as early as in 1962, whereby cheques on any of its offices for any amount were collected at par provided the receiver of the cheque too had an account with the bank. While many banks were constrained because of the fewer number of the branches, the advantage for the SBI was its ability to operate over a much wider network across the country.

the governor-general William Bentinck did not react in the same manner when his cheque was returned by the Bank of Bengal because his account was short by only four annas. It is worthwhile to state again here what he said when informed of the circumstance. He applauded and remarked: 'This was the bank to do business with, which would not violate its rules in the smallest particular for the governor-general himself.'

But things had changed now. The customer WAS the king.

In a circular letter dated 2 September 1969, addressed to all members soon after the nationalisation of banks, the managing directors of the banks pointed out that the pre-eminent position of the SBI could 'no longer be taken for granted' and that the new goals would have to be set and new challenges met to regain the position. They stressed the need to develop an attitude of 'positive helpfulness' towards the customer, further adding that growth in business was dependent on customer satisfaction.[4]

The chairman, R.K. Talwar stressed that a large number of complaints could be avoided if the 'man on the spot' was 'patient rather than impatient' and was 'persuasively firm rather than negatively rigid'. He added that he was not in any way suggesting 'a compromise on business policy, sound judgement and a proper appraisal'.[5] While discussing the emerging trends in banks' relations with the corporate customer, Talwar 'pleaded' for a relationship of 'enlightened proximity' between the bank and the corporate customer, rather than that of a moneylender and borrower.[6]

Besides evolving procedures for expediting tasks, like updating entries in savings bank pass books, collection of outstation cheques and issuing drafts, and many such, the bank also pointed out to its staff that the success of the measures depended eventually on their 'initiative and alertness'. In a circular in March 1972, the bank said: 'The magnificent reputation which our great institution has built over the years has been only for the reason that our aim has always been to offer nothing short of the best quality of service to our customers. This image must not be tarnished.'[7]

Customer satisfaction continues to remain a priority for the SBI. In today's age, when a customer can shift her loyalty with the click of a mouse, when customers can open an account in a bank through an app in a few minutes, it becomes all the more imperative that the listens carefully to customers' needs and complaints and responds well.

8

BUILDING STRUCTURES TO BUILD THE INSTITUTION

The Imperial Bank of India was initially headed by two managing governors. In 1934, one of the two posts was abolished and the post of a deputy managing governor was created. Their designations were also changed to managing director and deputy managing director. When the SBI was formed, the chairman was the head of the bank. Unlike the days of the Imperial Bank, which had a moving central office, the central office for the SBI was permanently located in Bombay. This step had not been taken well as the officers in Calcutta felt that the permanent head office in Bombay would diminish the importance of Calcutta. The *Amrita Bazar Patrika* on 29 November 1957 wrote that '... public opinion in this part of India will find it difficult to get rid of the feeling that the entire move is directed against Calcutta.' But all that was past now. The Bengal circle had been the largest of the three circles since the days of the Imperial Bank. Now more circles were needed to manage the expanding branch network. The first new circle to be formed was Delhi in 1958. The State Bank of India Act did not permit more than six local head offices (LHO) and the act was amended in 1963 to remove the restriction on the number of LHOs.

As the bank grew, it was important that a bank structure was put in place to manage the behemoth. We saw earlier how during R.K. Talwar's time, IIM Ahmedabad had been appointed to suggest the first organisational change. Talwar had expressed it eloquently when, during a senior management conference in the late 1960s, he said, 'My branch managers are lost. I want to find them.'[1] This had prompted the organisational restructuring for which IIM Ahmedabad was appointed as consultant.

When the consultants suggested that decision-making in the bank should be distinguished with three kinds of tasks central to an organisation—entrepreneurial, directional and operational—it was a new-fangled idea. They recommended that entrepreneurial tasks related with investments, return on capital employed, product diversification and innovation would be best performed by the board of directors. Directional tasks involving decisions on allocations of available resources, goals and targets for the executive system, periodic review of performance and long-range planning were the direct responsibility of the top management at the central office and the local head offices. Operational tasks were to be performed by the senior and operating management at the branches.

With the reorganisation, the top official of the branch, who was earlier called an agent, was redesignated as branch manager, while the agents of main branches were designated as chief managers. This was in 1972. A couple of years later, the secretary and treasurer were redesignated as chief general manager, and the deputy secretary (operations) and deputy secretary (planning and staff) were renamed general manager (operations) and general manager (personnel) respectively.

The growing complexity of the economic environment worldwide and its increasing impact on the business of banks in the twentieth century led to a few central banks and leading commercial banks of some countries to establish their economic research departments to complement their organisations.* In India, the RBI was the first to set up such a department of research and statistics on 1 August 1945. By the end of 1955, the SBI, too, followed suit and D.S. Savkar, an officer of the RBI's department of research and statistics, was brought on deputation as economic adviser to the bank.[2] Today, the research department of the bank plays a key role in a wide range of research and provides inputs to the bank management.

---

* It was Montagu Norman, the longest serving governor of the Bank of England who in 1928 appointed Walter Stewart, an eminent American economist, as economic adviser to the governors with the intention of building up a statistical and information system for advising the governors in 'the manner in which material should be collected and recorded' and also 'how the information ... could from time to time to be used to the best advantage in shaping the policy of the Bank of England'. See R.S. Sayers, *The Bank of England, 1891-1944, Vol. 2* (Cambridge University Press, 1976), Chapter 22, p. 621.

The bank had set up a public-relations department in 1963 itself and the first person appointed to head the department was Vadilal Dagli, financial editor of *The Indian Express*. He handled both publicity and public relations. A year later, the personnel department was set up under a chief officer. This department handled recruitment, training and industrial relations, which had undergone a qualitative transformation with regard to employee welfare. An increasing number of welfare measures were taken, which included setting up of housing cooperatives by employees, interest-free loans for housing to employees, assisting consumers' cooperatives set up by employees, setting up of holiday homes cum convalescence centres for employees, and cultural and sports activities.

The SBI also encouraged sports and sportsmen. It was a moment of pride for Talwar, when he felicitated Ajit Wadekar, the Indian cricket team captain and an employee of the SBI, after India's historic win against the West Indies and England on foreign soil in 1971. There were many other cricketers apart from other sportsmen who were employed by the bank. Cricketers like Nari Contractor, Eknath Solkar, Gundappa Vishwanath, Syed Kirmani, Roger Binny and Mohammad Azharuddin were all proud SBI employees. A name which few remember but needs to be mentioned is Subimal (Chuni) Goswami,* the mercurial footballer who led India to a historic gold medal in the Asian Games in 1962. Unfortunately, owing to changes in policy, the bank has not been recruiting sportspersons for the several years now.

The concept of convalescent homes was suggested way back in 1937, when the secretary of the IBIISA, Bengal circle urged the secretary and treasurer to construct a convalescent home at a healthy place within easy commutable distance from Calcutta for free use by the clerical and cash-department staff. It was argued that the staff members needed a place for rest and recuperation as they were suffering from mental depression on account of the severe economic burden, which in some cases had caused large indebtedness. The secretary and treasurer, however, found no justification for employees running into debt as they were paid handsomely in comparison to other banks and firms in Calcutta. He reiterated the bank's commitment for assistance in case of natural calamities and regretted his inability to construct a convalescent home. Incidentally, the IBIISA was

---

* Chuni was also a first-class cricketer, playing Ranji Trophy for Bengal.

formed in July 1920, even before Lala Lajpat Rai formed the All India Trade Union Congress in October that year. As there was no law in force regulating the activities of trade union organisations then, IBIISA was registered under the Benevolent Societies Act!

As recruitment and training became critical, a central recruitment board was created in 1964 for strengthening the recruitment of officers. The SBI probationary officers' (PO) exam is still an aspirational entrance exam for millions of youth across India. Even today, scores of training institutes coach young aspirants for the bank's PO exam. The State Bank of India Staff Training College, as it was known originally, was inaugurated in Banjara Hills, Hyderabad, on 2 December 1961. As the college grew in size and stature and the need was increasing each year, the bank finally bought 17 acres of land in Begumpet to create its own premises. The administrative block was formally inaugurated by Y.B. Chavan, union minister for finance, on 21 July 1972. The minister remarked, 'No more are the banks cold-blooded tradition-bound store houses of ledgers. They are now expected to be living organisms. Given certain social responsibilities and obligations, they have to function as instruments of social change. And this, really speaking, is the task and the function of the banks. ... when SBI is making a new experiment in the field of training I thought it was my duty to come here and focus the attention of the country as well as the banking system to what good work is being done in this particular institute.'[3]

Ten years later, the staff training college was renamed as State Bank Staff College. At the function marking ten years of the college, Talwar said, 'I do hope that when decades later the history of economic growth of our country will be written, you will have a good name to offer to State Bank of India and if that comes, I wish to record today that the credit will go to institutions of the type of which we have come to celebrate the first decade.'[4]

In the first course, there were 32 probationers who were recruited in 1960. The trainees were initially required to pay ₹7 per day towards cost of food and 25 paise for each bucket of hot water. When the trainees sought a waiver of these charges, the bank's managing director, then on a visit to the college, promptly sanctioned a stipend of ₹150 per month. In April 1963, the bank decided to bear all expenses connected with boarding and lodging and discontinued the stipend. The code of conduct at the college was strict and it reminded one of the army training institutes! Call letters listed the dress code: full suit for classes, white shorts and sneakers for morning workouts. No outings were permitted—no cinema, shopping, not even a visit to the hairdresser! 'I believe that during the time the trainees are at the college, they should eat, sleep, think and live banking,' stressed the then college principal.[5]

A Little Peek into the Past

The present-day system of probationary officers harks back to when candidates who were selected in Great Britain for staff appointment in the Imperial Bank of India were called probationary officers. The applicants were not to be less than 21 years nor more than 25 years of age. They were to have at least three years' training in one of the well-known British banks if they had no university degree, and not less than two years' training if they had a degree from one of the recognised universities of Great Britain or Ireland. They were expected to pass the examination of the English or Scottish Institute of Bankers. The candidates had to take inoculation for enteric fever before departure and sign an agreement for service and remain on probation for three years. Besides an allowance of 30 pounds as one-time payment, they would be provided with first-class passage to India. The initial salary was ₹500, a generous sum in those days. It was later revised upwards to ₹585 with scale of 585-35-725. In the days of the presidency banks, the bank was stern about rules of marriage. Only unmarried persons of non-Asiatic domicile were considered eligible for appointment as officers in the service of the Imperial Bank of India. Marriage without permission during probation could result in termination of service by the bank. Officers were required to seek permission for marriage from the bank's board of directors once their monthly salary reached the minimum princely sum of ₹700. Rules regarding borrowing and private trading were also stringent. No officer was allowed to overdraw his account with the bank or draw his salary in advance without first having it authorised in writing from the secretary and treasurer. They could not engage in speculating in stocks or shares or any securities or be connected with the formation or management of joint-stock companies.

At times the bank received recommendations or requests for jobs from Indian princes or highly placed government and military officials.

In one instance, an Indian prince of Madras requested the bank's managing governor in 1927 'to be kind enough' to appoint his eldest son in the bank's employment, adding that the family had 'sacrificed all its fortune for the good of the English and their thriving in India ever since the East India Company was formed'. The secretary and treasurer were then instructed to advise the prince courteously that 'the bank's Indian staff requirements were for the present satisfied and it had a lengthy waiting list of applicants.'

Later, to focus on agricultural finance, in 1981, the bank set up State Bank Institute for Rural Development attached to the State Bank Staff College. It was subsequently moved to new premises in the outskirts of Hyderabad.

Continuing with the growth and setting up of various departments, the electronic data processing centre was set up in Bombay in 1967. It helped in reconciliation of inter-branch transactions which were computerised.

The setting up of various departments for better efficiency, control, reporting and management is not complete, unless there is focus on proper audit and inspection. Of course, any amount of controls or mechanisms to control frauds may not be sufficient if the people who are responsible for the decisions are hand in glove with the perpetrator. It is to the SBI's credit that the bank, despite its size, has continued to function as a viable and robust organisation. While setting up the departments, it was reiterated that an inspection and audit was not an inquisition or a fault-finding mission but had to be seen in a constructive manner for improvement. B. Mukherji, the bank's managing director, wrote in an internal note in November 1963, that control was not 'an end in itself' and '... it had to be subordinated to the need for progress in business, qualitative and quantitative, so that on the whole the institution is better off. There must be scope for taking "calculated risks" for useful experiment in dynamic functioning. Control should not curb initiative and enthusiasm for progress and confine action to observance of form and routine. The cost of control, both actual cost involved in the process and indirect cost in terms of loss of business etc. should be taken into account and compared with probable losses avoided by the control measure and a correct balance struck between the need for caution and need for progress.'[6]

The bank inherited many systems and procedures from its forerunners. The first inspection manual was compiled in 1926 and it continued to serve as a guide for inspection and audit even after the creation of the SBI as the basic tenets of this excellently produced manual were quite relevant.

As has been observed in most frauds across various banks, the intent of audit and control is defeated when the individuals concerned are greedy and find ways to beat the system. Any organisation is made up of individuals and is as good as the sum of its employees. According to a news article that appeared in the *Business Standard* on 3 June 2019, the RBI estimated that there were over 6,800 cases of fraud totalling to more than ₹71,500 crores in 2018–19. There are many examples, one of them being that of Indian Bank, a bank more than 100 years old, which reported a loss of more than ₹1,700 crores resulting in its entire capital being wiped out in 1995–96. In the case of PNB, the frauds exceeded ₹13,000 crores. It is to the SBI's credit that it survives as an organisation known for its ethics and good practices. This has been so since the beginning. In the period between 1925 and 1955, more than 1,300 banks fell, half of them disappearing in a decade after the beginning of the Second World War due to over-speculation. The presidency banks then and the Imperial Bank later, in sharp contrast, inspired confidence in their depositors and shareholders. It was because of the sound banking principles followed since the early days.[*]

Since its formation in 1955, the SBI has scaled new heights in both traditional and development banking. The bank has moved beyond the role assigned to it at the time of its creation. By 1980, it had emerged stronger, preserving at the same time its premier status in all spheres. This was the year in which the bank launched long-range planning, becoming the first bank to do so. Long-range planning ensured creation of a strategic plan

---

[*] As many as 365 banks failed during the Second World War. The partition of India took another heavy toll on the banking industry, particularly in West Bengal and Punjab. Of the 634 banks that went out of business between 1940 and 1951, 205 collapsed after 1947. For quite a while, the RBI stood by as a silent spectator, being virtually toothless; it was only after 1949 that it acquired some powers of inspection and intervention though very limited in range and scope. From the early 1950s, the bank steadily armed itself with more and more statutory powers, as situations dictated, of which the most comprehensive were those vested in it by an Act of Parliament in 1956. (D.N. Ghosh, *No Regrets*, Rupa, 2015, p. 91)

aligning with the long-term business goals of the bank. On 24 April 1982, it inaugurated its 6,000th branch at Ghonda in Delhi.

※

In the mid-1980s, the SBI was among the top 100 global banks. In terms of assets, its ranking was 38 but its productivity and profitability were far too low, just a little above the 500th rank. In 1985, D.N. Ghosh was made chairman of the bank. A civil servant had been given the top post after many years. Ghosh was keen to understand the reasons for low productivity and profitability. He was not an outsider to banking, having interacted with many bank chiefs while he was a bureaucrat. He began a tour of various branches, as he writes in his memoirs, after taking blessings at Tirupati.

Ghosh launched the Commerce and Industry (C&I) project which was overseen by a group of senior executives. The business customers (C&I segment) needed a different kind of service and organisational innovations were needed to improve the bank's service to them. The group was assisted by a team headed by O.P. Bhatt, who would later on become the top boss (June 2006 to March 2011) and under whom the SBI would be revamped. SBINET was formed, which allowed voice, fax and data transmission to take place connecting the central office with 13 LHOs, 53 regional offices and 40 large branches. Ghosh also brought in P.G. Kakodkar, who was then chief general manager and would later became the chairman of the bank in 1995, for the project. Ghosh had seen multinational banks having dedicated research desks to appraise the officers. He had plans to set up a centralised research department to help the C&I team, the way some organisations like IDBI, ICICI and IFCI had. But it would not be cost-effective and hence the plan never came to fruition. Ghosh urged the colleges and training centres, numbering more than 50, to fine-tune their courses to emphasise how trainees ought to engage with the emerging environment and how it would impact the bank's business.

It was during Ghosh's tenure that the idea of getting into housing finance came up. The Housing Development Finance Corporation (HDFC) had existed for nearly ten years, having been set up in 1977. Ghosh set up a subsidiary, a joint venture with HDFC and a few other private sector groups as promoters, which was called Housing Promotion & Finance Corporation (HPFC), at Calcutta. The organisation was later liquidated and the SBI entered the housing-finance market under its own banner as SBI Home Loans.

Ghosh was against the portfolio management schemes run by the SBI and many banks. He believed that it went against the RBI directive on interest rate on deposits and suggested that the SBI should reduce its portfolio funds. He proposed that the bank should stop accepting new funds so that the entire portfolio would come to an end by June 1988.

Unfortunately, the RBI did not stop the practice and instead issued some guidelines in May 1989 and January 1991. We will later see how the Harshad Mehta episode nearly destroyed the bank.

Both SBICAP and the mutual-fund subsidiary, SBI Mutual Fund, came about during Ghosh's time. Today, SBI Capital Markets is one of the leading domestic investment banks, offering services which include investment banking and corporate advisory services, structured debt placement, capital markets, mergers and acquisitions, private equity and stressed-assets resolution. There is always a conflict of interest when a huge bank like the SBI has a subsidiary which advises clients for loans that are syndicated by various banks. But the SBI does maintain that no bank can blame the SBI group as each lender should and does conduct their own due diligence before sanctioning loans. There was an instance of Kingfisher Airlines where SBI Capital Markets was the advisor in restructuring the troubled airline's debts. The SBI was the lead lender among the 11 state-run banks and had an exposure of nearly ₹1,400 crores against the total of more than ₹7,000 crores outstanding debt.

The SBI has always been a pioneer in many areas, one of them being rating of its paper. In one of his visits to New York, where the SBI branch had raised short-term loans for Indian Oil Corporation through commercial paper, Ghosh found that it had been offered at a rate much higher than what many entities from several other countries could secure. The reason was that the bank had not been rated by any international rating agency. Ghosh realised that if the bank were to be rated, the rating exercise had to be preceded by a shadow rating of India itself, the country where the entity belonged. So, it was necessary that the rating agency rated India but that needed the permission of the government. Ghosh used his contacts to get a meeting with Rajiv Gandhi and impressed upon him the need to get a rating for the bank and the country. Ghosh was keen to expand the international presence of the SBI and this rating was crucial for it. Rajiv Gandhi gave his assent but Ghosh was in for a surprise. Moody's, the rating agency, gave a very cold response when contacted, stating their inability to do it as they were very busy with other assignments and that there was no chance for them to take it up in the near future. On persuasion, they blurted out that they did not rate a country where the per capita was less than US$ 500. Ghosh engaged Goldman Sachs as the advisor and they roped in Standard and Poor (S&P) as the rating agency. Ghosh refers to an interesting question raised by S&P about how the information from the branches reached him on time. The chairman mentioned that except for the branches in Arunachal Pradesh and those in Leh in Jammu & Kashmir, he got the information each Friday. That left just six or seven branches out. S&P was impressed. The country rating exercise was taken on hand immediately thereafter and Dr C. Rangarajan, then deputy governor of the the RBI, Shankar Acharya, economic advisor at that time, and Ghosh had to make several visits to S&P's office in New York. The exercise was completed to Ghosh's satisfaction and India got a rating of the middle point of the A scale, the same that China had at that time.

Later, in 1991, Ghosh would go on to set up India's first credit rating agency, ICRA. In an irony of sorts, ICRA would be acquired by Moody's, the same agency which had refused to entertain Ghosh!

In 1987, another important subsidiary set up—SBI Mutual Fund. Before that there was only UTI, and there was a lot of pressure from the UTI chief not to allow anyone else to manage funds. The SBI was the first organisation outside of the UTI to have an asset-management business. Today, it is a flourishing business not only for the SBI, but for dozens of other asset management companies operating in India, both with foreign and domestic ownership. Initially manged by SBI CAP, the mutual fund was vested into a new company in 1993. Later, it also entered into a joint venture with Societe Generale Asset Management of France, to attain leadership status in Indian mutual-fund industry. SBI Mutual Fund is one of the top ten mutual fund houses in India in terms of assets under management.

Ghosh had started the C&I project for business customers but he was acutely aware of the customer-service issues at branch level with complaints increasing each day. He realised that the problems lay in outmoded procedures and structural rigidities in the organisation of workflows, which were made worse on occasions by the quality of interface between customers and employees. Ghosh realised that banks world over were deploying technology to revolutionise the patter of customer service.

'The cabinet secretary had told me while I was leaving Delhi that even if I was able to improve the service marginally, I would have left a great legacy,' Ghosh writes in his memoir.[7]

Ghosh knew that the only way to make this happen was with the consent of the union. The management and the union were the two power structures which shaped the daily life of the bank. One area which was immediately tackled was delay in clearance of outstation cheques. The then deputy managing director of the bank, V.D. Dixit organised it by setting up an internal system of collection and dispatch of instruments to all centres connected by air, thereby reducing clearance time from two weeks to just three or four days. Ghosh knew that this was just scratching the surface and a drastic action was needed to make a significant all-round change.

Ghosh was looking for an early opportunity of going public on his commitment towards computerisation and sending a message throughout the organisation as to where he stood. An opportunity presented itself in mid-1987. During the silver jubilee celebration of the Hyderabad Training College, Ghosh had invited all past chairmen of the SBI. The RBI governor, R.N. Malhotra inaugurated the function. Ghosh used that opportunity to enunciate his approach towards technology. During his tenure as prime minister, Rajiv Gandhi was committed to computerisation. It was during Ghosh's time that the Institute for Information and Communication Management was set up in the SBI to develop awareness of what would be required by the Indian banking system, to train and educate people at all levels and to facilitate the changes which computerisation would bring about in the SBI. The unions, as always, opposed this vehemently.

However, Ghosh began negotiations with the unions and with his tact was able to convince the unions to come on board. The crunch came at the last stage when the unions demanded two advance increments to every employee. Finally, a settlement was reached for one advance increment. Referring to this, Ghosh says, 'The negotiations were being kept secret. According to the standing instructions from the government, the bank was required to obtain prior approval before according any monetary benefits to its staff.'[8] Ghosh took a risk that once the agreement became a fait accompli, the government would find it impossible to retract from it, except at the cost of a prolonged industrial agitation.

Ghosh considers the agreement with the union on computerisation, as his most memorable achievement. In his words, 'it was the springboard that helped my successors to catapult the bank into the technology age'.[9]

In a light-hearted moment, Ghosh recalls many telegrams worded 'good riddance' when he retired on 12 May 1989. He later realised that many people had been miffed because he had introduced a promotion policy at the middle level, upsetting a tradition that the bank had been following to fill vacancies at each level from a single batch, one level junior. Quite naturally, many people, upset at the policy, had shown their anger through the anonymous telegrams!

But Ghosh, in his short tenure, had left a lasting legacy.

Very soon India, under Manmohan Singh as finance minister, was to see a dramatic change.

The SBI was ready for the next phase of India's economic liberalisation which was to begin soon.

9

LIBERALISATION, THE HARSHAD MEHTA SCAM AND OTHER ISSUES

The year 1991 was a watershed year in India. Many people consider it as a turning point in India's economic march and some even rate it as the most important event since Independence.

The term 'licence raj' was coined in the 1950s by C. Rajagopalachari, a strong critic of Nehru, who predicted that corruption and inefficiency would follow when the government controlled everything. But the argument had not changed anything for decades. The crisis in 1991 was essentially that of balance of payments, which is considered today as the main reason for dismantling of what was called the licence or quota raj. Access to capital was becoming difficult and it was necessary to de-license industrial activity.

The Narasimha Rao government, which came to power in mid-1991, converted the crisis into an opportunity to change the economic architecture of the country with Manmohan Singh playing a key role as the finance minister. Many elements, some of which had begun even before the Rao government's assumption of power, came together to make it happen.

The licence raj had been something industrialists had been living with grudgingly. The Bureau of Industrial Costs and Prices* had conducted studies in the late 1980s on various commodities like steel, cement, etc., and recommended deregulation to bring India in line with the East Asian economies which were fast gaining ground. Rakesh Mohan from the World

---

* The Bureau of Industrial Costs & Prices was merged with the Tariff Commission in April 1999.

Bank, who had joined the industry ministry as economic adviser, did the draft work.

Mohan realised that the Monopolies and Restrictive Trade Practices (MRTP) Act and other technology controls and licencing regimes needed to be dismantled if the government had to liberalise. Mohan was given a free hand to draft an agenda for reforms by Ajit Singh, the industries minister in the short-lived V.P. Singh government of 1989–90.

The New Industrial Policy of 1990 was thus drafted. It looked at all things ranging from promotion of small and medium-sized enterprises (SMEs) to removing all unnecessary bureaucratic shackles, easing of raw material import restrictions, de-licensing of major items in imports and welcoming foreign direct investment into India. Political apprehensions shot the draft down in early July 1991 as there was no protection for certain industries where the field could not be opened up to all and sundry. Finally, with the right political packaging and with a long preamble to show some protection, the draft was presented to Parliament by P.J. Kurien. Thus, it was passed on 24 July 1991. While many changes were heralded with the reforms, some changes like the dissolution of the Planning Commission happened as late as 2014.

While India celebrated the reforms, a major jolt was waiting to happen. The Harshad Mehta scam, which was exposed in 1992, was one of the biggest frauds committed on the stock markets. The scam would severely hurt the SBI and its image.

⚘

The genesis of the Harshad Mehta scam, as it was called, began in the mid-1980s. There was diversion of funds from commercial banks and public sector undertakings (PSUs) using irregular ready forward (RF) transactions[*] in government securities, PSU bonds and UTI units. Quite obviously, brokers were in collusion with certain bank officials. It was brought to the notice of the RBI in a special report by Augustine Paul Kurias in October 1986.[†] Two banks stood out in the report—Andhra Bank and Syndicate

---

[*] Ready forward transaction is a secured short-term loan (15 days) from one bank to another. The collateral here is government bonds.

[†] Kurias later retired as principal of the RBI training college.

Bank, which were in the category of small public-sector banks but whose volume of transactions were substantially higher than the SBI, which had nearly 25 per cent of the total bank deposits. The report provided definite evidence of the genesis of the irregularities, if not illegalities, in the financial system as early as 1985. There had been an increase since the early 1980s in the RF transactions in government securities (in the investment portfolio of commercials banks) for various reasons. As a large part of the lendable resources were stuck in maintaining statutory-liquidity ratio and cash-reserve ratio, not to mention priority-sector lending requirements, the total available amount for improving performance and profitability was minuscule, thus forcing fund managers of the bank to find ways to come out with 'innovative ideas'.

The scam which unfolded later reached such proportions that a Joint Parliamentary Committee (JPC) revealed that between April 1990 and December 1992, about ₹36,000 crores of surplus investible funds from PSUs were diverted to the stock markets. One example was that of Syndicate Bank, which used the money from Oil Industries Development Board (OIDB). Even National Housing Bank (NHB) emerged a major player in securities transactions. It is another matter that NHB is wholly owned by the RBI and was set up in July 1988 to facilitate housing finance in the country.

In April 1992, the RBI found a shortfall of ₹649 crores in the SBI's investment portfolio. The bank did not have the securities for which it had paid its broker Harshad Mehta. Under pressure from the SBI, Harshad paid up around ₹620 crores between 13 April and 24 April. But the RBI dug deeper, and found that Harshad had paid ₹574 crores from his Grindlays Bank account. Of this, ₹489.75 crores was funded by NHB cheques drawn in favour of Grindlays Bank and credited to Harshad's account. That appeared to be a securities transaction between NHB and Grindlays, but NHB did not have any securities to show for it. The cat was finally out of the bag.

According to the Janakiraman Committee report of the RBI, the scam amount stood at ₹4,300 crores involving units of UTI. In today's terms, it would be in excess of ₹20,000 crores. While the kingpin is dead, the cases, even after almost three decades, are still going on.

Harshad Mehta: Rags to Riches to Ignominy

Harshad Shantilal Mehta was born in 1954 in Kandivali in Mumbai to a lower middle-class family. After some odd jobs, he started working as a salesperson for New India Assurance Company in 1981. When he started dabbling in stocks, he became a 'jobber'* and was soon trading in stocks himself. His favourites were Associated Cement Company (ACC), Apollo Tyres and Reliance, to name a few. He soon became very successful.

Around that time, the ACC share price rose from ₹200 a share to ₹9,000 in three years! Whatever Mehta touched turned to gold and he was called the 'Big Bull'. It is surprising that his lavish lifestyle, with a 12,000 sq. feet sea-facing penthouse in Worli and his Toyota Lexus and many other cars, was not investigated. He had even paid an advance tax of ₹26 crores before the scandal was out in the open. It was the investigative journalist Sucheta Dalal whose story exposed Harshad Mehta. She had seen him entering the SBI branch in his Toyota Lexus, which was just released in the market and had a price of nearly ₹40 lakhs.

Harshad Mehta used to broker the ready forward deals detailed earlier. He managed to convince the banks to have the cheques drawn in his name. He would then manage to transfer the money deposited in his account into the stock markets. Harshad Mehta then took advantage of the broken system. In a normal deal, there would be only two banks involved. Securities would be taken from a bank in exchange for cash. When a bank would request its securities or cash back, Harshad would rope in a third bank—then a fourth bank and so on and so forth. Multiple banks were thus connected in his scam.

A group of brokers, mainly rivals of Harshad, had short sold many shares, convinced that the exuberance in the stock market was not supported by fundamentals and that the rally would not sustain. Thanks to the banking funds at his disposal, Harshad was able to carry forward his buy positions and push prices even higher. The continuous rise in prices bled Harshad's rivals financially. To square up their short positions, they had to buy shares in the open market, which further fuelled the rally and cost them more money.

---

* Jobbers, also called stockjobbers, held shares on their own books and created market liquidity by buying and selling securities, and matching investors' buy and sell orders through their brokers.

Naturally, they were in a precarious position and faced ruin if share prices rose further. In January 1992, the RBI began inspecting the books of banks for irregularities in securities transactions. Unfortunately for Harshad, the BSE stopped trading operations on 16 April, as brokers went on strike protesting against the directive from the Securities and Exchange Board of India (SEBI) asking them to re-register and pay a higher registration fee. That prevented Harshad from being able to sell a part of his holdings and repay the SBI. Under pressure from the broking community, SEBI diluted the hike on 20 April.

It is generally believed that the bear cartel, aware of Harshad's problems, prolonged the strike by making other demands. Harshad is said to have approached a foreign bank with close ties to the bear cartel, offering a part of his holdings at a discount. But that deal did not work out.

Trading finally resumed on 27 April, but by then it was too late for Harshad. With news of the scam becoming public and the fund flow into the stock market drying up, share prices nosedived. From a high of 4,467 in the last week of April, the BSE Sensex crashed to sub-2,600 by August.

In November 1992, the CBI charged Mehta with 72 criminal cases which included bribery, forgery and falsification of accounts amongst other crimes. Many other brokers were also charged. There was another scandal which broke out, called the 'suitcase scandal' where Harshad Mehta alleged that he had taken money in a suitcase to bribe the Congress party. There was no evidence found for his claim but it did raise a political hue and cry. Out on bail after a few months, Mehta was the toast of the town and continued as an expert on market issues. It was only in 1999 that he was awarded five years' imprisonment. He secured bail once again and was arrested in 2001. Denied bail this time, he died in Tihar jail at the age of 47. While he had been convicted in one case, the civil suits against him and his family remain. The cases are a legal nightmare and may never see the light of the day fully.

A 2020 biopic titled *Scam 1992: The Harshad Mehta Story*, based on a book by Sucheta Dalal and Debashis Basu, became one of the most watched shows on SonyLIV and a line attributed to Harshad Mehta 'risk *hai to ishq hai*' became a catchphrase.

Earlier, Ghosh, as chairman of the SBI, had warned of likely irregularities. In a bank of the size of the SBI, there is always the possibility of an individual colluding against the system. A bank of its size and reputation survives and flourishes because to its thousands of loyal and conscientious managers.

Unfortunately, for India, the lessons learnt in the Harshad Mehta case were soon forgotten as the stock market witnessed another major scam, the main culprit this time being one Ketan Parekh, whom many consider to be a protégé of Harshad Mehta. There were banks involved in this too, some of them being UTI Bank, the Bank of India and Madhavpura Mercantile Cooperative Bank (MMCB). The extent of the fraud was estimated to be around ₹40,000 crores.

What Parekh did was essentially 'pump and dump' (make the price of a share go up and then sell it off by dumping it, making huge profits). During the days of the dotcom boom, when the prices of IT stocks were going up, people came to believe in what were known as the K-10 stocks of Parekh which were essentially in the ICE sector (information, communication and entertainment). Parekh was operating hand in glove with promoters of certain companies who wanted their stock price to rise in order to take loans against shares. Parekh began his manipulation of the stock markets in mid-1998 and this continued for another three years till the market crashed by 176 points on a single day, a day after the 2001 Budget was presented. While the SEBI and the RBI began investigating, the stock exchanges panicked with a run on the stocks leading to a major fall. Parekh had taken a pay order of ₹140 crores pay from Ahmedabad-based MMCB, which was discounted by Bank of India for ₹137 crores. The pay order bounced. Parekh had looted MMCB to the tune of a massive ₹1,030 crores.

The Serious Frauds Investigation Office (SFIO) found that Parekh had managed to rig prices of shares by circular trading, generating high volumes and prices by acting in concert with other brokerage firms across stock exchanges. He had traded mainly through Calcutta Stock Exchange. Taking advantage of weak regulations, he was able to manipulate prices. Tragedy struck when the bear cartel started hammering the K-10 stocks. Ketan Parekh was locked out of cash and a bank like MMCB, which had already extended unsecured loans, could not extend their credit further. The brokers holding positions on Parekh's behalf were forced to sell, which caused a massive fall. Ketan Parekh was banned from trading till 2017, but if rumours are to be believed he has been active all along!

Amongst all the gloom of the Harshad Mehta scam, one of the many positive outcomes of the reforms of 1991 was the permission given by the RBI to allow more banks. The RBI received 113 applications. There were many from large industrial houses but as expected, the RBI did not give licences to those. The Development Credit Bank, which was a cooperative bank earlier, was converted into a bank and nine more applicants were given the nod. These were HDFC Bank, ICICI Bank, IDBI Bank, UTI Bank, Global Trust Bank (GTB), IndusInd Bank, Centurion Bank, Bank of Punjab and Times Bank. HDFC Bank was set up by HDFC Limited. Developmental institutions like ICICI and IDBI also set up their banks. UTI Bank was later renamed as Axis Bank and is one of the top three private banks today. IndusInd Bank was set up by the Hinduja group while Bank of Punjab was started by Darshanjit Singh, son of Inderjit Singh, who was earlier chairman of the Punjab and Sind Bank. Ramesh Gelli, earlier head of Vyasa Bank, set up GTB.

Not all survived as successful institutions. Times Bank, set up by Bennett Coleman, the company which owns the *Times of India* newspaper, was acquired by HDFC Bank in the year 2000. Global Trust Bank was merged into the Oriental Bank of Commerce in 2004. Centurion Bank, which was set up by Devender Ahuja of Twentieth Century Finance Corporation, acquired the Bank of Punjab. The two merged entities were then absorbed into HDFC Bank in 2008. In 2003, the RBI issued a licence to Kotak Mahindra Financial Services to set up Kotak Mahindra Bank. It would soon rise to become one of India's most successful private banks. The formation of Kotak Bank was followed by Rana Kapur setting up Yes Bank in 2004. The fact that Yes Bank would later go through a crisis is a different story.

While new private banks were bought out by other private banks, later, in 2020, there was a merger of some of the older PSU banks into others. Oriental Bank of Commerce and United Bank of India were merged into PNB. Syndicate Bank was merged with Canara Bank, while Indian Bank was merged with Allahabad Bank. Union Bank merged with Corporation Bank and Andhra Bank. This left, after the merger, six merged PSU banks, namely the SBI, Bank of Baroda, PNB, Canara Bank, Union Bank of India, Indian Bank, and six independent PSU banks, namely Indian Overseas Bank, UCO Bank, Bank of Maharashtra, Punjab and Sind Bank, Bank of India and Central Bank of India.[*]

---

[*] United Bank of India was originally formed with the amalgamation of four banks—Comilla Banking Corporation (1914), Bengal Central Bank (1918), Comilla Union Bank (1922) and Hooghly Bank (1932).

10

A TIME FOR INTROSPECTION

The year 2006 marked two centuries of the founding of the Bank of Calcutta, which later became the Bank of Bengal. The story of how the three presidency banks eventually became the Imperial Bank of India and then the SBI has already been told.

It was in 2006 that Om Prakash Bhatt, who had joined the bank as a probationary officer in 1972, was made chairman. He had started his career in a rural branch in Maharashtra and had then risen progressively to become managing director of the State Bank of Travancore. Bhatt had been selected for the post of chairman of the SBI making many other contenders, who were senior or had better tenures, jealous. It was not an easy task for Bhatt, who had decided to transform the sleeping giant.

The SBI was quietly chugging along as a behemoth, secure in its leadership position and complacent about the fact that its main job was social banking, which many private banks were loath to touch unless mandated. The SBI's officers had never considered banks like ICICI and HDFC, both formed in 1994, and UTI Bank, which was formed in 1993 and renamed Axis Bank in 2007, as competition. But the fact was that ICICI Bank and HDFC Bank were already breathing down the neck of PSU banks, rapidly expanding branches and garnering business especially from corporates and the growing middle class which was eager for good, prompt and efficient service. Bhatt realised that the rate at which the banks were growing, the SBI may soon lose its leadership position.

Bhatt appointed McKinsey to undertake a bank-wide survey and come up with a strategy document. He had worked with the bank from grassroots level and was aware of issues that the bank was facing. He knew that without involving the 2,00,000 plus employees of the bank, any significant change was impossible. Customer service was one area of focus. The SBI could not afford to have queues of customers waiting patiently for their money to be withdrawn from the teller counter or their demand draft to be made ready. Private banks were talking of 'home delivery' while the SBI was stuck in its age-old practices. This had to change. There was a need for better products, quicker and convenient customer response time, better pricing—everything! Simple changes were not enough. What was required was a transformation—a 'parivartan' (complete change), which was the name given for the entire exercise. 'To reinvent yourself, you have to die first,' someone had quipped. Bhatt knew that the transformation had to be completed in incremental steps.*

Bhatt began by hosting an offsite of senior management at Aamby Valley, Lonavala in 2006. The offsite was not to discuss the business plan or review targets and performance appraisal, but for some deep introspection. Talking about the Indian economy, Bhatt spoke of the bank's failure to keep pace with the environment and how they had fallen behind the competition on various parameters like business growth, market capitalisation, market share, return on assets, capital adequacy, yields and many such parameters. Never had the SBI compared itself with competition and that had been a severe limiting factor for such introspection. The imagery of the tiger found mention in his talk. We have seen how the RBI had replaced the lion in the East India Company symbol with a tiger, which represented India better. Now Bhatt used the tiger as an analogy to talk of the danger of its extinction.

In his view, the SBI too was in a similar situation. While, like a tiger, it ruled the financial markets, it was likely to be overtaken by nimble new banks. The message was clear—the SBI did not have the wherewithal to serve the diverse needs of large corporates and had completely failed in attracting the growing upwardly mobile middle class which aspired for better service and products. Rural banking, where the SBI believed it had a leadership position, was a model which not viable according to the chairman. The

---

* In *Grit, Guts and Gumption* by Rajesh Chakrabarti (Penguin, 2010), about the O.P. Bhatt years, Ratan Tata comments on the dramatic revival of the SBI as 'one of the unsung success stories of Indian business'.

bank had not kept pace with the changes outside to provide training to its employees to be able to tackle competition. In fact, smug in their own world, they had never considered anyone as competition.

There was no doubt, the chairman proudly said, that the SBI was a bank of enormous strengths and that it was envied by one and all and had served the country for 200 years, in every nook and corner. The brand enjoyed a huge trust and was considered solid and dependable. As a banker to the nation, the SBI had pioneered growth in all sectors, including agriculture, large- and small-scale industries, government business, corporate loans and others. It also boasted of the largest network of branches and customers. Its management strength was exceptional and it had excellent corporate governance. No doubt, the SBI was put on a high pedestal by everyone in the industry. It was something to be proud of, the chairman reiterated.

The Changing Banking Scenario

At the time Bhatt was making plans to transform the SBI, the other banks were not sitting idle either. HDFC Bank was in the process of changing itself, while ICICI was growing at a breakneck speed wanting to catch up with the national leader. UTI Bank, under the ex-bureaucrat, P.J. Nayak, had also grown well. The Bank of Baroda, a public sector bank, was also undergoing rapid transformation.

HDFC Bank, the relatively new entrant, had made rapid progress since its inception, and was reinventing itself, something Bhatt was conscious of. After all, ICICI and HDFC Bank were charting their ways with new products and technology. HDFC Bank was headed by Aditya Puri, who was spearheading a new HDFC with a vengeance. HDFC was barely a decade old, but was already talking of reinventing itself and had embarked on digitisation to literally disrupt itself. It even had a product which could offer loan in ten seconds! The bank was readying itself for a digital strategy to drive the business, realising the threat of fintech companies which were on the horizon.

ICICI Bank and UTI Bank (later, Axis Bank) were not far behind, opening branches and offering products to suit the new-age customer. The Bank of Baroda, under the leadership of Anil Khandelwal, was spearheading a transformation similar to what was happening at the SBI.

Khandelwal had started his banking career as a probationary officer in the Bank of Baroda in 1971 and had risen up the ranks like most other chairmen who had headed PSU banks. He was different from the others given that he had spent most part of his career in human resources (HR). He had a brief stint as head of Dena Bank before being made chairman of the Bank of Baroda. Khandelwal, like Bhatt, realised that the Bank of Baroda was considered a socialist relic in post-reform India but he also knew, as an HR practitioner, that change was possible only if the employees were empowered and owned the change. He involved branch managers by showing them reports by financial analysts which were trashing the Bank of Baroda and advising their investors to avoid the bank's stock. It was a direct appeal to the employees' pride. Who would want to work for a bank which was not considered good by investors? In a programme called 'manager to messenger', he introduced a concept where the bank branch remained opened from 8 a.m. to 8 p.m. The staff was not given any extra salary or bonus but had agreed to do it on their own. They even designed their own marketing events.

Khandelwal also introduced reforms, which included rebranding of the Bank of Baroda, establishing new next-gen branches, retail and SME loan factories (one-stop shop). He encouraged employees to talk to him through Sampark, a hotline to the chief managing director, and started Samadhan, a counselling service in metro cities. His talent hunt exercise named 'Khoj' was a huge success. The efforts showed results and the Bank of Baroda doubled its business in just three years while completing technology upgradation providing anytime-anywhere banking facility through online banking. The transformation story was mentioned in a *Business Review* article entitled 'Leadership Lessons from India'. The story was also covered in a book co-written by four Wharton B-School professors, *The India Way: How India's Top Business Leaders are Revolutionizing Management.*

What Khandelwal and Bhatt were trying was a belated acknowledgment of what R.K. Talwar had done decades ago. Under Talwar, the concept of employee participation was introduced. In 1973, the State Bank of India Act was once again amended. It provided, inter alia, for representation of employees, one each from staff and officers, on the central board of the SBI and on the board of each of its seven subsidiaries. Talwar felt that such participation did not end with the induction of employee representatives on the boards of the management. True employee participation, Talwar felt, meant that every branch employee would 'share responsibility' for formulating branch objectives and strategies as also their successful execution.

Bhatt was conscious of the rapid changes being made by private banks, especially HDFC and ICICI, and aware of the transformation of PSU banks, like the Bank of Baroda. Challenges and threats were also opportunities for the SBI to copy and renew itself and maintain its leadership position.

It was in Aamby Valley that the top brass of the bank had been shown the mirror for the first time. The open and frank discussions initiated by Bhatt encouraged all to open up and freely air their views. They all agreed that for a transformation to take place, and for the SBI to regain its lost glory, it had to make a structural as well as a cultural change at all levels. But first the top management itself had to lead the way.

Any HR exercise is a complex affair. Changing the culture of a behemoth like the SBI is not easy. To add to it, unlike private banks, the SBI was a public institution and could not pay top-notch salaries. There were many other such constraints. After Aamby Valley, the deputy managing directors of the bank took the discussion forward and met the 9,500-odd branch managers in all fourteen circles. The idea was to communicate the transformation exercise in person. It did not end there. It was followed by a meeting of chief general managers (CGMs) in Mumbai, general managers (GMs) and deputy general managers (DGMs) in Hyderabad. The DGMs were nearly 300 in number. The discussions were also of a different kind.

In the CGM meet, the focus was on planning while for the other meetings, it was more on strategy. Such meetings were taking place for the first time. People learnt about what the top management was thinking and this helped create a team spirit. A sharp focus on business development was a clear outcome. People also realised that the SBI, which prided itself on a virtual monopoly in rural India, was losing ground there to the likes of ICICI and others.

The chairman himself met nearly 1,800 assistant general managers (AGMs). The idea was to involve them in the transformation and carry it down the line. It was not an exercise from the chairman's office but something which was to be done by each employee. Even the two unions, those of staff and officers, were taken on board at a three-day meeting held in Jodhpur, starting 15 December 2006. It was again something that the unions had never experienced before and many ideas and issues were discussed openly in a spirit of teamwork. All agreed that the leadership and prominence of the SBI had to be regained. A joint communique was issued on the last day of the conclave with the chairman, managing directors, the general secretaries and circle general secretaries of the All India State Bank of India Staff Federation and All India State Bank Officers' Federation as signatories calling upon each other and every employee to render the best customer service so that the SBI could emerge as the best bank in customer service by March 2007.

It was the first instance of an organisation the size of the SBI and that too a PSU issuing such a statement. It spoke from the heart. It hit the nail on the head without insulting anyone. It was a message of working together to making it happen. It is worth reading for its simplicity, honesty and its appeal:

Dear Colleague,
Message from Jodhpur

1. *We all know that the Bank is passing through an unprecedented phase of formidable challenges. Our premier position as the 'number one Bank of India' is threatened by our competitive pressures. Over the years we have been steadily losing our market share from about 35 per cent in the 1970s to around 16 per cent in 2006. Our vast network is failing to attract the new and demanding young customers. Our new technology platform and various new business process reengineering initiatives are still in the process of implementation. Our business per employee and profit per employee is one of the lowest in the industry. All of us agree that we the custodians of our 200-year-old glorious institution, it is up to all of us to regain our premier position.*

2. *This is indeed a daunting but not an impossible task; and the onus of winning this battle lies on all of us. To win the battle we need to transform the Bank. But let us begin with transforming ourselves. Let us be more open and friendly. Let us undertake to take a few simple steps today:*

   a) *Discipline at work is paramount to ensure customer satisfaction. Let us be punctual at our desks, ready to serve the customer in time. Can we all resolve to start from our house a bit early so that our branches could open before the stipulated time? Let us give wide publicity to this in local media. This will lead to immense customer delight.*

b) *Let us present a happy and smiling face to our customers to begin a pleasant business interaction. Can we be smartly dressed, well-mannered and approach customers politely and courteously. Let us be conscious of the customer's overall needs rather than only the transaction at hand. We depend on the Customer and the Customer has wide choices today. Let us expand our Customer base.*

c) *In today's competitive environment, each one of us working in the Bank be a marketing man. Let us, therefore, ensure that we understand the details of all our products and every need of the customer and present the entire bouquet of products to him. Can we empathize with the smaller customer who has been loyal to the Bank for decades? Let us be true ambassadors of our Bank.*

d) *Shall we now resolve that we will exhibit perfect understanding of our customer needs and resolve to meet his needs and requests in a time bound manner? Even though complaints in the area of misbehaviour have come down, let us completely shun it even in the rarest of rare occasions. Let us endeavour to see that every customer who walks into our branch walks out full satisfied. Let us accept the theory that the Customer is always Right.*

3. *Therefore friends, irrespective of our cadre or position in the Bank, let us come together with a single mission to give the best customer service and make our Bank the 'Best Bank in Customer Service' by March 2007. Let us walk hand in hand together.*

   Together we can surmount the biggest challenges.
   Wishing you Godspeed in your endeavours.
   With New Year Greetings to you and your family members.

In mid-2008, the bank wanted to come up with the new vision statement. It was short, but compact and one that communicated the bank's vision clearly. A questionnaire and a survey were both initiated. The employees had to choose the vision statement from a set of three options. An overwhelming 1,41,000 plus employees responded. The final vision statement was unveiled in July 2008. It was what the bank employees wanted—to put the customer first. It was a winner! It read, 'My SBI. My customer first. First in customer satisfaction.'

Most organisations display the vision statement as a poster that can be seen in every office or branch. But Bhatt was not going to sit easy merely by highlighting the vision statement. He wanted to see that it was implemented at every level. It is thus not surprising to see the SBI managers routinely working extra hours or on holidays in the far-flung places of Jammu and Kashmir, Ladakh, Naxalite-ridden Chhattisgarh and other areas, to name a few, often times at risk to their lives. They do not get any additional salary but the motivation to satisfy customers makes them do this.

Employee Empowerment

Today, HR leaders talk of empowerment. But not many in the private sector face the problem which the SBI had faced—that of empowering the subordinate staff who comprised nearly 20 per cent of the total manpower and consisted of security personnel, messengers and general attendants or peons. They did the jobs of moving files from one desk to another, offering water and tea, and general housekeeping. How could they be involved in banking duties? The security personnel welcomed customers into the bank. The neatly dressed messengers would help customers with forms, provide brochures, assist them in dropping off cheques and pass book printing and so on. These were small steps but they made a huge difference—not only did they made the subordinate staff feel empowered, the staff also felt they were part of getting business for the bank and providing customer delight. Even today, we continue to see in many multinational organisations subordinate staff serving water and tea, while they could perform more meaningful jobs. Clearly, the SBI, with its radical thinking, was leading the way in 2008.

Vineet Nayar, CEO of HCL Technologies, pioneered the radical thought, 'Employee first, customer second'. The SBI was following a similar philosophy. It realised that in order to make the customer happy, it was important to make the employees happy. Many changes were happening in a short period. Take the case of felicitating performers who had achieved the membership of the Chairman's Club. This was a yearly exercise for top performers and those who reached the SBI Hall of Fame were felicitated in the SBI headquarters in the chairman's office. Bhatt decided to change that and the awards were given in the sprawling lawns of the SBI chairman's home, Dunedin, in Malabar Hill. Previously, no one except the top management had had a chance to visit the chairman's residence. The employees' families too were invited. For most achievers, it was a day they would never forget. People remember how they were treated and here was an example being put into practice.

Dunedin

The bungalow is one of the most cherished heritage structures of the SBI. Named Dunedin after the Gaelic word for Edinburgh (Dun Eideann), giving it a Scottish feel, the bungalow is a magnificent affair. It was bought in 1928 from Shirinbhai Ahmedbhoy Currimbhoy. Those visiting are impressed seeing the stately rooms, the charming wooden staircase, splendid furniture and two impressive pieces, namely a Bluthner grand piano and a John Roberts billiards table. There are many other antique pieces, including a lovely clock from the celebrated watch-making house of James McCabe of Royal Exchange, London. The clock stands beside an antique oak sideboard with intricate carvings. There is a lovely garden as well with mini waterfalls, a gorgeous vertical garden, green lawns, fountains with statues and small ponds, which has won numerous awards. A small gazebo tucked in a corner invites one to have a cup of coffee there. Some film buffs may recall that the Hindi film *Professor*, starring Shammi Kapoor and Kalpana, was shot there with the permission of the then chairman, P.C. Bhattacharya.

Equally impressive was Kinellan, the bungalow on Napean Sea Road occupied first by the secretary and treasurer of the Bank of Bombay and then by managing director of the bank. The bungalow was purchased from Dawoodbhoy Fazolbhoy in 1918 for ₹4.5 lakhs. The bungalow originally consisted of a drawing room, a dining room, five bedrooms, a billiards room and a small study along with the usual kitchen, pantry, etc. In 1957, the bungalow, with some alterations, was made into a twin bungalow to house the two managing directors as per a suggestion made the previous year by H.V.R Iengar, the chairman to H.M. Patel, the secretary in the ministry of finance. Later, to provide for the residence of senior officers, a multi-storeyed building in lieu of Kinellan was constructed. It is currently a 13-floor building. The old bungalow thus does not exist anymore.

Employee Motivation

Another instance of employee delight was in clearing the backlog of promotions. Any delays here were a sure cause for employees feeling demotivated. The entire backlog was cleared within a year. Stock options were unheard of in public sector organisations, but played a crucial role in employee motivation in private enterprises. The SBI managed to convince the RBI with a rights issue and decided to award part of the pie to the employees. The bank did not need the money but got a commitment of ₹10,000 crores from the government. The SBI announced that every employee could participate in the stock purchase scheme. A personal loan too was extended for those who wanted to fund their purchase.

Small things make a huge difference, especially when a small percentage can mean hundreds of employees for an organisation like the SBI. Earlier, when an employee retired, he or she often times had to forego the last leave travel concession just before retirement as the employee would be busy making post-retirement plans. The bank extended this facility to three months after retirement. What sounds like a simple idea in theory made a huge difference in practice.

At times, a small directive from the chairman's office is enough to initiate a change which though minor is critical to the image of the bank. It was found that the business cards used by employees did not follow the exact design and colour code. While this seems innocuous, it does reflect poorly on an organisation of the stature of the SBI. An official circular from the chairman's office streamlined the issue, which had been left unnoticed for years.

Innovative solutions were used in recruitment. For example, there was a shortage of nearly 20,000 people at various levels in 2007. Not only was it a logistical nightmare, such an exercise had not been carried out for any organisation. Using online methods, more than 24 lakh applications were scrutinised, and more than a lakh interview calls set up. A few years later, the SBI advertised for another 11,000 positions and received 36 lakh applications. Clearly, while private banks and other industries were hiring, the SBI was—and continues to be—a dream employer for millions who aspire to wear the SBI tag on their sleeve! In an interview to a newspaper, one of the deputy managing directors was quoted saying, 'It might even earn us an entry into the Guinness Book of World Records.' There were more than 300 applications for each post. Keeping in mind the changing scenario, it was made clear to the prospective candidates that even clerical posts carried responsibility for making customer calls and cross-selling products.

While recruitment at entry level is a dire need, every HR person is concerned with developing managers to create a leadership pipeline. Luckily, the SBI's hierarchical structure had helped to develop leaders over the course of its lifetime. Even people like Bhatt had cut their teeth at a branch level and had been rotated across functions and geographies. By the time they took over the top post, they were well aware of most of the functions and divisions of the bank. But with the changing external environment and the changes happening since the opening up of the economy in 1991 and the advent of private banks creating a tremendously competitive landscape, it was necessary to equip the middle management and above with cutting-edge management skills. As is the case for every issue, the problem in the SBI was of huge volumes. The bank entered into tie up with the Indian School of Business, IIM Ahmedabad and Duke University in the USA to train AGMs.

Any banker will tell you how deposits are an important component of their business. Bhatt launched a triple D, 'Do or Die Deposit' campaign. Using mass contact and involving literally everyone at the branch, it turned out to be a super success. The efforts bore fruit and the declining trend of the bank's share in deposits and advances, which had been a regular feature for many years in the past, showed an upward trend. It was not as expected but still positive. During the later downturn in the late 2000s, when there was a flight of deposits in private banks, the SBI actually received more than ₹1,000 crores each day for weeks on end.[1] This showed the stability of the SBI and the trust it enjoyed and had enjoyed for more than a century. The share of deposits recorded rose more than 2 per cent in the October–November period of 2009. 'No other bank has such a per day record and the figure is increasing,' said Bhatt, in an interview to a newspaper.[2] 'SBI has more than 43 per cent market share among 200 banks in the country and the market cap of SBI recorded more than that of Citibank,' he added.[3]

Structural Changes

Bhatt changed the organisational structure of the SBI by creating three new business groups within three months of assuming office. The groups were treasury and markets (now called global markets), corporate strategy and new businesses, and rural and agribusiness (now rural business). Till then, rural business was considered more of a necessity due to the government directive. But Bhatt was aware of the gold mine at the bottom of the pyramid and expected a rural boom over the next few years. He was of the opinion that the SBI had to be prepared to take advantage of it when the time came. It was in any case an inherent strength of the SBI. The goal was to be the banker to every Indian. The treasury and markets group was set up as a profit centre. The SBI, after all, sat on a huge treasury and was a powerful force in the money markets. Bhatt also worked on innovative ideas like a 'bank within a bank' by creating a super circle of excellence (SCE) comprising select branches across the country with best growth potential. The aim of the SCE branches was to excel in service, in retail business growth and in cross-selling and also be an initial window for all new products being launched. They were to become the best domestic banks in the area of their operation.

Even in the international area, the SBI realised that while Indian companies were going out and buying foreign companies, the bank was lagging behind. In 2006, the contribution of foreign operations to the SBI balance sheet was in single digits. The target was to raise it to a quarter of the bank's earnings in the medium run. As one CEO had quipped while expanding into foreign shores, 'Foreign branch should not be a hobby but a serious business.' The SBI too took the foreign operations not as a 'side business' but as a part of the core strategy.

The bank was the largest lender to corporates but was rapidly losing business to private banks who had better products and service. While they had all the necessary reasons to succeed, yet they were losing business. A mid-corporate group, focused on accounts between ₹50 crores to ₹500 crores, was set up under a deputy managing director, instead of a chief general manager. Larger clients required wholesale banking and it needed coordination between the corporate banking group which serviced the clients, the treasury group, and the investment banking group of SBI

Caps. McKinsey provided some solutions in architecture, after which the wholesale banking group was launched.

The SBI rode on these changes coupled with the performance of Indian economy as a whole.

How does a giant like the SBI change its IT infrastructure to ensure that it meets contemporary needs? Bhatt took a bold decision, realising that stopgap and quick fix solutions would not suffice, and suspended the roll out of the Core Banking Solution (CBS) for three months in September 2006. This time was used to streamline all the problems associated with CBS. The time taken for the roll out to 1,000 branches before the suspension was 295, which fell to 92. Later, in February 2010, the SBI celebrated a grand event at the Brabourne Stadium to announce the coverage of CBS to 18,000 plus branches, not to mention the 20,000 plus ATMs. At that time, the system was handling more than 4.6 crore transactions per day.

Mergers

Bhatt also began what would be a long process of amalgamating the seven associate banks into the SBI. The first among them was the State Bank of Saurashtra (SBS) in 2007. The SBS itself had a history of merging many banks into it. On 1 April 1902, the Bhavnagar Darbar Savings Bank was established in Bhavnagar, a princely state in the Saurashtra region. Maharaja Sir Bhavsinghji Takhtsinhji Gohil and Sir Prabhashankar Pattani, the Dewan, were the founders of the bank. The main objective was to encourage thrift amongst the people of the princely state and provide a safe place for their deposits. In 1950, the Bhavnagar Darbar Savings Bank was formed into a statutory corporation called the State Bank of Saurashtra, under the Saurashtra State Banks (Amalgamation) Ordinance, 1950 with four other Darbar banks owned by erstwhile princely states, namely Rajkot State Bank, Porbandar State Bank, Palitana Darbar Bank and Vadia State Bank, also getting merged with it. The bank became an associate bank of the SBI on 1 January 1960.

Once again, Bhatt's corporate development officer (CDO), Bharati Rao, was given the charge of the amalgamation. The SBS had 460 branches, of which 395 were in Gujarat. It was a win-win situation. The SBI got a huge reach while the employees of the SBS would benefit from the SBI's better

HR policies. Merging two running entities is not an easy task for anyone. While luckily both the SBS and the SBI were on the CBS, their products, parameters and procedures differed. Rao worked with five different teams which focused on IT systems, accounts, HR, network rationalisation and other areas. A major HR issue cropped up when it was decided that the officers of the SBS would lose a few years of seniority. Quite expectedly, the officers' association moved court. After months of litigation, the courts decided in favour of the SBI.

It was during Bhatt's tenure that merger of one more associate bank, the State Bank of Indore, would take place. As with the case of all associate banks, the Bank of Indore too had a long history. The territory around Indore was ruled by the Holkars since the time of the Peshwas. It was in 1920 that the Bank of Indore was set up under a special charter from Maharaj Tukoji Rao Holkar III, who ruled the state from 1903 to 1927. Indore State awarded the bank a monopoly for ten years. It granted the bank certain concessions and subscribed to its share capital. At the time of merger with the SBI, the bank had 470 branches. But there was a difference in the merger of the SBS, which was a wholly owned subsidiary, and the State Bank of Indore, which had 98 per cent ownership with the SBI and the rest held by private parties. The SBI has already announced a share swap ratio of 34:100 for the merger, i.e., for every 100 shares of the State Bank of Indore held by its minority shareholders, the SBI would give 34 SBI shares. The SBI issued 1.6 lakh shares of ₹10 each to the minority shareholders. The merger itself was not a smooth affair as had been the case with the SBS. The union was left-dominated and, as expected, opposed the merger. But in the end, the SBI prevailed and the merger went through, much to the benefit of all stakeholders.

The merger of the SBS and the State Bank of Indore into the SBI provided, in some sense, a way forward for other banks. This does not mean the journey was easy as each bank would have its own challenges. In 2017, the SBI merged five of its associate banks into itself. The banks were the State Bank of Bikaner and Jaipur, State Bank of Mysore, State Bank of Travancore, State Bank of Patiala and State Bank of Hyderabad. Each of these banks had a long history of its own and had played a unique role in the building of a nation. The State Bank of Mysore was started in 1913 by

Maharaja Krishna Raja Wadiyar IV,* at the instance of a committee headed by Sir M. Visveswaraya. It was called Mysore Bank then. The State Bank of Bikaner and Jaipur came into existence in 1963 when two banks, namely, the Bank of Bikaner (established in 1944) and the Bank of Jaipur (established in 1943), were merged. The Bank of Bikaner was founded by Maharaja Ganga Singh of Bikaner. The Bank of Jaipur was founded in 1943 under the leadership of the industrialist Ramnath Anandilal Podar on invitation by the then princely government of Jaipur. The State Bank of Travancore was established in 1945 as the Travancore Bank Ltd., at the initiative of the Travancore Dewan, C.P. Ramaswami Iyer. Following popular resentment against his dictatorial rule, the bank never credited his role. Instead, the bank considered the Maharaja of Travancore, Sri Chithira Thirunal Balarama Varma, as the founder, though the king had little to do with its founding. The Maharaja of Patiala State, Bhupinder Singh, founded the Patiala State Bank in 1917 to foster growth of agriculture, trade and industry. The bank combined the functions of a commercial bank and those of a central bank for the princely state of Patiala. The bank had one branch at Chowk Fort, Patiala. The formation of the Patiala and East Punjab States Union in 1948 led to the bank being reorganised. It was brought under the control of the RBI and renamed as the Bank of Patiala.

It was during Bhatt's time that the world saw the financial crisis of 2008, dubbed the worst since the Great Depression of the 1930s. In the USA, more than 8 million people lost their jobs, while close to four million homes were foreclosed due to inability of the borrower to pay back. The main cause of this complex failure was the propensity of banks and other financial institutions to dabble in high-risk mortgages. The so-called housing boom had been around for more than a decade since 1994 when the house ownership rate increased from 64 per cent to an all-time high of 69.2 per cent in 2004. The major contributor to this was subprime lending, which offered loans to literally anyone willing to buy a house. As expected, borrowers started defaulting once the initial grace period ended

---

* At the time of his death, he was one of the world's wealthiest men, with a personal fortune estimated in 1940 to be worth US$ 400 million, equivalent to US$ 8 billion in today's prices. He was the second-wealthiest Indian, after Mir Osman Ali Khan, Nizam of Hyderabad.

and many refinanced their mortgages to tide over things for a while. By then the housing prices were reducing and thus the ability to refinance became more difficult. It was the sharpest fall in housing prices since the 1930s. This resulted in many foreclosures creating further downward pressure on housing prices. The value of the mortgage-backed securities was eroding rapidly. This, in turn, affected the health of the banks which had funded them. This vicious cycle caused the mortgage crisis.

The collapse of Lehman Brothers, one of the most venerated firms, sent shock waves across the financial sector. Lehman Brothers had been in existence since 1844 having started as a general store founded by a German immigrant, Henry Lehman, in Montgomery, Alabama. While the USA was already facing a housing boom which most had not read as a bubble, Lehman and many other banks aggressively got into mortgage-backed securities and collateral debt obligations. By 2007, cracks in the housing market were visible and soon the house of cards came tumbling down. Among many changes, Bear Sterns was acquired by J.P. Morgan and Merrill Lynch by the Bank of America.

The impact of the subprime crisis was not felt much in India in general and did not affect the SBI.

⊗

In October 2013, Arundhati Bhattacharya became the bank's first female chairman. She was the 24th chairman and remained in office till October 2017. In 2016, she was listed as the 25th most powerful woman in the world by *Forbes* magazine. She is the only Indian corporate leader listed on *Fortune*'s world's greatest leaders list (she was ranked 26). Like most other heads, Arundhati too rose from the ranks. She had joined the SBI as a probationary officer in 1977 at the age of 22 and went on to head the bank decades later. A few of the women-centric policies which she introduced merit mention. She introduced a two-year sabbatical leave policy for the bank's female employees to be used either for maternity or elder care. Even large multinational corporations do not have such policies for women employees. She also started free vaccination against cervical cancer for all the female employees of the bank. There have been noises in Wall Street about women not being able to break the glass ceiling. Rarely do we find examples of women heading such large banks in the USA, but India is different. Shikha Sharma headed Axis Bank for nine years from 2009 till 2019, while Chanda Kochhar headed ICICI during the same period. Sharma and Kochar, like Arundhati, had risen from the ranks, having joined ICICI as management trainees.

The year 2009 was a watershed year as one more woman, Naina Lal Kidwai, was elevated to head HSBC's India operations as Group General Manager and Country Head. Women continue to dominate Indian financial services scene with Kalpana Morparia heading J.P. Morgan. (Ms Morparia announced her retirement in December 2020.) She cut her teeth at ICICI joining the organisation in 1975 and rising up the ranks. Madhavi Puri Buch is a whole-time member of SEBI while Ashu Suyash heads ICRA. Even in public-sector banks, we have had many women at the top positions. Usha Ananthasubramanian headed Allahabad Bank while Archana Bhagwat was MD and CEO of United Bank and Vijayalakshmi Iyer was CEO of Bank of India. Kaku Nakhate is the country head for Bank of America Merill Lynch. The list goes on.

As an industry leader in various categories, it was not surprising to see the SBI entering associated areas of business, be it mutual fund (it was the first player after UTI to enter the business), credit cards, life and general insurance and others.

The SBI made a foray into insurance as soon as the industry opened up in 2000. SBI Life is a joint venture with BNP Paribas Cardif. It competes with 23 other insurance companies. In the general insurance business, the SBI began operations in 2010 with a joint venture with Insurance Australia Group, which later sold its stake to a few funds. Insurance again is a hugely underpenetrated market, despite the efforts of the LIC and the GIC over past many decades. Despite there being 34 companies offering general insurance today, the penetration of the products continues to be in single digits in many categories.

In March 2020, SBI Cards received a lot of attention as the company came up with a public issue which was overwhelmingly subscribed. SBI Cards started its operations in 1998, as a joint venture between the SBI and GE Capital. GE Capital sold its stake to the SBI and CA Rover Holdings, a subsidiary of Carlyle Group, in 2017. In the initial public offering (IPO), the SBI offered 4 per cent of its share while CA Rover offered 10 per cent. The issue price for the IPO was ₹755. Credit cards comprise a major chunk of unsecured loans, the largest being personal loans. With the Indian economy growing and the use of electronic payments increasing in the aftermath of demonetisation, the credit card market is expected to grow further. Credit card spends in the year 2019 were around ₹6 lakh crores and are growing at a rate of 32 per cent year on year. The spends are expected to exceed 15 lakh crores by 2024. The number of credit cards at 5.2 crores[4] are still a small percentage of the population. Currently, as is the case with many other services, the credit card penetration in India is a mere 3 per cent while debit cards are at 65 per cent. This is not surprising, given the savings-oriented approach of Indians who shun credit usage. But it is changing slowly. As with other categories, the SBI has a huge market share and is the second largest player in the industry, HDFC Bank being the largest.

Frauds, Defaults and Banks Going Under

Even a layperson cannot ignore the issue being raised about defaults, non-performing assets (NPAs) and outright frauds which have been orchestrated by some individuals who borrowed thousands of crores and fled the country. And there is anger on the streets when a bank like the Punjab and Maharashtra Co-operative Bank (PMC) fails as lakhs of middle-class depositors and their life savings get affected. History helps us to understand some of the changes better. In the 1950s, just after India got independence, a large number of legal entities were engaged in reckless lending, leading to a speculative culture, with the RBI barely having any control. There were around 54 state-owned or controlled banks in 1952. The banks varied in size—the Bank of Baroda was the largest with deposits running into several crores, while the Bank of Barwani had deposits of only ₹3,000!

Quite naturally, there was a consolidation effected through a stronger RBI and compulsory merger of 737 such legal entities to a manageable number of 94.*

---

* Some trivia: some of the state-associated banks were privately owned. A case in point is that of Krishna Ram Baldeo Bank in Gwalior, which was owned by the ruler himself. Some state banks were constituted under the act passed locally. One example is that of Bank of Baroda which was incorporated under the Companies Act of the Baroda State, while on the other extreme we have Sri Ramchandra Laxman Bank, Durgarpur, which was set up on the basis of a verbal order. Likewise, the Bank of Patiala which was set up on the basis of a firmaan by the ruler!

Going Back into History

One of the structural weaknesses of the Indian banking at the time the SBI came into being in 1955 was the large number of small and often uneconomic banks. Amalgamation of these small banks was one method by which a certain degree of strength could be imparted to them. But the fear of unemployment and consequent payment of compensation to surplus staff made amalgamation a rather unattractive proposition. The AIRCS committee had recommended that the SBI be created by nationalising the Imperial Bank of India and amalgamating with it ten major state-associated banks and a few minor ones, like Manipur State Bank, Sangli Bank, Bank of Baghelkhand and Mayurbhanj State Bank and a few others.* The RBI was in favour of nationalising the Imperial Bank but wanted to keep the issue of amalgamation of state-associated banks in abeyance. While the government of India was initially enthusiastic about an immediate takeover of the state-associated banks, it subsequently accepted the RBI's view that takeover of the Imperial Bank was the first step towards setting up and 'integrated commercial banking institution.' The bill, however, included an enabling provision authorising the new institution to own and manage institutions as subsidiaries.

As per the provisions in the State Bank of India Act, the RBI forwarded a list of minor state-associated banks to the SBI for consideration. A committee was formed to consider the issue of acquiring the business of certain minor state-associated banks. Accordingly, the Cooch Behar State Bank (est. 1949, taken over in 1958), Manipur State Bank (est. 1948, taken over in 1959), Mayurbhanj State Bank (est. 1938, taken over in 1961), Bank of Baghelkhand (est. 1933, taken over in 1961) and Bhor State Bank (est. 1844, taken over in 1962) were inspected by the committee and schemes for amalgamation sent to the RBI for approval. Bank of Aundh (est. in 1938) was taken over in 1963. Raikut Industrial Bank (est. in 1920) was taken over in 1967, Kamala Bank (est. 1963), in 1967, Bengal Duars Bank in 1967 and Krishnaram Baldeo Bank (est. 1958) in 1973. Apart from

---

* Of the ten banks listed by the AIRCS committee for takeover, the Bank of Baroda was left out at an early stage, as it was no longer associated with the business of the state. The Bank of Rajasthan opted out of the voluntary takeover proposal and, with the approval of its shareholders, agreed to discontinue its association with government banking business. Later, in 2010, the Bank of Rajasthan was merged with ICICI Bank.

amalgamating the above banks under Section 35 of the State Bank of India Act, certain other minor banks were also amalgamated under Section 45 of the Banking Companies Act (later renamed as Banking Regulation Act), which empowered the RBI to apply to the central government for an order of moratorium on a banking company if there was a good reason to do so. The section also empowered the RBI to prepare a scheme for its 'reconstruction' and amalgamation with any other banking institution. Under this section, the Unity Bank, Madras was amalgamated in 1962, Allahabad Trading and Banking Corporation (est. 1883) in 1965, Bank of Behar (est. 1911) in 1969, National Bank of Lahore (est. 1942) in 1970.

Bank nationalisation was a major step taken essentially to address the issue of commercial banks stepping into the agricultural sector. There was a fundamental disequilibrium between what the banking system was structured to provide and what the economy needed. As we saw earlier, the demands arising out of the impact of the Green Revolution could not be met by the cooperative sector alone and banks needed to step in.

The world of state planning collapsed in the early 1990s and India migrated to a market-oriented competitive system. This was not without hiccups and issues of NPAs were raised but largely ignored. When the development finance institutions were dismantled in the early 1990s, all too sudden, the commercial banks, with little in-house expertise of dealing with the appraisal and viability of large-scale projects were severely handicapped. All this while they were being flooded with large investment proposals from businesses now freed from the licensing raj and were now wanting to expand with reckless abandon. The in-house expertise of the banks to appraise such projects was questionable and they had to depend on outside support. Soon, asset-liability mismatch arose. The seeds of quite a few of the large NPAs we see today were sown at this time.

In the early days after independence, compulsory acquisition saved us while in the next crisis the government stepped in with bank nationalisation.

In the current situation, a catharsis is due. 'Shedding the ownership of bulk of the PSBs [public sector banks] while keeping a few in overall national interest is a way forward,' suggests a senior retired banker, who did not want to be named. 'This will contribute substantively to the cleansing of the system with supportive policies for the development of a vibrant capital market.'

It is not the mandate of this book, the magnificent history of the SBI, to analyse the current situation of defaults and bank failures. There could be many reasons for the origin of the mountain of debts we are witnessing now—the decision to close the development finance institutions, the RBI policy or the lack of intervention, not to mention greed and corrupt officials. It sounds almost simplistic when the RBI admitted that it has noticed three major irregularities in the operations of the multi-state PMC. These include major financial irregularities, failure of internal control and systems and wrongdoing and under-reporting of its lending exposure. Needless to say, the RBI needs to revive its own capabilities to regulate and ensure financial stability. The banking sector spread of 1,20,535 branches,[5] of which 35,649 are in rural areas,[6] is essential for India's progress and to fulfil its global aspirations. It simply cannot be ignored.

Having said that, let us turn back to our story of the SBI.

11

GOING FORWARD

Every event that threatens to overturn a business also comes with opportunities that otherwise would have been difficult to imagine. The recent COVID-19 pandemic, still raging in all parts of the world, has been a boon for many companies which are in the last-mile delivery business like Zomato, Swiggy and Big Basket, to name a few. Similarly, it has had an impact on the speed at which customers have adapted to digital banking. What was earlier possible but not done through an app, is now being pursued with a vengeance. With social distancing becoming a norm, there is a huge demand for e-commerce and digital financial services. Sheer necessity has brought about this change. Before the pandemic, disruptive events like the demonetisation exercise carried out nationwide had brought into focus the need for net banking. Today, we see a large number of shopkeepers accepting payments digitally.

With technology come challenges. The outages in the data centre in November 2020 forced the RBI to ask HDFC Bank to stop issuing new credit cards. In 2020, the SBI had 61 such outages. Now with digital transactions on the rise, there is an increasing load on the bank's IT infrastructure with billions of transactions. Apparently, an hour's outage affects nearly 4 lakh UPI* transactions. Imagine the chaos that outage for a few hours can create. Moreover, the bank's legacy systems are failing to keep

---

* Unified Payments Interface (UPI) is a system that powers multiple bank accounts into a single mobile application (of any participating bank), merging several banking features, seamless fund routing and merchant payments into one hood.

pace with the rapid changes in technology. For the bank, the cost of a digital transaction, be it one rupee or one lakh, is the same. While the customer is moving to digital transactions creating an opportunity for banks, it comes with its own set of hurdles to overcome. Banks are cognisant of that. It is just that the legacy systems in which they have invested hundreds of crores cannot be junked overnight.

'If it was sitting outside banks, my valuation would be ... maybe US$ 40-50 billion for YONO, which the startups get,' said Rajnish Kumar, the then chairman of the SBI, in an interview to the *Mint* newspaper in October 2020. He was talking of the app You Only Need One (YONO), which the bank had launched in November 2017.* YONO is a super app which swallowed all of SBI's 50 plus apps.

Rajnish Kumar believes no one knows the true valuation as the app sits within the bank. With the kind of valuations which are being talked about, YONO would probably find itself among the top five most valuable start-ups globally, with only Bytedance, the Chinese internet giant, ride hailing firm Didi Chuxing and Elon Musk's space transportation company Space-X valued higher. In India, the most valuable start-up was Paytm, valued at US$ 24 billion or so.† Surprisingly, the SBI itself is valued at US$ 24 billion. Now

---

* A little about the YONO app. Customers can withdraw cash from ATMs even without the debit card using the YONO app. The app can be used to conduct banking activities, investing, buying insurance, paying bills, booking IRCTC tickets, getting loans or even do shopping. On one single app, the customer can manage all her money related transactions and anything to do with her finances. For basic banking transactions such as checking account balance, creating a fixed deposit, adding beneficiary, etc., the customer does not need to log on to the net banking of the SBI. The app helps. In addition, one may request cheque books, debit cards or use the emergency services to change ATM PIN, block debit cards or stop cheques, by accessing the YONO app. It is a single window view for all investments, cards, insurance and banking transactions. This saves the hassle of accessing different websites and places to know the current financial standings.

† SBI YONO is reimagining banking to thwart disruption by fintechs, which are gradually eating into the market share of banks. A recent Federation of Indian Chambers of Commerce & Industry (FICCI) and Boston Consulting Group (BCG) report was entitled 'India FinTech: A US$ 100 Billion Opportunity'. There are already many billion-dollar fintechs in the market. BharatPe, a payments start-up which also lends (₹1,200 crore loan book), has reached a billion-dollar valuation in just three years. Bangalore-headquartered Cred, a credit card bill payment platform that rewards people for paying on time, has achieved a billion-dollar valuation in a similar time period. Razorpay, a digital payments facilitator for

it looks like a distant second compared to YONO. At some stage, the bank may even look at hiving it off into a separate subsidiary. Unlocking surely has value, which was seen when SBI Cards was listed in March of 2020 and now has a market cap of a whopping ₹1,00,000 crores, compared to the SBI's market value of ₹3,71,487 crores.[1] The recent example of Reliance hiving off its Jio platforms has helped it to raise US$ 20 billion with a valuation of over US$ 60 billion (these are estimates).

As per the *Mint* report, the bank has been adding 70,000 users on the YONO app daily, taking it to more than 7 million. The bank took the help of McKinsey and IBM to create the app. The bank is clear—its strength lies in the trust the customer reposes in the bank. While using the app, the bank wanted to ensure that the customer is able to feel safe, apart from the convenience of using the app. YONO has partnered with over 80 e-commerce players in more than 20 categories. It is not a simple app for logging in to transfer money. From cash to cars is what the app is designed to help the customer transact or buy.

An article in *The Ken* quotes Ravindra Pandey, the deputy managing director (strategy) and chief digital officer, while talking of the sheer size of YONO, 'There are thirty million users and more than a crore of daily login on the app.'[2] The app has helped SBI disburse more than ₹24,500 crores while investments in mutual funds alone is in excess of ₹1,600 crores. The app helped to open nine million bank accounts in three years and sell 3,50,000 credit cards, 5.9 lakh life insurance policies and 17.5 lakh general insurance policies. The thirty million customers, while huge, are still a fraction of the 448 million SBI customer base. (Since the publication of the article, the customer base has increased to 45.92 crore as of March 2021, as per the SBI annual report.)

The SBI has a long way to go when it comes to mobile banking, mainly due to the fact that a large user base still prefers to visit the bank and may not be internet and mobile savvy. Banks like HDFC Bank, which digitised with

---

businesses, is valued at US$ 3 billion. PineLabs, a merchant payments solutions company, is valued at a billion dollars. The number of Indian fintech unicorns will more than double over the next few years, says the FICCI-BCG report. YONO has been designed to offer customer convenience and innovative products to target customers who opt for products from players such as Cred or Pine Labs. (Anand Adhikari, 'SBI YONO is the startup you didn't see coming! It's worth billions now,' *Business Today,* 11 July 2021).

a vengeance under Aditya Puri, have nearly 90 per cent of its transactions through the mobile phone. For the SBI, the number would be around 55 per cent.

But unlike most start-ups, which have been losing money,[3] YONO has been profitable and in the quarter ending June 2020, it made a profit of ₹200 crores. Though the bank's annual report does not state any numbers, the bank expects the app to deliver a profit of ₹1,000 crores for the year ending March 2021, as per a Credit Suisse report.[4] The investment of nearly ₹800 crores would thus be recouped. Such numbers alone make the SBI a very valuable entity.

Dinesh Khara, chairman of the bank, in an exclusive interview to Fortune India, said, 'Our corporate internet banking wasn't as popular as our retail internet banking. But with YONO business, I think corporate clients will also come on board, so I expect that it (YONO user base) will go beyond that [90 million].' As of March 2021, YONO had clocked 70.5 million downloads, across Android and iOS devices, with 37.1 million registrations and 10 million average daily logins. In financial year ending March 2021, over 100 merchant partners were live on YONO's B2C market place platform, clocking 11.92 lakh transactions worth ₹641 crore in gross merchandise value.[5]

'YONO has been successfully launched in the UK, Mauritius, Maldives, Bangladesh, Sri Lanka and Canada. As of 31 March 2021, over 40,000 overseas customers have been onboarded on the YONO platform. We are on course to launch YONO in Singapore, Bahrain, South Africa, and the USA by the end of FY2022,' informs the SBI annual report of 2020–21.

YONO is mentioned 91 times in the SBI's latest annual report, showing its importance for the bank. It might transform the SBI, the giant bank, into a league of its own. A cursory glance at its Annual Report of 2020–21 already makes a casual reader wonder at the size of the giant.

The numbers are staggering. With more than 22,000 branches, 60,000 plus ATMs and 70,000 plus outlets of Banking Correspondents, the bank serves nearly 46 crore customers. The SBI continues to hold its eminent position with a share of more than 23 per cent in deposits and nearly 20 per cent in advances.[6]

The SBI and its subsidiaries continue to do well. We had seen how SBI Cards has already gathered a significant market cap, with its 1.2 crore credit cards in the market.[7] Even SBI Life holds a leadership position being the number two private life insurer, serving millions of customers with its 947 branch offices. There are many other subsidiaries of the bank, but that is beyond the scope of this book.

With domestic deposits of nearly ₹36 lakh crores and domestic advances of ₹25 lakh crores, it is not easy for the chairman to make the elephant dance. But the SBI has been surprisingly nimble, thanks to the hard work of its 2.4 lakh plus workforce, of which nearly a quarter are women. The current and past chairpersons, highly regarded in the industry, have continued their focus on building the SBI.

The history of the SBI is that of a rich heritage of more than two centuries. It is a remarkable journey of resilience, coming out stronger and better each year. Resilience is a strong pillar of the SBI. We saw how remarkable people not just heading the bank but even at the lowest rung have been making a difference, as they believe theirs is not just a job but a cause worthy of spending their life for. The unflinching dedication and commitment of the people is a pillar which the SBI is very proud of. The YONO platform proved to be the perfect medium to serve customers in the digital space in which the boundaries of 'physical' were pushed to 'phygital'. Technology thus completes the third and a very important pillar for the bank.

The SBI, with its roots going back to 200 years, may be old, but with each innovation, it is reinventing itself.

The words of R.K. Talwar ring true: 'It is the biggest bank for the smallest man.' It has come a full circle with the opening of its branch at the Rashtrapati Bhawan on 24 July 2021. It is the SBI's first branch in the president's estate. President Ram Nath Kovind is the first customer of the branch but the branch, despite being within the premises of the Rashtrapati Bhavan, would be accessible to all those who are not residents of the estate. The SBI is truly a bank for all—from the first citizen of the country to a common man.

As the current chairman, Dinesh Kumar Khara says confidently, 'The elephant is ready to dance.'

The SBI is surely poised to not only take off into a higher trajectory, but see another 200 years!

NOTES

The Origins of Banking: An Introduction

1. Dr Y.V. Reddy, at a seminar on 'Harmonising the Role and Operations of Development Financial Institutions and Banks', on 28 June 1999. Quoted on the Reserve Bank of India website, https://rbi.org.in/scripts/BS_SpeechesView.aspx?Id=25.
2. Ibid.
3. Bakhtiar K. Dadabhoy, *Barons of Banking* (Random House India, 2013), Introduction, p. xxv.

Chapter 1: The Turn of the Nineteenth Century

1. A.K. Bagchi, *The Evolution of the State Bank of India: The Roots (1806–1876), Vol. 1* (Oxford University Press, 1987), p. 221.
2. Ibid., p. 222.
3. Ibid., p. 365.
4. Abhik Ray, *Banking Beyond Boundaries* (Penguin Viking, 2011), p. 17.

Chapter 2: Banking in the British Raj Post 1857

1. Frank Lawrence Owsley, *King Cotton Diplomacy: Foreign Relations of the Confederate States of America* (University of Chicago Press, 1931).
2. A.K. Bagchi, *The Evolution of the State Bank of India: The Roots (1806–1876), Vol. 2* (Oxford University Press, 1987), p. 214.
3. Ibid., p. 233.
4. Report of the Bombay Bank Commission, p. 32, quoted in A.K. Bagchi, *The Evolution of the State Bank of India: The Roots (1806–1876)*, op. cit.
5. Ibid., p. 280.

6. Ibid., p. 398.
7. 'Origin', Punjab National Bank, https://www.pnbindia.in/origin-of-PNB.html.

Chapter 3: The Turn of the Twentieth Century

1. A.K. Bagchi, *The Evolution of the State Bank of India: The Era of the Presidency Banks (1876–1920)* (Sage Publications, 1997), p. 66.
2. N.K. Sinha, *The Economic History of Bengal, Vol III*, 1970, Chapters VII and VIII, quoted in A.K. Bagchi, *The Evolution of the State Bank of India: The Era of the Presidency Banks (1876–1920)*.
3. A.K. Bagchi, *The Evolution of the State Bank of India: The Era of the Presidency Banks (1876–1920)*, op. cit., p. 231.
4. Ibid., p. 286
5. Ibid., p. 568.
6. Ibid., p. 595.
7. Abhik Ray, *The Evolution of the State Bank of India: The Era of the Imperial Bank of India (1921–1955)*, op. cit., p. 20.
8. Sumit Sarkar, *Modern* India, Chapter V, p. 169, quoted in Abhik Ray, *The Evolution of the State Bank of India: The Era of the Imperial Bank of India (1921–1955)*, op. cit., p. 32.
9. Abhik Ray, *The Evolution of the State Bank of India: The Era of the Imperial Bank of India (1921–1955)*, op. cit., p. 32.

Chapter 4: The Imperial Bank of India

1. Abhik Ray, *The Evolution of the State Bank of India: The Era of the Imperial Bank of India (1921–1955)* (Sage Publications, 2003), p. 484.
2. Ibid., p. 505.
3. Ibid., p. 77.
4. Ibid., p. 123.
5. Om Prakash Gupta, *Central Banking in India, 1773–1934* (Hindustan Times Press, 1934), Chapter 5, p. 144.
6. *Royal Commission on Indian Currency and Finance, Vol I*, p. 35, para 87.
7. Abhik Ray, *The Evolution of the State Bank of India: The Era of the Imperial Bank of India (1921–1955)*, op. cit., p. 124.
8. Ibid., p. 165.
9. Indian Legislative Assembly Debates (Official Report of the First Session of the Third Legislative Assembly), Vol IV, 1927 (Government of India Press, 1927), pp. 3455–3474.

10. Jawaharlal Nehru, *An Autobiography*, Ch XLVIII, p. 386, quoted in Abhik Ray, *The Evolution of the State Bank of India: The Era of the Imperial Bank of India (1921–1955)*, op. cit., pp. 229–230.

11. Abhik Ray, *The Evolution of the State Bank of India: The Era of the Imperial Bank of India (1921–1955)*, op. cit., p. 302, footnote 24.

12. Ibid., pp. 432–433.

13. Ibid., p. 139.

14. Ibid., p. 583.

15. Ibid., p. 584.

16. Ibid.

17. Ibid., p. 585.

18. Ibid., p. 590.

19. Ibid., p. 592.

20. Ibid., p. 609.

21. Ibid., p. 627.

Chapter 5: Dawn of a New Avatar

1. Abhik Ray, *The Evolution of the State Bank of India: The Era from 1955 to 1980* (Penguin Portfolio, 2009), p. 29.

2. Ibid.

3. Ibid., p. 36, note 2.

4. Ibid., p. 43, note 1.

5. H.V.R. Iengar, *Monetary Policy and Economic Growth* (Vora & Co., 1962), p. 124, quoted in Abhik Ray, *The Evolution of the State Bank of India*, op. cit., p. 37, note 25.

6. Ibid., p. 48.

7. AIRCA, Vol. II, The General Report (Bombay, 1955), Ch. IX, p. 27.

8. State Bank of India Bill, 30 April 1955, Lok Sabha Debates (New Delhi, Lok Sabha Secretariat, 1955), p. 7194.

9. Ibid., p. 76.

10. Ibid., pp. 79–80.

11. N. Vaghul, *R.K. Talwar: Values in Leadership* (Parksons Graphics, reprint courtesy Shrenuj and Company Ltd, 2012), pp. 23–26.

12. Ibid., pp. 26–27.

13. P.K. Mohanty, *Down Memory Lane: A Collection of Anecdotes from SBI*, quoted in Vaghul, R.K. Talwar, op. cit., p. 151. Unfortunately, the name of the successor is not mentioned.

14. Abhik Ray, *Banking Beyond Boundaries* (Penguin Viking, 2011), p. 54.

15. Abhik Ray, *The Evolution of the State Bank of India*, op. cit., p. 149.
16. Abhik Ray, *Banking Beyond Boundaries*, op. cit., p. 150.
17. Ibid., p. 148.
18. Ibid., p. 150.
19. Ibid., p. 55.
20. Ibid.

Chapter 6: The Growth Years

1. Abhik Ray, *The Evolution of the State Bank of India: The Era from 1955 to 1980* (Penguin Portfolio, 2009), p. 171.
2. Ibid.
3. Ibid., p. 178.
4. Ibid., pp. 183–184.
5. *History of RBI*, Volume III (1967-1981) (Reserve Bank of India Publication, 2005).
6. D.N. Ghosh, *No Regrets* (Rupa Publications, 2015).
7. Ibid.
8. D.N. Ghosh, 'Bank Nationalisation: The Original Sin?', *The Quint*, 11 July 2019.
9. Ibid.
10. Ibid.
11. Ibid.
12. *Free Press Journal*, 2 July 1955, quoted in Abhik Ray, *The Evolution of the State Bank of India*, op. cit.
13. Ibid.
14. State Bank of India, *Colleague*, A Quarterly House Magazine of the State Bank of India and its Subsidiary Banks, Vol. III, No. 1, January 1971.
15. Speech of Chairman P.C.D. Nambiar at the 25th AGM of shareholders held at Bombay on 31 March 1980, in *The Chairman*, p. 166, quoted in Abhik Ray, *The Evolution of the State Bank of India*, op. cit.
16. V.S. Natarajan, 'Satbarwa: The 5000th Office', *State Bank of India Monthly Review*, December 1978–January 1979 (State Bank of India, 1979), p. 17.
17. Abhik Ray, *The Evolution of the State Bank of India*, op. cit., p. 292.
18. In his speech at the 26th AGM of shareholders held at Chandigarh on 31 March 1981, *The Chairman*, p. 178, quoted in Abhik Ray, The Evolution of the State Bank of India, op. cit.
19. Speech of P.C.D. Nambiar, chairman, at the 25th AGM of shareholders held at Bombay on 31 March 1980, in *The Chairman*, p. 168, quoted in Abhik Ray, *The Evolution of the State Bank of India*, op. cit.

20. Abhik Ray, *The Evolution of the State Bank of India*, op. cit., pp. 342–343.

21. Annual policy guidelines for the State Bank of India for the year 1976.

22. Speech of R.K. Talwar, chairman, at the 21st AGM of shareholders held at New Delhi on 30 March 1976, in *The Chairman*, p. 139, quoted in Abhik Ray, *The Evolution of the State Bank of India*, op. cit.

23. Abhik Ray, *The Evolution of the State Bank of India*, op. cit., p. 348.

24. Speech of R.K. Talwar, chairman, at the 21st AGM of shareholders held at New Delhi on 30 March 1976, in *The Chairman*, pp. 138–139, quoted in Abhik Ray, *The Evolution of the State Bank of India*, op. cit.

Chapter 7: Focus on the 'Aam Aadmi'

1. Speech of J. Matthai, chairman, at the first AGM of shareholders held at Bombay on 29 February 1956, in *The Chairman*, p. 7, quoted in Abhik Ray, The Evolution of the State Bank of India: The Era from 1955 to 1980 (Penguin Portfolio, 2009).

2. Speech of H.V.R. Iengar, chairman, at the second AGM of shareholders held at Bombay on 28 February 1957, in *The Chairman*, p. 13 quoted in Abhik Ray (2009)

3. Abhik Ray, *The Evolution of the State Bank of India*, op. cit., p. 592.

4. Ibid., p. 633.

5. Speech of R.K. Talwar, chairman, at the 21st AGM of shareholders held at New Delhi on 30 March 1976, in *The Chairman*, p. 142. The need to impart proper training to the employees in handling customers was one of the recommendations which emerged in the course of deliberations at a workshop on customer service organised by the National Institute of Bank Management (NIBM) in Madras in December 1969. Talwar participated in the concluding session of the workshop. See 'Customer Service: Summary of Deliberations and Recommendations of the Workshop on Customer Service held at Madras from 17 to 20 December 1969' (NIBM, 1970), pp. 24, 33.

6. R.K. Talwar, *Banker and Corporate Customer* (The A.D. Shroff Memorial Trust, 1974).

7. Abhik Ray, *The Evolution of the State Bank of India*, op. cit., p. 634.

Chapter 8: Building Structures to Build the Institution

1. Abhik Ray, *The Evolution of the State Bank of India*, op. cit., p. 721.

2. Ibid., p. 767.

3. Ibid., p. 880.

4. Ibid.
5. Ibid., p. 87.
6. Ibid., p. 803
7. D.N. Ghosh, *No Regrets* (Rupa, 2015), p. 296.
8. Ibid., p. 302.
9. Ibid., p. 303.

Chapter 10: A Time for Introspection

1. *The Financial Express*, 29 March 2009, quoted in Abhik Ray, *Banking Beyond Boundaries* (Penguin Viking, 2011).
2. Abhik Ray, *Banking Beyond Boundaries* (Penguin Viking, 2011), p. 123.
3. Ibid.
4. 'Customer Priorities – Credit Card Users in India', report from ReserachAndMarket.com, 2 November 2020.
5. As of end March 2019, as per RBI report dated 24 December 2019.
6. Saloni Shukla, 'Govt asks banks to open 15000 branches in FY 21', *The Economic Times*, 17 January 2020.

Chapter 11: Going Forward

1. www.screener.in, based on stock price on 26 August 2021.
2. 'SBI's one app to rule them all', *The Ken*, 12 October 2020.
3. Digbijay Mishra and Ashwin Manikandan, 'IPO-bound Paytm's revenue drops 14% in FY21, losses narrow to Rs 1,701 crore', *The Economic Times*, 5 June 2021.
4. V. Keshavdev, 'YONO to be the Super App; won't be spun off', *Fortune India*, 12 August 2021.
5. Ibid.
6. SBI annual report, 2020–21.
7. From the SBI cards website, www.sbicard.com.

ACKNOWLEDGEMENTS

It would have been impossible to come out with this book without the extensive use of references from the following books, with kind permission from the State Bank of India.

The Evolution of the State Bank of India, Vols 1 and 2 (authors: A.N. Bagchi and Abhik Ray), Vol. 3 (Abhik Ray and others) and Vol. 4 (Abhik Ray)

Banking Beyond Boundaries and *SBI's Living Heritage; Edifices and Beyond*, both authored by Abhik Ray.